ADVANCE PRAISE FOR

Take the L

"Beautifully vulnerable and epically cool, Eyal Cohen's brilliant *Take the L* pulls us along threads of understanding about men, women, love, and New York. Cohen's storytelling mixes in conversations with other authors, other literature, and the truths surrounding how love works, or doesn't, or might yet. Who knows, maybe we'll never look at the letter "L" the same way again without thinking of everything it could represent. We will pick up many books this year, and we may not finish all of them. But this one? Finish this one—and be all the better for it."

—Michele Parker Randall,
author of *Museum of Everyday Life* and *A Future Unmappable*

"A lively, frank and inventive rumination, experimental in the best sense. If you've ever wondered what goes on in the mind of an intelligent, sex-obsessed, bookish young man of today's generation who is trying to figure out the meaning of love, this is the ideal place to start."

—Philip Lopate, writer, essayist, film critic, poet,
author of *The Art of the Personal Essay*,
To Show and To Tell, and *The Contemporary American Essay*

"With remarkable wit and intensity, *Take the L* cracks open the soft center of the masculine soul. In this era of accelerated romantic connections and breakups, here is a story of how love can transform one's perception of the entire world. *Take the L* got under my skin and opened my mind. A wholly original and necessary read."

—Wendy Walters, Associate Professor at Columbia University,
author of *Multiply/Divide: On the American Real and Surreal*

"A whip-smart series of awkwardly hilarious, earnest and insightful essays about love, masculinity, youth, age, and the search for meaning, Eyal Cohen's *Take the L* strikes at the heart with a subtlety that's hard to pull off."

—Jinwoo Chong, author of *Flux* and *I Leave It Up to You*

"*Take the L* is a brave, bold, and immersive journey through masculinity, desire, loneliness, and need. Unafraid to play with difficult questions, and determined to expand the range of what men can write and talk about, Cohen's writing invites the reader into his heart and mind. In addition to exploring his own experiences with humor and humility, Cohen gives us a window into the current landscape of being a man with feelings in America today."

—Gila Ashtor, Columbia University, author of *Homo Psyche*

TAKE THE L

Take the

L

How Men Understand,
Withhold, and Express
Their Love

EYAL COHEN

SENTIENT PUBLICATIONS

First Sentient Publications edition 2025

A paperback original
Book design by Timm Bryson, em em design, LLC
Cover Design by Laura Waltje

Library of Congress Control Number: 2024949302

Publisher's Cataloging-in-Publication Data
Names: Cohen, Eyal, 1994-, author.
Title: Take the l : how men understand , withhold , and express their love / Eyal
    Cohen.
Description: First Sentient Publications Edition | Boulder, CO: Sentient
    Publications, 2025.
Identifiers: LCCN: 2024949302| ISBN: 978-1-59181-344-6 (print) |
    978-1-59181-345-3 (eBook)
Subjects: LCSH Love. | Man-woman relationships. | Men—Sexual behavior.
    | Men—Conduct of life. | Men—Mental health. | Masculinity—Social
    aspects. | Interpersonal communication in men. | Self help. | BISAC
    FAMILY & RELATIONSHIPS / Love & Romance | SOCIAL SCIENCE
    / Men's Studies | SELF-HELP / Personal Growth / General
Classification: LCC HQ1090 .C64 2025 | DDC 306.7—dc23

10 9 8 7 6 5 4 3 2 1

SENTIENT PUBLICATIONS
A Limited Liability Company
PO Box 1851
Boulder, CO 80306
www.sentientpublications.com

FOR DES & DAPHNE,

whose love could, can, and will never be surpassed

RECIPE

The person is real, and the feelings are real—
but you create the context. And context is everything.

—CHUCK KLOSTERMAN
Killing Yourself To Live, p.232

AN OFFERING

I don't recall braiding many challahs in my lifetime. Given the fact, though, that I grew up with guttural capabilities from day one and with no foreskin from day eight, I must've weaved at least a handful.

Most likely, I'd guess, as an Israeli kindergartner during some pre-Shabbat activity. Two decades later, when I was a teacher in a private, Jewish middle school in Orlando, the school hosted a Friday baking day event, but only the girls and their mothers participated. Had I not held great disdain for institutional religion beforehand (working there was merely a vocation, not a passion), that gender-non-inclusive event would've been the catalyst.

Boys (yours truly, at least) also love carbs. If you want us to be able to realize our feelings without having to rely on a woman, then from a young age, we need to knead. Maybe if boys (yours truly, at least) were encouraged to engage, try, and fail while growing up, then men could confidently pursue their loves today being able to say, *We've weaved.* As the old saying goes: 'Tis better to have weaved and lost than never to have weaved at all.

Given the scarce experience yours truly has, had I to weave a challah now, I'd probably keep it simple. Three strands. Each, though, constructed differently:

(1)

Improvised—as things unfold, in the present tense—out of whatever I have to work with.

(2)

Based on how I've seen people around me—friends, family—make one.

(3)

A more methodical approach—baking is a science, after all. I'd find some smart people, people who've not only written recipes, but described how each ingredient works, and follow their words. At least until I figure out what I want to say.

The point would be to see if I can slowly braid all three, weave them together till they're combined into one. Ideally, hopefully, by the end of the process I'd be left not only with something I love, but with a better understanding of what goes into it, and how it's made.

Step One

Assemble the Ingredients

(1)
L for Love

The first time I see L is when I bump into her on the west sidewalk of Broadway on April Fools' of 2021.

It isn't happenstance. We already went through the customary conversational rigmarole that comes along with matching on a dating app, then decided we'll meet tonight. But in what I will later learn to be very on-brand for who she is and how we'll entwine into each other's lives, everything is a bit helter-skelter.

The names of several bars in the six-block span that separates our apartments were thrown around, but we never quite set on one. With the scheduled meeting time just around the corner, I figured I'd leave my apartment and simply walk in her direction, assuming our paths would eventually cross, which they do.

(2)
Love on a Friends and Family Discount

There were ten of us at the dinner table: three married couples in their fifties, one couple in their mid-to-late twenties, a widow in her seventies, and yours truly. Behind us was the kids' table. Despite being the youngest of the adults, I had no interest in joining the *grape juice instead of wine* crew.

It was Rosh Hashanah in September 2021, which I flew down from New York to Florida for. I was there to celebrate with Dani, my best friend, who was one half of the couple in their twenties.

The evening's host was an eccentric man who, three minutes after our introduction, invited me into his bedroom and handed me an authentic ivory sculpture he got on a trip to West Africa. This man's morning routine, which he relayed to us in great detail over the course of the meal, includes reading the same two chapters of a book every single day. As the evening went on, between bites of challah and pomegranate seeds, Mr. 2-Chapters prompted each of the happy couples at the table to share the three things they love most about their partner.

(3)
All About all about love

If it didn't help me find a wife, I thought bell hooks's *all about love* would at least get me onto the @HotDudesReading Instagram page. I picked up the first book in hooks's acclaimed trilogy, *Love Song to the Nation*, while perusing my bookstore, buying it along with *Bad Feminist* by Roxane Gay and Paul Beatty's *The White Boy Shuffle*. The latter was the only one I intentionally sought out, since I was making my way through Beatty's brilliant banter. My eyes were drawn towards the other two books on the "Literary Favorites" table by their exteriors: *all about love*'s bright red surface, *Bad Feminist*'s glistening white cover adorned with a capped and bolded Times New Roman fuchsia font. Either, I thought, would be a good accessory to hold as someone snaps a candid image of me on the subway, helping me achieve my lifelong dream of becoming a Hot Dude Who Reads.

I decided, perhaps uncannily, to look at what's on the inside before fully committing. I randomly opened hooks's book to page 37, where at the top of the page my eyes landed on the words, "Males learn to lie as a way of obtaining power," and I could hear the cash register *cha-ching* itself.

(1)

I sent a snapchat to a few friends before I left my apartment tonight to meet L. Twenty-six may render me too old to use the app, but I can at least say I don't use, like, the dog ears filter. I just send funny shit to my friends.

When I walked out of my room earlier in my gray, woolen quarter-zip handed down to me by my roommate, I saw that he and his girlfriend were occupying the shower. I've lived with the couple for more than a year, so knew I wouldn't have access to the bathroom cabinet anytime soon. I had yet to apply deodorant or cologne, and with the meeting time promptly approaching, I was faced with a decision. The mirror selfie I sent my friends posed the question of whether I should arrive at the date late or unscented. Two friends replied immediately with a closeup of their face offering opposing answers. I screenshot both snaps and sent the conflicting suggestions to a group chat of the three of us.

Being raised in a household that dearly valued punctuality, particularly when making a first impression, and since I had showered before getting dressed anyway, I grabbed my leather jacket and left my apartment sans Old Spice or my 2014 Black Shot Pull&Bear cologne.

Walking down Broadway, phone in my pocket on Do Not Disturb, I wasn't aware my two friends had started a debate about their conflicting priorities. Later tonight, when I'll stand in L's room as she'll go to get us cups of water, I'll check my phone and see that my friends' conversation quickly transitioned into the pair of them calculating, through a comparative analysis of their impression of me, the probability of me getting laid tonight.

(2)

Mr. 2-Chapters, an aura of effortful nonchalance around him at the head of the table, spent parts of the evening auctioning off his beloved mother: an eccentric woman in her own right who had been widowed two decades prior. Being the only other single adult at the table, I found myself spewing an array of lighthearted and amicable responses about my open-minded but strict parenting ideals to the host's repeated inquiries as to whether I'm interested in being his daddy.

His mom pleaded he shush, despite that she undoubtedly enjoyed the attention. She, in turn, revealed some of what dating in your seventies looks like. My personal favorite anecdote was about when her elderly date claimed he wanted to better understand what she was saying and suggested they go back to his place so he could grab his hearing aid. Had that magnificent line worked, and that hard-of-hearing hombre been her +1 for dinner, I'm certain one of the triad of things she'd have said she loves about him— alongside his undeniable and impressive smoothness—would have been how good a listener he is.

Alas, it didn't work, and thus I was left rejecting uncomfortable offers to be a fifty-year-old's daddy as I sat cross-legged, observing, listening to people proclaim their love, silently sipping on a bottle of Heineken that was perspiring, allegedly, at a similar rate as the men at the table.

The host informed Dani and his girl that they would commence the love-professing round, then repeated the same joke—*Better start thinking!*—approximately fifteen times to the middle-aged husbands at the table, as if their ability to appreciate and articulate their love waned away along with their hairline and good posture.

On the one hand, sure. Of all the demographics, heterosexual businessmen who were born in the 1970s could be perceived as most inept when it comes to eloquently expressing their love. Especially in front of an audience. Then again, Jerry Maguire, a slick sports agent, told Dorothy she completes him in front of her Divorced Women's Club. Harry Burns, a political consultant, told Sally in the middle of a New Year's Eve party that he loves that she gets cold when it's 71 degrees out. Admittedly, it was Nora Ephron, a woman, who wrote Harry's confession for him, but then we could also say it was Richard Curtis, a man born in the 1950s, who was responsible for Anna Scott proclaiming she's also just a girl, standing in front of a boy, asking him to love her. I guess, though, none of these proclamations of true amour came after two decades worth of marriage. Or at a Rosh Hashanah dinner table. Anyway, Mr. 2-Chapters endeavored to milk every last drop of the already barren comedy cow that is *Men don't know how to express their feelings.*

There's a section in bell hooks's *all about love* where she discusses the need for open and honest communication between two deeply loving grown folk, the kind rarely seen on television or at the movies. Apparently, hooks was not an avid fan of corny, cliché, Caucasian romcoms. Or she knew better than to try to comprehend how men love by idealistically drawing onto real life from a scripted feel-good fable. She asks, "How can any of us communicate with men who have been told all their lives that they should not express what they feel?" But surely even the most narrow-minded and stereotypically macho men can come up with three nice things to say about the person they chose to share a life with, which, in fairness, all the men at the dinner party did eventually do.

The ensuing minutes after Mr. 2-Chapters's "three things" prompt proved to be rather awkward, as he aggressively put each couple on the spot. Dani and his girlfriend did well, considering the circumstances, appreciating each other's kindness and humor, along with the trust they gain and give one another. I don't quite recall what the other couples said, though I remember with imperial confidence that no answer was anywhere near romcom ending-scene worthy. While part of my feigning interest in the answers derived from their banality, my mind mostly drifted elsewhere because I was thinking about what my answers would have been if the person

I wished was there sat next to me. The one whom, now, I cannot envision ever struggling to croon over, nor express my feelings towards, the only toil being trying to decide which of her countless idiosyncrasies to leave out of the top three.

If she were there doing what the bottle of Heineken was: resting in my hand, appeasing my mind.

(3)

I first encountered bell hooks about six years ago. It was in undergrad, when I cited her work for a rhetorical analysis of Frederick Douglass's speech, "What to the Slave Is the Fourth of July?" My initial artifact proposal for the assignment was Al Pacino's iconic pregame speech in *Any Given Sunday*, which was rejected by my professor—a wonderfully intelligent and sarcastic white-haired man who would twiddle drumsticks between his fingers as we'd chat in his magnificently dusty and cluttered office—with a gentle scribble on a note that read, *Try again*, implying he, much like Pacino's players, wouldn't budge a single inch.

I returned to my college dorm, googled "famous speeches," figured everyone else in class would be talking about MLK's dream, and landed on Douglass's address, which in turn led me to hooks. Citing her in my first draft, I capitalized her name. I didn't have the faintest idea who she was, nor that the option to not capitalize your name even exists, so assumed whichever scholarly database I retrieved the information from must've made a mistake. My professor handed back my draft with lowercase "b" and "h" in red pen over the name I typed, which baffled me, but given my trust in that man, I uncapitalized her name for my final submission. In *all about love*, hooks says that "trust is the heartbeat of genuine love," so, Dr. McFarland, wherever you may be, know that I genuinely love you.

As my academic stint ended, hooks and I went our separate ways, and my interests mostly entailed sports and alcohol and the relentless pursuit of getting laid (guys who want to license this phrase as a tentative memoir title, DM me). Those three endeavors monopolized the attention of my social circle, comprising mostly my college soccer teammates and our fellow kin, a circle in which the words *bell* or *hooks* didn't tend to appear. Except, of course, when her first name signified the arrival of a pizza at the door, or when her last name was used as a phrasal verb, paired with the directional adverb that's an all-time Pixar classic, *Up*, to describe a dude's successful night out. (*Hooks up*. Stay with me, please.)

The closest we ever came to literature and cultural analysis would be when joining cognitive forces to decipher messages from someone one of us was texting. If ever there was a group of people equipped to decrypt subliminal female words, comprehend a woman's intricacies and yearnings even better than she can understand herself, read between a lady's lines, it was us: a bunch of dudes who played fantasy football and considered the addition of Tabasco to a takeout burrito to be nothing short of a culinary tour de force.

(1)

My third date with L, on the first night we meet, is six blocks away from my apartment, back at her place. Our first, after bumping into each other on Broadway, was a drink at a bar/café in which we were the only customers and which, a few months from now, will go through a total renovation and rebranding. The second was at a cocktail bar that, despite being at full capacity, felt to me as if it, too, was occupied by two patrons and two patrons only, who shared overpriced drinks and a (highly recommended) salted pretzel with honey yogurt and feta.

I'm not big on sharing food. Certain social circumstances, though, require me feigning lightheartedness and amicability about meal sharing. The conditions under which I find it most acceptable to share food are when the quantity can be divided evenly between the number of sharers. There's no problem splitting eight slices of pizza between two people, but if there are three feasters, I'd argue the group must revert to fifth grade math class and find the least common multiple, which, in this hypothetical case, would mandate ordering three boxes of pizza. (Side note: given the abundance of branches twenty-four's factor tree has, three boxes would be suitable for groups of one, two, three, four, six, eight, twelve, and twenty-four people, rendering the order size to be, ironically, prime.) Even harder to adjudicate is the apportioning of non-sliceable food, but before I digress into the utter impossibility and insanity of attempting to allocate each member of the group an equal portion of the chicken tikka masala, lamb vindaloo, and rogan josh ordered, I'll return to the point.

The power dynamics associated with ensuring I get just as much as everyone else at the table, the fear of not being awarded my fair share, and the lack of control that stems from my fulfillment being dependent on the person sitting next to me at the table all occupy too large a section of my brain, and prove to be too much of a handful for me to feel appeased.

In a chapter about mutuality, bell hooks talks about how men's use of power dynamics in their relationships makes them feel "safer" as they operate within paradigms of one-up and one-down, in which the rules of the game are known. This sadomasochistic struggle for domination coupled with the fear of the unknown, she writes, is what stymies our ability to trust that mutual satisfaction and growth can be the primary foundation in a relationship. "The practice of love offers no place of safety," hooks claims, contending that to practice love we must risk loss, hurt, pain, and being acted upon by forces outside our control, which, I would argue, may include not having precisely fifty percent of the pretzel you choose to share with someone.

The question of what made me feel so comfortable with L from the very second I bumped into her on Broadway, when we both laughed at the impromptu yet planned moment before embracing each other for the first time, is a difficult one to pinpoint. It feels a bit like an algebra problem from a high school textbook: the book is giving me both the question and the answer, since the process of deciphering is the actual challenge.

Standing by the island in her kitchen, I feel like I'm still in the early pages of weaving my way through the how and what. But were I to flip to the solutions page, the answer, the manifestation of the sensation I felt with L, could be seen earlier this evening. It'd be the image of our drinks at the center of the table, her nonchalance in alternating which she sipped from, my sense of freedom in ripping off part of a pretzel, gripping and flailing it as I put the finishing touches on a long-winded joke, my blissful ignorance of her cutting off a pretzel piece for herself, tilting the plate to swipe the final bits of feta and yogurt, and how I could not care less what percentage of it I got. It was as if we'd been doing this for decades already. As if we were already fluent in each other's individual predilections and knew the boundaries—or lack thereof—of us as a duo.

It's easy to say this in hindsight, at the end of the evening, but I knew it even before we met, and I'll say this to L next week: I knew the date would go well. I knew there wouldn't be a single awkward silence. I knew whatever jokes I'd come up with would work. I knew I would want to see her again. So much is about to transpire, and me being a guy who had yet to have L in his life will become a distant, hazy memory, but the sensation of how confidently I felt about her and us before this date will remain so clear, lucid. There was a degree of casualness in the lead-up to our date—a perfectly timed and unscented one. Not in the sense that I didn't take it seriously, but that I knew it'd take no strenuous effort to be genuinely happy with the person I'm about to meet. All I'd have to do is be myself.

I was even more certain that regardless of how much of this person I'd get to learn about tonight, I'd end up craving more, which I do, now, at L's place, when we're about to cross into the second day of April together. Perhaps the date of the month has something to do with it, but the way everything feels so perfectly safe, riskless, and fulfilling makes me feel like the world is playing a prank on me.

(2)

Had she been next to me at the dinner party, though, and 2-Chapters had put us in the love-professing spotlight, I wouldn't have said what I truly felt. There's a certain inauthenticity in being forced to exhibit attentiveness, intimacy, and care within that public context. Especially when surrounded by people you don't know. Even the act of vow recitation at a wedding—a moment purposefully dedicated to attesting unadulterated love for another human being—doesn't feel wholly genuine to me when done in public. That's why, perhaps, I shouldn't criticize the couples for not conjuring up Nora Ephron-esque "watch and sob while eating ice cream" sentimental statements. Especially on the spot. It's not like any of them were able to sit down, take their time writing, and slowly build up towards articulating the three features that encompass their love for this person of theirs. Heck, given enough time, maybe they could have even ended up weaving the three things, like strands, into one intertwined confection.

Perhaps, too, I shouldn't be the one to dispute love's inevitable demise, being a 27-year-old with one committed relationship under his belt. A relationship with a girl I met in undergrad in Florida, which came to an abrupt ending just short of its twelve months mark (a date I know precisely thanks to a Wells Fargo statement for our first date at Chili's). Perhaps I shouldn't argue against the premise that young love's elation and immaculateness don't last, as the idea is often propagated that the magic eventually and inevitably fades. A Louis CK skit comes to mind (is he still canceled?), where he says love is worth doing since it's the best part of life, but you shouldn't be greedy and insane by expecting it to last: *It's like going to a horror movie, and in the first minute you're like, "I think they're all gonna be fine." No, they're all gonna die, and you're gonna hate the person you love right now... Love + time − distance = hate.*

(3)

The boys and I relied on each other to ascertain what ladies lust for or what dudettes desire because we weren't mind readers, like Mel Gibson in *What Women Want*. I remember watching the movie as a prepubescent boy, long before I grew an affinity for alliterations and Mel Gibson began verbalizing his antisemitism. I found Gibson's character's newfound ability to read women's minds to be an absolute gold mine. Since my baritone had yet to materialize and my balls had yet to drop, my infatuation with his telepathic skills had less to do with using the ability to trick women into bed, and more with money-making schemes (a Jewish instinct, Gibson would call this).

Gibson's love interest in the movie was played by Helen Hunt, who ironically was the catalyst for my eventual sexual awakening. Hunt's wet T-shirt scene in *As Good as It Gets*, which I watched while sharing a couch with my grandparents, set in motion a lifetime of concealing erections and suppressing the urge to proclaim, while seeing any shade of an areola, *Oh my fucking god it's a tit*.

Throughout puberty, the boys and I explored and conceptualized the chaotic, carnal carnival of the world as a group. Years before we began collaborating to analyze the prospect of obtaining sexual gratification from someone else, we joined forces to learn how to satisfy ourselves. When one boy discovered hand lotion, we all reduced friction. When one guy had a wet dream, we all needed a new pair of underwear. When one of us figured out how to set the internet browser on the family computer to incognito mode, we all unlocked a universe of X-rated possibilities. As the old saying goes: Give a boy a tissue and you clean him for a day; teach him how to use a gym sock and you crust him for a lifetime.

My dad tried, around those days, to talk to me about hair popping up in new places or new sensations my body may be encountering, but I abruptly blocked each of his attempts. I never felt comfortable learning about the world of salacity from an adult authority; I much preferred exploring it in parallel with my peers.

In *The Right to Sex*, Amia Srinivasan writes, "While almost all of us today live in a world where porn is ubiquitous," myself and the generation I am a part of is "the first to have come of age sexually in that world." There was a sense of security—I felt, at least—around my conversations with my friends, enabling us to openly talk about what our bodies and minds were going through—to come of age together as if we were some organically organized orgasming organism. In *all about love*, hooks writes, "There is no better place to learn the art of loving than in community," and the double entendre of the term "art of loving," in the case of a community of horny young boys taking their first sexual steps, could not be more apt.

This salacious education within male socialization is the foundation for the conflation of sex and love. "The vast majority of males in our society are convinced that their erotic longing indicates who they should, and can, love," hooks tells us. To be fair, she has a point. I know I love Liverpool Football Club because every time I watch them run onto the pitch in their red jerseys, my testicles tingle.

The pitfall, though, is that the confusion of sexual attraction and romantic connection leads men to commit to relationships in which all they find is physical gratification. Subsequently, they venture out to seek emotional affirmation and cheap dopamine outside their romantic relationship. Most stereotypically, perhaps, in golfing, fishing, a really well-mowed lawn, or their fantasy quarterback having a three-touchdown game. Or, I guess, someone thirty years their junior.

When it comes to sex, men are conditioned to believe there's a certain power dynamic that commodifies it. Renowned American writer and activist Rebecca Solnit says, "Accumulation of this commodity enhances a man's status, and every man has a right to accumulation, but women are in some mysterious way obstacles to this, and they are therefore the *enemy* as well as the *commodity*" (emphasis my own). Both Solnit and

Amia Srinivasan speak to the way this "gendered socialization" regarding sex is ingrained into facets of westernized and capitalistic societies, and whose casualty is primarily women.

Self-asserted masculine studies scholar Eyal Cohen builds on these notions in his work, arguing that "Guys use sex as a social- and self-barometer of masculinity, so given the value attributed to 'being a man,' this creates a flawed method of gauging self-worth." Moreover, Cohen contends, "the detrimental byproduct that arises from the conflation of sex and love is that the power dynamics men grow up wrongly attributing to sex are then applied to their romantic endeavors."

Cohen, who happens to be me, combines Solnit's claim about the monetization of sex as a form of social capital in early male socialization with hooks's claim about the confusion of attraction and affection, contending that this all leads to guys' commodification of love. This commodification and the ensuing dynamics don't manifest themselves only across genders (in cis straight relationships), but also between guys as another barometer of masculinity. Romantic love becomes something to be obtained and owned. As the process of maturation takes place, the possession of love—much like indulgence in sexual activity did in earlier days—becomes the stepping stone that enables guys to climb the social totem pole, and boys to become men.

(1)

Far before sex becomes a threshold (be it for masculinity or within a relationship), a simple kiss is one. We've all, I'm sure, at some point, encountered that hesitancy of *should I kiss them or not*. I've certainly found myself in such moments while walking someone home, standing a half-lean away from them outside their building, or sitting alongside them with our bodies parallel but our necks straining to face each other. In those moments, the festering, cyclical thoughts about what will transpire next preoccupy my brain to the point where I feel dissociated and absent from the here and now.

At the end of this first night, when I sit at the foot of L's bed having just spent close to half an hour at a kitchen island seamlessly chatting with her roommate as if we'd long been acquainted, nothing feels uncertain. It's inevitable that we'll kiss. It's a concoction of affirmation, appeasement, serenity, and eagerness. It's exactly where I'm supposed to be and who I'm supposed to be with, and despite knowing how perfect the next moment will be, I'm in no rush to leave the here and now—when she's already fluent in my sarcasm and I'm already fluent in her smile. Regardless of how highly valued a commodity physical contact may be, being an arm's length from her, in a room dimly lit by streetlights peering through curtains, our smirks indicating we're sharing a wavelength, is equally as immaculate, satisfying.

It's as if there's a bottomless well of words and jokes next to me at the edge of this bed, and I can subsist on them, and with her, for the rest of my days. It's both a power trip and a fall into submission. Total control and absolute fragility. It's like being both a resistible force and a movable object: a cat and a mouse, the pretzel and the feta. Whatever cliché you want to use. I could never speak for her, but I can only hope L feels the same way.

Eventually, of course, we meet in the short distance between us. She slowly raises both arms, wraps her hands around the back of my neck, chuckles in the darkness, edges towards me, nods her head, and softly mouths, *Come here.* As I mirror her movement, as I string my arms around her waist, as the minuscule space still between us evaporates completely, as the world in which we don't know what each other tastes like ceases to exist, as our bodies so seamlessly entwine into each other, my beaming smile disappears, for my lips have a new occupation.

(2)

After years of fishing onions out of my Bolognese, stacking up greens on the side of the plate, and feeling self-conscious when dinner party hosts would go out of their way to find something I could eat, I stopped being an absurdly picky eater. For close to two decades my family tried to broaden my palate, claiming I'd like one food or the other if I just gave it a chance. They suggested I simply take a page out of Nike's hyperbolic and reductive slogan, as if any task can be accomplished by just doing it. Oh, you want to climb Mount Everest? Just Do It. You want to condense atmospheric moisture at a greater rate than that at which it evaporates? Just Dew It. You want to figure out how you and the rest of the male species understand, withhold, and express their love? Just read bell hooks and pretend you have any idea what the fuck you're talking about.

I eventually grew out of the picky eating habit, but only after leaving home and doing so on my own terms. A part of my reluctance to yield, as a teen, came down to my unwillingness to change in front of people who know me. That would have indicated an admission that they were right all along, which, by virtue of, would have meant I was wrong.

On a recent visit home-home (one "home" signifies where one currently lives, two stand for the place where one grew up and molded the childhood trauma they carry into adulthood), I saw old friends, all of whom are in long-term, committed relationships. While they enjoyed scrolling through my dating app profile, scouring and scouting what's out there, they all asked some form of a *Why don't you settle down?* question. I looked at my friends, the brothers I grew up in parallel with, whom I went through every step of life with, and stared with adulation at their unadulterated, adulthood joy. Not in possession of love but possessed by it. Enamored and settled and living in communion with their person in homes where they own kitchen tables. Tables which they never sit at the corner of. Tables where they never need to let their mind drift to envision their co-owner, because they're right there next to them: ever-present, ever-available to be crooned over, hear the three things they love most about them, no prompting needed, should my friends wish to do, which I hope they do, both now and in the future, when they'll have two decades worth of marriage under their belt.

I didn't argue against my friends' line of questioning. They merely wanted—presumably still want—me to find my seat at the grownup table. My single lifestyle, at the ripe age of 26, apparently already considered by some to be immature, as overused as a Hollywood trope.

The previously referenced Mel Gibson in *What Women Want* (whom I promise I have no particular affection for, and, frankly, prefer his role as the butt of Ricky Gervais's jokes over any of his movie parts) plays on the trope of the unabashed bachelor finally growing up. The stud who goes through life seducing women, spending his life between one nightstand and another, till he matures and realizes it's actually love, not sex, that should be his goal and purpose, his path to true happiness. Ryan Gosling in *Crazy, Stupid, Love*, Jason Sudeikis in *Sleeping with Other People*, and Owen Wilson and Vince Vaughn in *Wedding Crashers* (best post-2000 rom-com out there, non-debatable) all spring to mind as other examples of men who arrive at this realization, which, ubiquitously, is prompted by the meeting of *the* woman.

And it's important, I'd argue, with my shaky understanding of how grammar and language work, that the article is "the" and not "a." Their eyes are opened by the one, specific woman who enables them to see what they really want. The happy endings for all these men, all these movies, come after the man decides, or, rather, it is decided for him, to stop chasing happy endings in the proverbial sense of the word.

(3)

Sex dominates numerous discourses, perhaps none more than that of
young men. That's probably why I've talked and written about sex at great
length. Jokes, mainly. The topic still carries some taboo, and the naturally infused tension around it makes it perfect for comedy (this is Jimmy
Carr's claim, not mine). I once spent 5,000 words of an essay analogizing
an orgasm to a punch line for the numerous parallels they share: performance, elation, timing, set up/foreplay, hitting the spot, etc.

The word "essay," as its French origin suggests, means "to try." What
I was trying to do with those 5,000 words was use humor as a form of
critical thought to understand what sex is in my mind, since no matter
how comfortable I may seem writing and joking about sex, I feel anxiety
around the actual act. Most likely that's the real reason I write about sex
so much, and that humor I just confidently defined as "critical thought"
is, in fact, a smokescreen. Or a defense mechanism. Or a spoonful of
sugar that helps the medicine—or man—go down. Or all of the above. I
walked away from that essay with two takeaways.

The first was about the gap between the act of sex (or absence of it)
and the manipulation of its discourse. Once, as a group of my college
friends was sitting in a testosterone-scented room, exchanging sexual
bragging stories, one friend whose inexperience must've weighed heavy
on him, shared a story about a girl giving him head eight times in one
night. Eight times. In one night. Jaw-dropping.

His story was clearly fabricated. Without trying to psychoanalyze him,
I'm sure it stemmed from feeling the need to make his voice heard, lest
anyone think he doesn't have the adequate sexual experience to partake
in a conversation reserved only for Men. By "Men," I, of course, mean:
Men. Cis males. Wearing a shirt with cut off sleeves and telling you to
straighten your back at the gym. Chewing on a toothpick. Checking a
fantasy football line-up during dinner. Profile picture hoisting up a fish.
Drinking a Miller Lite at the table instead of getting up to dance at a

wedding. "I have a sister so I'm a feminist." "Guys grow up playing more sports, which improves our hand-eye coordination, which is why we're better drivers." "I'm not trying to explain it to you, but." "I thought we were just having fun lol." You know, Men.

The act of sex is commonly confined to a bedroom to which only two people are privy, but the narrative outside the room isn't always just theirs. In the wrong hands, the narrative turns dangerous, in the form of slut- and virgin-shaming, as both labels impact the societal perception and evaluation of people—particularly teens and young adults—according to what they're alleged to have done or not done in the bedroom. Simultaneously, the fear of being branded with either label pressurizes people to take actions detrimental to themselves or others. Specifically, because there's a gap between the physical performance (or lack thereof) in the bedroom and a testosterone-scented room, and due to sex's functionality as a barometer within male social groups (not only but predominantly), men have space to create whichever façade they feel best boasts their "manliness," regardless of the casualties they accumulate along the way. Not to mention, of course, the indisputable fact that men have long acted on their privilege and power in ways that are emotionally, mentally, and physically harming.

Maybe had the gap between the act and the discourse not existed, and that which transpires in the bedroom been constantly displayed for all to see, sex wouldn't be that big a deal. But we don't talk about it in that open, honest way, so the gap does exist. Within it, pressure percolates at a rate vigorous enough to prompt a guy to fabricate a story about a time when he got head eight times in one night, bro.

Maybe we don't have to share any and everything we do in the bedroom, but maybe we—experienced and inexperienced alike—need to be a bit braver and broaden the spectrum of what's *allowed* to be shared. Have the courage to speak and the courage to listen. Maybe we need to use the comfort of the testosterone-scented room, the sense of security we have with each other, to cultivate healthy conversations and foster communal growth, especially when sometimes that room is the best we got. Those guys we conceptualize the world of salacity with should be the same ones we understand compassion alongside, yet unfortunately, these rooms sometimes teach us the exact opposite. The narrative can change only from the inside, so maybe it's about figuring out how to normalize vulnerability and openness there. Maybe, I'll naively say, despite what we've been doing since a young age, it's time we turn off incognito mode.

The second takeaway from the essay I wrote was about the vulnerability required inside the bedroom. It's not only the exposure of parts of our body we've been historically taught to conceal, but—and I am obviously talking about a healthy sexual relationship—the relinquishing of control over your own body. Allowing someone else to have access to the way your body feels and allowing your body to freely respond to what they do, takes, well, real balls. Sex could be daunting for anyone, I'm sure, but I can only speak for guys who've felt the pressure of not having had sex yet, or those who are familiar with going through prolonged periods of time without intercourse. There's an added pressure of inadequately performing, or lasting, in the bedroom, which stems from the inverse correlation of time between not having sex and having sex. No matter how hard you think about your grandmother or Thanksgiving dinner or the electoral college, there's an inevitability to the outcome's rapid approach, at times even before skin-on-skin contact ensues. And in the back of our minds, on top of disappointing the person we're with, there's the fear of other people finding out, and the inevitable ensuing mockery for prematurely arriving.

Now, listen. I'm not here to tell you it's fun to cum in your pants. To any inexperienced young dude reading this, if, when you finally get your shot with a member of your desired sex, you proceed to use your underwear as a canvas for a semen-based Jackson Pollock imitation, know that it's not that big a deal. As you miserably try to prolong the imminent, thinking about child hunger or SAT essay prompts, I hope you think of me, too. Maybe not me. That sounds weird. Scratch that last one off the tape. But in case you do find yourself stained and embarrassed and thinking you've reached a low point, I hope you recall these words and know while it may be a low point, it is, much like you, a rapidly fleeting one. Plus, even during the worst possible cum-in-pants scenario, you still get to orgasm, and that's, like, a pretty decent solace. More importantly, though, if you did things the right way and are with the right person at the right time, and you're simply a victim of your own biological lack of stamina, then just know that it's fine. Be honest, be upfront, and never ever forget the value of putting your finger on the problem. Preferably in circular motions.

The importance of normalizing vulnerability and authenticity within the rooms we grow up in can also be applied to the vulnerability associated with losing control of your own body inside the bedroom. I'll speak for myself, at least, when saying there's intimidation in this loss of control, one that has often prompted me to perform in bed. I don't mean "perform" as in put on a show, but I also do, in that an ideal show is one where both people arrive at the punch line without the need for any mansplaining.

What I don't mean is pretending to be someone else out of fear of being myself. "Sometimes we worry so much about what frightens us," Lisa Taddeo writes in the prologue for her book *Three Women*, which brilliantly explores concepts of sexuality and desire, "that we wait to have an orgasm until we are alone." The book talks about the desires of women specifically, but the line stuck with me.

Not to be too presumptuous, but I know that it's much easier for me, as a man, to orgasm than it is for many women. I'm not here to complain. I have eternal gratitude towards any woman, Steven Gerrard goal, or Chipotle bowl that has led me to climax, but even when I do, I struggle with the act of letting myself go—allowing my body to just perform as it wants to, move in ways I feel like moving, and externalize the sounds I'm prompted to emit.

In *The Right to Sex*, Amia Srinivasan talks about societal perceptions created by pornography. For straight boys and girls, there's been put "a script in place that dictated not only the physical moves and gestures and sounds to make and demand, but also the appropriate affect, the appropriate desires, the appropriate distribution of power." That's probably true, but for me, it's a slightly different form of pressure. It's a feeling more akin to a Freud quote Lisa Taddeo uses in *Three Women*: "The behavior of a human being in sexual matters is often a prototype for the whole of his other modes of reaction in life." Sigmund gets me.

It can be a beautiful thing, sex, but only when it's mutually honest. And honesty, for me, requires a level of comfort built on trust, over time. Honesty, for me, has been sparingly offered to others over the course of my life. The fact that even after twenty-seven years I still struggle to expose honest facets of myself to myself, let alone to others, probably explains why I feel anxiety about the exposure that healthy and happy sex mandates, which, come to think about it, sort of makes sex synonymous with love.

(1) (2) (3)

L and I don't have sex on this first night, which I'm glad about. But I am staying over. *There's no pressure or anything,* L says to me as we prepare for bed, *but you can take your jeans off if you want.* I don't do so immediately, partly because I don't want to seem too eager to do so, and partly because I don't want L to think I'm only doing so because she surfaced the idea.

We chat for a little while longer, and when all that's left to do is sleep, I awkwardly blurt out, *I'm gonna take my jeans off now,* and we both do some version of a chuckle. I wiggle out of the denim and I think everyone involved is relieved when I toss my pants aside and the AirPods case in my pocket makes a thud against the hardwood floor.

I turn towards L, in bed, and see her face barely illuminated by the streetlights peering in through the curtains, just like, I assume, my face is. My right arm wiggles into the crevice between her neck and the pillow, her nose an inch away from mine, and as I wrap my bare left leg around her right one, I bend my knee backwards so my ankle hooks her leg to nestle in between my two legs. My thigh gets to feel the warmth of hers, and we fall asleep like this, weaved together like a two-braided challah.

The next morning, L heads to roast coffee beans in the kitchen, and my friend asks me to spill some in the three-man group chat from the previous night. I reply that there are no beans to spill and follow it up with a text that will end up being the final one I ever send in this conversation, which reads: *She's the one, boys.*

Step Two

Mix Ingredients Up

(3)

It's been more than two decades since hooks asserted, "As it stands, men tend to be more concerned about sexual performance and sexual satisfaction than whether they are capable of giving and receiving love." To an extent, of course, that still rings true. Plenty of guys still commodify sex and consider it the be-all and end-all of their life. But the "Greed" chapter in hooks's book is dedicated towards this idea of love being something one craves as a product, an emblem of the capitalistic society we live in, which deems love to be the *correct* goal men should aspire to. Drawing on this, and to paraphrase the aforementioned notions of Eyal Cohen, what becomes the social- and self-barometer of masculinity is love. Or, at least, the performance of it. That leads me to ask, *where does the difference lie between the peer pressure inducing guys to have sex, and the one imposed on us to find love?*

But that's a counterproductive question for me to ask. Smothered in deflection as a defense mechanism, emblematic of males' redirection of a conversation when it tries to push us out of our comfort zone. The real question I want to grapple with is how do I, self-asserted masculine scholar that I am, understand, withhold, and express love. So I won't shout into the abyss about how hard men have it, nor will I allow the pent-up testosteroned teen in me to expostulate at you to just leave me alone, dude, because, man, I don't have to love if I don't fucking want to, bro.

Instead, I'll stay focused on love—the one, specific kind of it.

(1)

The ensuing days, after our first night together, are some of the most emotionally intense of my life. Without trying—or being able—to tell L's side of the story, I'm quite certain she feels the same way. We see each other the next day, and the one after, then repeatedly as the second month of spring stretches out.

We go out to eat at this American bar/restaurant underneath my apartment. I'm not sure how, but I somehow misread the menu and think that a beer costs twenty-odd dollars. We order food—her a vegan burger and me a blackened Cajun one—then I walk upstairs and grab two beers from my fridge. We slyly sip on them on the outside deck as she hands me a bite of her fake patty and, despite an obvious yearn in her vegetarian eyes, she declines a bite of my real one. The shift manager eventually walks up to our table and confronts our cheapskate asses, reminding us that it's against NYC law to bring alcohol into an establishment or something like that. We apologize and feel justifiably embarrassed and guilty, while at the same time giddy by this conjoined culpability.

The bond, for me, feels rapid and intense. We fly past mundane small talk and almost instantly stretch a canvas to paint for each other who we were until our paths crossed. As we do so, her paintbrush begins to stroke my part of the fabric, permanently leaving her mark on who I am. With every failed attempt at making chai, with every empanada she picks up for us and we leave cold on a plate on the island because we stay warm in each other's arms in her bed, with every pill she hands me when I get sick, and every time I place the toothbrush she gave me on top of her bathroom cabinet, I feel our paint strokes edging towards each other, the artwork fusing into one.

One lazy morning, I linger in her bed while she's on a work call in the kitchen. I have no deadlines hanging over my head, nowhere to be, not a care in the world. Late spring rays of sun glare through the window, along with a light breeze and the customary honking Broadway tends to emit.

The noise, though, is deemed inconsequential in my too-blissful-to-give-a-damn condition. The color on the walls—apt for a millennial girl in the big city—is some version of cream. The duvet, desk, wardrobe, dresser—much like her—are all bright. Trust me when I tell you I wish there was another way for me to describe this, but the scene feels as picturesque and heavenly as picturesque and heavenly get.

I shuffle from under the duvet and make my way to the foot of the bed where her bookshelf stands. I assume that eventually, whenever L is done with her call, she'll open the door and peer at this person who's occupying her space, who's on the edge of his seat waiting for two things: hallway footsteps followed by the creak of a door.

I don't want to be on my phone when she walks in. I want to impress her at every turn and opportunity. The clothes I wear, the conversation topics I choose, the food I order. I don't want her to walk in and see me aimlessly scrolling through one social media or another, so figure I'll nibble on a book instead. The prospect of being some man of literature, a hot dude who reads, along with the insight into her personhood a peek at her bookshelf will provide, entice me.

There was a moment, I don't remember when it was exactly, could have been a different lazy morning or at the end of a drunken evening, but we wound up talking about one of the books on her desk, *The Secret Lives of Church Ladies* by Deesha Philyaw. I hadn't read it, but in perfect timing it had come up in a conversation I had with a professor a day or two prior. The professor told me some fact about the short story collection, which I then regurgitated to L (with credit to the professor, don't worry). Being this man of insight, this man who can read and debate the same books she does, who can enlighten her about something she and I share an interest in, felt like it was my calling. Perhaps my memory is tricking me as I write these words, perhaps I'm staring back at our moments together with glasses too rosy, but when I told L that Philyaw's book getting nationwide recognition despite being picked up by a (relatively) small publisher like West Virginia University Press was an emblem that commercial success doesn't hinge on being signed by one of the "Big Five" publishers, she gave me this look that affirmed me in a very specific way. It was as if I were able to not only impress her, but nestle myself slightly more into her life, expand the role I'm lucky enough to be awarded by her, and develop and grow parts of me I wanted to become.

On this lazy morning, at the foot of her bed, I pick out Haruki Murakami's *Men Without Women*, partially because I've never read his work but mainly because the short story collection has a pink and yellow glossy cover. I rest horizontally in the middle of the bed, open the book at random, and land on "An Independent Organ." I get through about eleven pages of the story of Dr. Tokai, a 52-year-old plastic surgeon and life-long ladies' man. I enjoy the pages I read. I get the Murakami hype. When hallway footsteps followed by the creak of a door interrupt me, in the best way possible, I make a mental note of where I pause and set L's copy of the book aside, unaware I'll never pick it back up.

The look on her face when she opens the door and sees me reading her book tattoos itself on my mind. I'll never forget how she drops her head and releases an almost embarrassed chuckle into the palm nestled into the oversized sleeve of her sweatshirt. This moment, just like all the others we're sharing in these early days, is unexpected, incomprehensible, and rapturous, to the point where her only possible reaction to seeing this bearded man lying horizontally in her bed, occupying her space, reading her book, is to laugh. I somehow manage to contain my giddiness at how well my plan worked, at the person I'm becoming under L's influence, then signal a silent invite with my eyes, which she duly, blissfully accepts. The palm in her sleeve is free to land on my chest, as her face finds a new spot to nestle into.

(2)

I got into an argument with a friend, once, about the merit that the song "I Don't Want to Miss a Thing" deserves. She wasn't a friend yet, actually. It was the night we met at a grad school orientation event. It was before the two of us and a handful of others began meeting on a weekly basis to drink crucial alcohol and answer trivial questions. This argument was before I found out whiskey sours were her go-to, that we watched the same British panel shows, and that she knew a disturbing amount about 1980s music. These facets of her that I gratefully and fortunately got to learn about all took shape over the course of our friendship.

Our argument about Aerosmith's greatest hit (apologies to any "Dream On" fans) was before our group's disdain for Paul the Trivia Guy's niche questions grew so vigorous that we began hosting our own trivia nights. Before we spent days building IKEA furniture and evenings making pot-stickers. Before we met at an apartment where we had gin and tonics to pregame a school reading event I did, after which my kind friend told me, and I quote, that it was *So good*, despite my inclination that it wasn't. Long before I found out that I can construct a FRIHETEN any day of the week, but ask me to seal a dumpling and watch the filling spill onto the boiling pan. Long before I realized that these facets of my self, developed alongside others, have become inextricable from them; attached to them not like a dumpling, through a light coat of water over half the dough, but with an Allen key Tightened for good.

The grad school program we were in, my Aerosmith-hating friend and I, was a Writing MFA. When I submitted my application, I had to indicate whether I was interested in joining the fiction or nonfiction program (poetry was an option too but let's not kid ourselves). I had to google both terms because I didn't know the difference. Like, yeah, fiction is fiction, but nonfiction has the word *fiction* in it, and that just felt counter-intuitive. They could've called it something that makes more sense, like real-tion or fact-tion or do-this-instead-of-going-to-therapy-tion.

In the first week of the program, I had to break social ice during my campus tour and my orientation and my workshop and my seminar and my other seminar. The answer to all the introductory prompts and questions seemed to be some type of book—your favorite, last one you read, one that challenges the way you view the world, etc. Given that I read one book in the ten years that preceded that week, I used it to pick at the ice on every occasion, each time from a different angle. I hoped that there was no overlap of characters between my tour and my classes, and that if there was, people wouldn't notice I'd been contorting the same John Irving novel for days.

That same week, I sat with a couple of fellow new students who were sharing a joint—which I was offered but graciously declined—on our campus's lawn when one of them mocked a guy in our program who didn't know who a member of faculty was. *Forget that,* I could have told them, *I heard there's a guy here who doesn't even know the difference between fiction and nonfiction.*

Or I could have told them that I, too, had no idea who the fuck Paul Beatty is but I could recite Liverpool's starting lineup from the 2005 Champions League final in my sleep, and who's to say which of those two is a more valuable piece of information. I didn't say that. I acted bemused and feigned contempt and raised my eyebrows in dismay while, on the inside, feeling like The Sellout.

My solace, in those early and ignorant days, was a newly formed group of friends, writers—who I didn't think of as such—with whom I spent time contemplating trivial questions, playfully treating silly arguments as if they're the last battle between good and evil before the Day of Judgement.

Have you even fucking seen Armageddon? I asked my friend on that first night. We'd scraped just enough cash between us to share one food truck Philly cheesesteak on a concrete bench at 4 a.m.. I hoped that the reminder of how Bruce Willis took Ben Affleck's spot on that asteroid would conjure some sentimentality from her towards the song.

Look, I get it, she said, *really. It's a good song. But also, it's not that good.* We agreed to disagree, finished our drunken sub, drunken subway'd back to our respective NYC apartments, and put the argument to bed.

Months later, I googled "Top love songs of all time" for some awful joke I was trying to make. When I found a classic Steven Tyler power ballad ranked #1 on a list, the argument resurfaced. After months filled with trivia and dumplings and whiskey sours, I sent the list to my friend, and she laughed. She said she'd thought about the argument a lot, and believed she was being unnecessarily judgmental to the many people who just want to jam out to a lovely message. *YOU taught me that,* she texted back, before joking she now listens to the song three times a day as a reminder of her hubris.

She changed her mind. That's natural. Everyone does that. I guess, though, maybe because of where I came from, or maybe because of where I went to, or maybe both, or, maybe, neither of those and, actually, because of *who* I left and *who* I was now around, I felt like I was relearning that our opinions change because we change.

After inhaling the toxins from a proverbial and literal locker room for so many years, the dissonance that came from landing in rooms that debated literature and declared pronouns and respected opposing opinions felt, in a way, jarring. So, when my friend changed her mind, when she admitted—albeit about the most trivial of matters—that she was wrong and I was right, she was exemplifying the most basic form of vulnerability and friendship, one I was, perhaps, conditioned to see being countered through microaggressions that steadily expand. SHE taught me that.

After officially putting a bow on our argument, and having told my friend that I looked up that list for a silly joke I was trying to make in a silly essay I was trying to write, she asked whether I would send it to her, which I said I would, of course, if she shared some of her writing in return. At the time, I was working through an alleged "essay collection about toxic masculinity" while she was trying at a novel about a group of girls living in a psychiatric hospital. Both of us, when sending the email that included our creative endeavors in deciphering our genders' psyche, jokingly referenced that Aerosmith song in the subject line.

Our opinions change because we change. I knew that even before this lesson, but it also felt as if something opaque had instantly become so clearly clear. Life is about picking the people we want to see grow and change—those who make room instead of limit space, those with whom arguments can turn humorous—and embrace every facet of themselves they choose to share, trusting that they'll do the same for us.

(3)

There's nothing revelatory or unique about arguing that "masculine" and "emotional" are, stereotypically, antithetical adjectives. Back in 1951, philosopher Theodor Adorno, in his book, *Minima Moralia*, distinguished between the "tough guys" and the "intellectuals" in Oxford. The latter, he claimed, "are equated almost without further ado to those who are effeminate." I'll expand upon Teddy's claim by saying that if intellect is considered feminine, then emotional vulnerability is as far away from masculinity as a floating asteroid is from earth. "In the end," Teddy adds, "the 'tough guys' are the ones who are really effeminate, who require the weaklings as their victims, in order not to admit that they are like them."

Us, Men, can always identify the weaklings. They're shorter, fatter, slower, need glasses, not as good at sports, read novels, attracted to guys, go to therapy, can't hold their liquor, meditate, own metallic water bottles, can't grow a beard, live gluten free, wear dresses, pursue the arts, put on nail polish, don't eat meat, use umbrellas, call their mother, fall in love, prefer oat milk, care about their grades, watch romcoms, and, of course, the worst one of them all, cry. The social conditioning boys go through at a young age teaches us that crying is a sign of weakness and vulnerability, which is influential since we simultaneously grow to believe that another boy's weakness is an opportunity for us to pounce on them. Pushing them further down the totem pole, by virtue, lifts us higher. Maybe guys don't identify weaklings. Maybe, just maybe, we create them.

My earliest memory of crying is from when I was six-years-old. I was at judo training, carrying a bigger kid for some drill, till his weight proved to be too much and he fell on top of me, cracking my collarbone. I wailed wildly while my nine-year-old sister crouched next to me and whispered, adamantly, *Stop crying*. Later, my right arm in a sling, lingering in the backseat of dad's car, she told him how everyone could hear me, and how embarrassing it was.

A year later I watched a Pokémon episode where Butterfree flies away from the group to start his own family and when they say goodbye Pikachu cries and Butterfree cries and Ash has tears in his eyes and watching it I felt a lump forming in my throat and tears welling in my eyes and my dad and sister were in the living room with me and I was so fucking embarrassed at being so emotional about an animated TV show that I wished I could fly away but I couldn't so I made sure my family couldn't see my face and I closed my eyes and inhaled the tears and swallowed the lump and clenched my fists till I was sure the tears and the lumps and the feelings were buried deep down in a place that animated shows or friends or family can't reach because access to that place will be, even for me, blocked.

The association of tears with weakness, alongside the inherent human urge to not want to be ridiculed or pushed down, have created a generation of dudes who won't let anything out; who let things fester and rot till they inflict not just themselves, but the relationships with those around them. This suppression of emotion encourages and glorifies individuality, and propagates a façade of faux heroism and the idea of being a macho man.

The new generation of men, bell hooks claims, was more than happy to be told they did not have to be the big, strong man, "but the only alternative to not turning into a conventional macho man was to not become a man at all, to remain a boy." Those are the stereotypical options offered to us: macho man or immature boy. Couple these ideas with social constructs that have historically empowered men, abated their culpability, and enabled them a privileged leeway, and you may begin to decipher why a man wouldn't want to grow or open up, and why he can get away without having to do so.

Maybe, though, I shouldn't pretend I'm some German philosopher who has any base for this theoretical framework. Maybe I shouldn't try to presume how other men felt growing up, nor try to speak for them. Maybe I can just say that a lifetime of shutting down questions about the way I feel has left me searching for answers in childhood memories, Jewish dinner parties, Japanese animated shows, and books with glistening covers. I could even come up with a metaphor of how, as a growing boy, whenever someone dared nudge me out of my emotional comfort zone, all I had to do was stick my head under the blanket and pretend I'd never heard anything. How I grew up to be an alleged man who's still covered by an abundance of sound-proof layers of fabric, blocking not only sound, but air, too, from penetrating through the blanket my fists are still clenching so tightly, as I slowly suffocate underneath it.

Adorno, in *Minima Moralia*, suggests that the only thing that can break the archetype of manliness is a "whiskey soda: the carefully recorded fizzing of the mineral water says what the arrogant mouth does not." In college, a couple of days after my team's season ended in heartbreaking fashion, my teammates and I went out drinking. As soon as my roommate and closest friend had a few beers, he began to sob. *It was my man who scored*, my friend blurted that night, *it was my fault*. We tried to explain to him that that's not how it works, that we win and lose as a team, but to no avail. His sober mind had been carrying the weight of believing that it was his mistake that cost us, but it took his drunken, non-arrogant mouth to verbalize the feeling. He needed alcohol to relieve whatever was constraining him, and once that happened, he was able to look us in the eyes and confess. We affirmed him, as we were supposed to, and he was able to begin the process of letting go.

I've always found alcohol to be magical for the way it enhances, reveals. A few sips, and a version of a man, one kept under layers of insecurities and blankets, constrained by his sober self, breaks free.

Guys cry. Of course we do. Alcohol didn't create a crying version of my friend out of thin air. His sobbing self was a version of him he'd always had, somewhere in his subconscious, that he elected to keep at bay till the beer liberated him. Made him candid, the can did. And that could be daunting. We don't know what part of us will come out when drinking, and there's no resealing a Pandora's Box once it's opened. Yes, revealing its contents may bring you closer to someone, but there's also intimidation in inviting intimacy.

There's a chance Adorno would argue that my team didn't lose when the player my friend was marking headed the ball into our net. Maybe Teddy would say that, actually, we lost the following week, when our team went out drinking again, and the night's theme was preventing my friend from having too many beers. We had no interest in dealing with a crying woman again.

(2)

I had a whiskey with a rabbi once. I call him a rabbi because he's a rabbi, but he's not my rabbi. He's my friend. He just happens to be a rabbi.

I told him about how when my grandfather died—my first real encounter with loss, aged 23—all I could do was think about how I was *supposed* to feel about my grandfather dying. *I should probably sit and cry,* I thought, so I sat on my bed by myself and cried. When the rabbi asked me why I felt that way, I shrugged and said I'm not sure, but it feels like something is blocked. Realizing the whiskey was taking over, I whisked the conversation elsewhere, with a rye smile.

He never asked what I meant by *blocked.* Theodor Adorno would've probably used some fancy word like *repressed* or *dissociated,* when I just mean it feels like I'm checking the weather app instead of sticking my head out the window.

I never told the rabbi that my grandfather died in South Africa, and I was given the opportunity to fly there for his final days and funeral but turned it down. I gave some shitty excuse or another, when in reality, I was terrified of my image of the most perfect man I'd ever met becoming tarnished. A man who taught me manners, card games, and when to flip a piece of steak. A man who matched Zara shorts with me (looked way better on him). A man whom I once saw kiss his wife when he came home from work, more than forty years after they got married, with a passion I can only dream of sharing with someone one day. The thought of seeing that man on a deathbed or in a casket panicked me. I didn't think I'd be able to contain myself, my emotions, my tears, and I thought such a loss of control would let out a part of me I was nowhere near ready to reveal to myself, let alone others. So, I let my fear prevent me from going to take one last look; see, for the final time, the most beautiful man I've ever known.

I never told the rabbi how I received the news of his death in the middle of an afternoon library session. My dad messaged me, *Chamud, give me a call when you can.* Given that my dad had spent the previous few days at his father's deathbed, and he hadn't called me by that nickname since I was a child, I knew what the message actually said. I didn't tell the rabbi that my girlfriend at the time and I had a double date to the movies scheduled for that night, with one of my best friends and his now wife, both of whom I love dearly. I didn't tell him that I didn't cancel the plans because I didn't want to tell my friends the reason I wanted—and probably needed—to cancel. I just blocked whatever needed blocking and went to watch *Kingsman: The Golden Circle*. After the movie, my ex-girlfriend and I got in her car and when she twisted the key in the ignition, Sam Smith's "Too Good at Goodbyes" comically and ironically came on the radio. We hugged over the parking brake and, with my face hidden and with the aid of Sam Smith's tenor, my eyes teared up. We separated, I inhaled and blocked, then we drove to our friends' place where I smoked weed for the first time in my life and felt nothing.

I never told the rabbi I wrote a eulogy for that great man—words fawning over his love of whiskey, memories I made and values I learned while teaching him how to safely remove a USB, and songs that'll forever remind me of him. I sent the eulogy to my father and he read it at the funeral. My words, his voice. I knew putting words on a page was child's play. Crying them out loud would've been a whole nother game—one I was too scared to play.

I never told the rabbi how my grandfather was too sick to speak on the phone in his final days, so my goodbye to him was in the form of a voice note. I never revealed that when my phone lit up with a response, I left the voice message untouched for a day, then a week, and a month, and a year, till three years since his passing had passed, and I still had control of a part of him that was alive.

I opened that message, eventually. The Covid pandemic leaving me confined alone could probably serve as the most logical explanation for why I felt the need for some familial contact, a warm voice. Logic and proportion, though, as Jefferson Airplane sing in "White Rabbit," are destined to fall sloppy dead.

By the time I opened that message, I had already replaced the proverbial locker room with a literal nonfiction workshop, which, just like everything else those days, had turned remote. Social life was more challenging to cultivate online, which is why my newly formed group of grad school friends had to disperse, until all of us—apart from one—finally reunited, more than a year later, on a sunny Saturday morning, at Harlem's 125th Street train station, in a moment that felt like the opening scene of a movie, a 1980s cult classic proving to be the breakthrough role for some actor like Jeff Goldblum.

(1)

The train pulls into 125th, zooms by the five of us. I see ourselves, fleetingly, as if filtered, on the darkened windows. The gaps between the cars flicker our image like the break between slides on an old-time projector. The last car stops in front of us, stilling our tinted reflections. The sound of steam. We all hold. I fix my eyes on the darkened versions of ourselves in the window. A last puff of a cigarette. A final sip of coffee. The doors open. *One day*, I think, *we're all going to write about this.*

We take our seats in the car, and I stare out the window. If this had been a 1980s movie, this is when the opening credits, in a yellow font that's bound to become obsolete, would roll over the screen and the sound of train tracks would slowly dissolve into the melody of a violin as I'd watch Harlem morph into suburban upstate.

Getting dressed this morning, I thought about a question I recently asked. I'm due to fly to a friend's wedding soon, so inquired with another friend about the dress code. *Tailored pants and a button-down shirt*, he told me, and I pondered his answer this morning as I donned a pair of black pants and a navy button-down. I wondered whether it's possible to look the same at both a wedding and a wake. Individually? Maybe. As a group, the way we looked through the reflection of that last train car, I didn't think there was any doubt as to where we were going.

A conductor approaches to claim our tickets, remarks, cheerfully, on our fancy dress, asks us where we're heading, and even though we all write for an alleged living, none of us have a single word to say.

As we walk over from the train station to the house, I remind myself of a piece of advice my rabbi friend gave me once. When dealing with a crying child, it helps to get them to look up. Something about the upward tilt of the head helps collect the tears at the bottom of the eyelids, preventing them from streaming down the cheeks. I've never been to a wake. When I came to terms with the fact that I'll be attending one, I googled it to have an idea of what awaits me. I read that, traditionally, the body is present, so I prepared myself to tilt my head up, brace, block. The thought of seeing my friend as anything other than the vibrant ball of light she was panicked me, and I feared not being able to contain myself, my emotions, my tears. I still thought such a loss of control would let out a part of me I was nowhere near ready to reveal.

The casket isn't there when we arrive. After a quick reception catered mostly by Dunkin' Donuts, people begin taking their seats in white folding chairs, vaguely six-feet apart, in the back garden. I walk to the front, where the spread is set up, and grab four water bottles. By the time I return to the garden, all the seats are occupied, so I stand at the very back, place myself on the outskirts of the pain. It'd be easy to liken this image of me standing in the back to that of a pebble dropped into water, with the ripples being the levels of pain felt—the further you are from the center, the more the ripple wanes. But I'm not quite sure that that's the case. It's more like the now-debunked Mona Lisa effect. Wherever you are in this back garden, it feels like the sorrow is staring at you and you at it, for yourself, as only you could.

Still, it feels appropriate to have my vantage point distract me from my pain by having me see others'. I see those ahead of me, closer than me, do their best to both succumb to and withstand the pain. This moment and this pain are mine, and forever will be, but on top of that, they are ours, and forever will be.

Just before the service begins, I hand two of the water bottles to my friends, and they tell me there is an empty space next to the boyfriend. He's on the other side, on a garden bench that can just about squeeze two people onto it. We've never been overly close, me and him, but have always gotten along well. A minimal yet perfect form of rapport exists between us: a handful of reoccurring jibes guys use to bond, *and one* anecdotal moment we shared on a basketball court. I sit on the garden bench and find myself, through logistics and life's happenstance, closer to him than anyone else in the world. Our knees touching, we listen to a reverend then a mother then brothers then an aunt then a father then a recording of a high school *a cappella* rendition of "Landslide," all the while he's trembling, shaking me with him. As jarring as this moment may be for me, I can't conjure what it must be like for him, nor what I can do to try to help. I hand him water, put my arm on his shoulder, then his thigh, try to offer stillness in a rickety moment, a grasp in an ungraspable moment.

The mic is then offered to anyone willing, and a high school friend walks up to tell us how my friend was like a diamond. Not because she was tough or shone bright or was sought after, even though she was all of those things. She was like a diamond, her friend says, because each time you looked at her, you could see a different side, and she reflected back something else. She took you in then handed back a shinier, brighter version of yourself. The friend can feel that she needs to wrap up, but I can tell she has more to say. It is a battle between her refusal to let go of this moment, where the existence of her friend is close enough for her to get away with talking about her in the present tense, and the lump forming in her throat, reminding her it's time to stop, to let go.

She lets go. Because the boyfriend approaches the mic next, she takes the garden bench seat he just vacated. As she sits down next to me, her shoulders clench, as if she's trying to squeeze and shrink herself till she disappears. My left arm—subconsciously—rises to embrace her, and her head lands on my chest as she continues to condense herself. It's cold and it's windy on this northeastern early spring morning, and I hope the gusts of wind hit only me. I feel as close to this woman who I've never met before as I have to anyone I've ever known, just because I happen to be in this place, at this time. We embrace for two lifetime seconds, then let go. I offer her water, she declines, graciously, and we never speak again. At the mic, the boyfriend reads aloud emails he'd received from my friend. *Her voice needed to be heard today,* he'll tell me after, and he'll be right. There's beauty in the contrast between the mundaneness of an email and the magnitude of this moment. He's offering us the lightness of words in this heavy moment, and I'll forever be grateful that he's doing so.

I consider approaching the mic. I could tell the story of how my friend once shared an excerpt of her writing with me, and added the note, "don't want to close my eyes." I could say that when I emailed back some of my writing, my subject line was "I Don't Want To Read A Thing." I could explain how these references to this long argument we once got into about a classic Steven Tyler power ballad was what I wish for every person sat on a white folding chair in front of me. How I wish that they'll all get to experience moments in which they can accentuate something trivial with someone special. How I hope they'll all get to form and share relationships—big and small and short and long—that can be encompassed and manifested through six words that bring out the most genuine of smiles.

I could go up there and share how during a round of homemade trivia, in the Literary Music category, my friend instantly recognized the song I chose to play: "White Rabbit" by Jefferson Airplane. *I chose the same song,* I could tell people that she said that night, *but I had a feeling someone would pick it, so I have a backup.* How that moment signified her ability to always think of the whole, her constant consideration of others. How I wish everyone would have friendships like ours—ones whose value does not waver by opposed opinions and does not depend on the sharing of the same thought.

I could go up there and fawn over how I learned that a whiskey sour was her go-to, things I learned while teaching her, and songs that'll forever remind me of her.

But I don't. I just silently sit and brace and block; hope my presence proves worthy; offer water or warmth; leave my own cold for later.

One day, I figure, if I'm man enough, I'll put all these words onto a page and cry them out loud.

꧁꧂

The sun is still up when the group of us makes it back to 125th station in the afternoon, and Lenox Ave is engulfed in the sound of 90s hip hop. We end up parked at a high-top table, sitting on barstools with no back-rests, leaning on each other. If the morning was cinematic, the evening is cathartic. Phrases like *We need to do this more often* slip between sips of beer and wine. Whether uttered to another or to ourselves, I'm not sure. People say these things all the time, and they often fall flat, but I hope they'll hold strong. I think we all know that being together is as close as we'll ever have to being with her.

After a couple of rounds, one of us wants to get up and dance. She forages for a partner, unsuccessfully. I tell her I'd need ten shots of tequila before she'd see me out there, and she turns to look for the waitress. We all laugh and my friend keeps probing till she says, *You know who would definitely come dance with me,* and we all know the answer, so we let a silence take over from our sigh.

A couple of us do end up dancing. Not me. I just cross my legs and set my elbow on the table and rest my jaw on the base of my palm and sip from a green glass bottle of Heineken and watch my friends smile as they sway to the tune of "California Love." I put my phone away and embrace the waning rays of sun beaming through the glass and the music, till I can feel their warmth inside, underneath the layers of blankets, where I keep that part of me that's blocked. And as the version of me sitting on this barstool feels the merit of cherishing a moment, all I can think of is how *I don't want to close my eyes.*

Had this been a 1980s movie, this could have been the final scene. Perhaps there'd even be narration over the music, one where I reach some profound conclusion about how even images around caskets or death-beds, as difficult and as tarnishing as they may seem, can carry beauty, so long as you're surrounded by the right people.

I have love for the people who are in this scene with me, and I am glad to be around them, but the profound conclusion won't come till later, after another person—one, specific one—will enter the frame.

(1)

While at the final pitstop of the night with my friends—a god awful
American sports bar by West Harlem Piers—L and I text and plan for
me to come over. I rush my hugs goodbye, then begin walking north on
Broadway. She's been downtown somewhere, so I lean against a lamppost
one block up from the 137th station and wait. I stand there in my black
pants and navy button-down until someone wearing a soft, ribbed black
sweater enters the frame; someone I hug and lean against instead.

The focal point of our kitchen island barstool conversation isn't my
friend or the day I've had. Maybe L doesn't want to probe or push me into
talking about it, if I'm even able to do so. Most likely, though, if I have to
guess, I'm adamant on being distracted—in the best way possible—by L.
I want to replace the day I've had with hers, listen to her thoughts and
feelings as they are certainly better than my own, clear space in my brain
and absorb more of her. I hope to bring a smile to her face by making
jokes so bad they're good, hope that the extent of the world could be this
island and the two people inhabiting it.

What we do talk about is music, and when we get in bed L prompts
me to play my Liked Songs playlist on Spotify. I'm not embarrassed by
my taste in music (some songs, maybe), but the 1000 song playlist is a
bit of a clutter. It's all my favorite genres and moods and bands and sing-
ers and covers and performances thrown into one. It goes from Frank
Sinatra to J Balvin to string quartets to Eminem to old Israeli folk bands
to—unabashedly—Nickelback to the Pitch Perfect soundtrack to Adele
(whom L drastically underrates, rendering her music the punch line for
an unfunny number of my jokes).

Four or five shuffled songs in, worried some weird song will come up
and alter the mood, lying in bed under a white duvet in a dark room, I
ask L to turn DJ.

After careful consideration, as I watch her squinting at her phone, inquisitively searching, she plays The Weeknd's album, *After Hours*.

Maybe there's something to be said here. Some comparison of my musical disarray with L's choice to play a specific album, carefully curated by the same mind, sung by the same voice. Maybe this contrast is the metaphor that explains why we're too different to ever work out. Me just letting songs come on, letting life happen, casually pressing the skip button whenever something that isn't to my liking comes up. Her, on the other hand, with her lyrical and emotional ducks in a row. Perhaps, though, this difference is the metaphor explaining how we're a perfect match. Some Lily and Marshall olive theory shit. It all depends on whose words I want to follow, as I'm still in the process of figuring out what I'm trying to say.

We lie in bed. Me on my back; her, to my right, at an angle on her side, resting against my body, her arm draped across my chest, her head in the crevice just under the collarbone I once cracked, the top of her head tangential to the chin hiding behind the stubble of my beard, her hair like a soft, black quilt, keeping me warm. We don't speak. We simply exist in a universe whose extent is a bedroom, dweller is a single body made of two, and soundtrack is The Weeknd's light, lyric tenor. We listen, and I feel my fists' grip of the blankets loosening. Not by the music, but by the person who's playing it. With her warmth and presence, with how much I want her to be with me and me to be with her in this moment, L uncovers a side of me nothing else ever has, or could. At the end of a day where I braced and blocked, tilted my head, and wordlessly said goodbye to a diamond of a friend, I finally let go. Maybe L knew what the music would do to me. Maybe it doesn't matter what she played, so long as she was the one I'm listening with. Maybe this is her way of saying, without probing or pushing, that it's okay. All of me is.

She killed herself, I say in the dark, breaking a long silence with welling eyes. It's the first time I cry these three words out loud, finally taking a moment to look at how this sorrow is staring at me; how I see it, at this outermost ripple.

Lying here, honestly, my eyes closed, my mind racing, my heart raging, asking why and what, seeking solace in not carrying any blame, I find so much weight on my shoulders, and fear they'll crack. Sensing guilt, my head atilt, till my eyelids prove no match to my tears, tearing layers of blankets from the inside, I finally let in some air that enables me to breathe, then exhale a lifetime of suppression into three words. Say them not to L, but into the space she created for me; for us. A space I could never create for myself and that I never thought I'd let anyone see me in.

L doesn't say anything. She just wipes my tears, kisses my cheek, and strings her arm around me tighter. She brings herself closer, inks herself into my life in ways I don't know if either of us will ever understand.

(3)

Much of the opening parts of *all about love* are dedicated to the language we use about love. It's important to hooks, and therefore useful to me, to establish early on the difference between the feeling of love and that of emotional investment. She quotes M. Scott Peck, who said that most of us confuse loving with cathecting: the process of investment wherein a loved one becomes important to us. The pair are not mutually exclusive, of course, but hooks encourages a specificity of language so we can distinguish between the types of love in our life, so we can do the necessary work to thrive in and enjoy particular incarnations of those different loves.

Later in the book, when discussing romantic love, hooks brings up John Welwood's distinction between a "heart connection" and a "soul connection." Welwood defines the former as a special way of clicking that could take us on the path of love, but one that is "usually not a difficult process," and can be had with many people. The latter he describes as a "sacred alliance whose purpose is to help both partners discover and realize their deepest potentials." A soul connection, he adds, enables us to love someone not only for who they are, but for who we could become under each other's influence. A soul connection isn't easy—it requires work. But it is the base for a true love in which individuals "feel in touch with each other's core identity." Sometimes, a soul connection happens without us even knowing why, rendering us unable to put the feeling into words, at least until after the fact.

One night, in L's bed, back in the early days of her being in my life, she lay in my arms, lifted her head from my chest, stared directly into my eyes, and said, *I'm scared by how much I like you.* I smirked, stared back, and said, *Me too.* My words were true, but I knew they were far from convincing. Given time, I could have probably come up with more telling words to reply, and, instantaneously as the words came out of my mouth, I regretted how banal my response was in this moment that should've connected our souls. I just didn't know any better words to talk about love, which was ironic, because I was learning them as the moment happened.

In her book, hooks goes on to talk about the way many men in her life have been wary to talk about or admit to love, as they believe women make too much of the feeling. Simultaneously, most of the theorizing and philosophizing about love has been done by men. "Whenever a single woman over forty brings up the topic of love," hooks writes, "again and again the assumption, rooted in sexist thinking, is that she is 'desperate' for a man."

But that's not necessarily the case. "It turns out, in fact," Pauline Harmange writes in her book-length essay, *I Hate Men*, "that single women who don't have children are the happiest demographic of all." She goes on to quote Paul Dolan, professor of behavioral science at the London School of Economics, speaking about his book *Happy Ever After* at the 2019 Hay Festival:

You are a single woman of 40 who has never had children — "Bless, that's a shame, isn't it? Maybe one day you'll meet the right guy and that'll change." No, maybe she'll meet the wrong guy and that'll change. Maybe she'll meet a guy who makes her less happy and healthy, and die sooner.

Men playing the role of purveyors and experts of a product they wouldn't dare consume themselves feels incredibly on-brand. But much like single women over forty may write about love without being desperate for a man, single men in their mid-to-late twenties may write about love precisely because of how desperate they are for that soul connection. The one, specific one, they've lost.

Writing this, I'm desperate to face L again as we're both sitting on kitchen island barstools with our legs entangled. Tilt my torso forward, land my forehead on her shoulder, feel her fingers run along the top of my spine, breathe her collarbone in, look down and see our thighs alternating from left to right: hers, mine, hers, mine. Beyond them, our feet leaning against each other's footrest, our soles connecting with the metal, our souls connecting just out of sight. I thirst to lie in bed all morning. Skip breakfast, then lunch. Subsist on blissful kissed existence. Move strands of hair, one at a time, off her face, curl them behind her ear as she speaks, each strand removed and word spoken elucidating a face and a facet, a person and a persona, each more beautiful than the other. See her chin resting on her crossed arms atop my bare chest, feel the weight of her head and warmth of her palms as we exchange stories and questions; laying, as we lie, groundwork for inside jokes and shared memories, an infinite amount of space in my brain to absorb it all: her outfits, the way she pronounces the word "brothers," which of her friends she goes to for what, the dreams—big and small, how I can't decipher a single word she sleepily mumbles into the pillowcase we're sharing yet she still makes perfect sense, where the best sweet potato pie in town is, how she laughs when my joke is funny, and how she laughs when it isn't.

When hooks talks about true love, she says that "embarking on such a relationship is frightening precisely because there is no place to hide." This would've been a perfect quote to say to L as we lay in her bed and she told me she's scared by how much she likes me. But, at that point, I hadn't started reading and learning from *all about love* so all I ended up doing was keep my feelings, my real feelings, to myself. What I was beginning to learn about was the fear of love. How the exposure that love requires can be paralyzing, overwhelming, and lead us to make decisions we'll gravely regret.

(1)   (2)   (3)

Back at L's place, that first night, when I stood in her bedroom as she went to get us something to drink, I whipped my phone out of the back pocket of my jeans and deleted the dating app. I no longer had a need for it.

I've never been a fan of the apps. Or, I should say, I've always deemed it impossible that I'd find my person on the apps, despite the plethora of joyful couples who meet on them these days, how socially acceptable they've become. My single friends who've had success with them all had different approaches. One would go on multiple dates a week, one would give their matches a five-message limit to ask them out, one would delete the app after every successful match that's switched to text. That last one, a guy, claimed it's impossible to commit to one person when offered such an abundance of choice, hence the necessity to remove the distraction. His argument echoes the famous line of thought sparked by research conducted by Sheena Iyengar and Mark Lepper in 2000 about the paradox of choice. The more options we're presented with, the harder it is for us to decide. My aversion to finding love on the apps, though, has stemmed mostly from the hopeless romantic in me who's always wanted a meet-cute story.

Why have I been using them then? Because despite their superficiality, they are the norm these days, and even if I've not been set on finding love on them, I've been keen on meeting people, dating, figuring out who I am and who I click with. For someone who's never been able to walk up to someone and spark a conversation, the apps made it easy to connect with people I'd never meet in real life. Even if I'd have sat across from L in a coffee shop somewhere in the six blocks between our apartments, knowing myself, I'd have never walked up to her, made some witty remark, and wound up going on three dates with her in one night.

Nostalgia is a powerful drug, Kate Christensen said, so perhaps when I'll end up looking back at these early days I spend with L, combining hindsight's lessons along with my propensity to romanticize, my eyes will inevitably turn too glossy. Perhaps the very same glossiness will be what sends me down a slippery slope. Time will tell. What I can say with certainty is while I undoubtedly feel the intensity of my time with L in these early days, I am not able to comprehend the feeling, nor recognize how it is what I truly want—intense, seamless, natural.

She tells me she'll be leaving town for a week or two. By the time she's scheduled to return, I'm meant to have flown home-home to attend a friend's wedding. When she leaves, I prepare myself for a month apart, which, after how intense everything has been up until now, feels very much like going cold turkey. The main problem is that we never really speak about what's happening between us, or whether either of us is in a place in our lives where we want to enter a committed relationship, despite all the signs that suggest we should do both—speak, enter. Still, even if we've not had "the talk," she's been open with her feelings towards me. She's told me how she feels and what she's been through, all of which I've affirmed and reciprocated. I've told her—not convincingly, perhaps—that I feel the same way, which I more than do, but I don't lower my guard enough. I recognize how she feels, but maybe a part of me takes it for granted, doesn't recognize how imperative it is that both deeply loving grown folk initiate open and honest communication with one another. I never make myself approachable enough and her comfortable enough to ask, really ask, what's going on with me. Maybe she's wary that the fact I haven't initiated the conversation means I'm not interested in putting into writing what's already been so clearly spelled out. Maybe that leaves her lying in bed, toiling over my unknown location, suppressing an urge to reach out, timid it'll push me away. I don't know. I don't know what she makes of my guardedness, mainly because of a mindset I've been carrying for over a quarter of a century.

I've always believed the decision to bottle up my emotions is my own. Since I'm the only person who suffers from the festering's repercussions, I'm the only person who should be taken into consideration. If I want to hold on to my anxiety and avoid sharing the weight of my troubles, that's my choice. Half the reason for this mindset is an archaic, patriarchal performance of masculinity, which Jared Yates Sexton so brilliantly dissects in *The Man They Wanted Me to Be*. "Realizing I could be vulnerable and that my suffering wasn't a sign of weakness, but actually a display of strength," Sexton writes, "made all the difference in the world." He encourages all of us to remind our father, brother, cousin, or friend who may "inexorably believe in traditional masculinity… that it's okay if they aren't always the stoic patriarch." He's right, Sexton. There's a flawed perception of heroism and manliness that I associate with the active choice to hold onto pain, as if suffering and strength are synonyms. I think back to my days playing soccer, competing with my teammates over who can hold a plank the longest, the winner—the alpha male—lauded for holding onto the pain the longest, despite the fact all of us end up crashing on the floor.

The second half of the reasoning is my adamant inclination to not be a nuisance in anyone's life, even on the smallest of levels. I stay out of your way when you pick your vegetables at the grocery store, lower my headphones' volume so god forbid no one on the subway will be troubled by hushed reverberations of my music, don't tell the waiter about the mistake in my order, and never reply in a group chat with a message meant for only one person. I'd much rather stand silently and awkwardly in the corner of a room than risk imposing myself into a conversation. If I'm wary of being obtrusive by engaging in small talk at a dinner party, then sharing with someone—even if I subsist on blissful kissed existence with them—that I can't fall asleep without two swigs of gin, is far beyond the realm of feasibility. People have so much going on in their lives— their own fears and worries and dilemmas—so why on earth would they need me to pile onto their troubles with my own.

I know, of course, and hooks and Sexton and anyone who isn't a stoic patriarch knows, too, that my withholding is, in fact, selfish. By withholding, here and now, I'm affecting L. I'm hurting her by not sharing that it's hard for me to make sense of my feelings because as we meet my mind is occupied with the upcoming graduation that means the end of my visa in the US, my friend's sudden and premature death, an apartment lease coming to an end, and the worthlessness I feel about my mother having health issues 6,000 miles away.

I do have some shit going on, but I'll look back at these reasons through glossy eyes as weak excuses. Not because they aren't taking a toll on me, but because my decision to keep them hidden from a person I feel so close to is a sign of weak, stoic patriarchy. I'm not prepared to let her near, and soon enough I'll be mangled over how far away she is.

Every second I spend with L is a blissful escape from the shitty, real world, and I don't want to tarnish our time with any gloom or negativity. I feel as if I've walked into her life and—please pardon the self-aggrandizing—made things better. I've made her laugh and smile with my words, I've listened to her troubles, and I've made her bed. (Once, maybe a week or so after we bumped into each other on Broadway, I told L I had known I'd want a second date even before our first. When she initiated a conversation asking what I meant, she prefaced it by saying *Can I first just say you made my bed so well this morning, like damn*, which made me feel affirmed and giddy in ways I can't quite explain.) I've been someone, I feel, she can lean on. I don't want my words to become a burden, make her wary of sharing her troubles with a person who has plenty of his own, unveil the corners of my life I have untucked, present myself as too fragile for her to lean on.

When she tells me she's leaving town, and I prepare my mind to exist without her, a part of me begins thinking this is it. A month apart from each other, most of it in different time zones, with no established, spoken commitment to rely on, surely signifies the end. She's too gorgeous to not have people line up out the door for her, too intelligent to not have people crave her opinions, too caring and compassionate and kind to not have every single person in this world desire her care, compassion, and kindness. I don't trust that what we have, who I am, is good enough for her to commit to when she has such an abundance of choice. I'm sure there are some psychoanalysts out there who would suggest some form of self-defeating personality disorder, or cynics who would label me as just another man who's feigning victimhood, but since I don't have a PhD in psychology and am doing my best to remain non-cynical, I'll just say I decide to retract my bet before the roulette ball is done spinning, foolishly thinking that'll prevent me from losing.

So, when she tells me she'll be back in town ahead of schedule, before my flight home-home, I panic. I have the option of seeing her, but after a week of trying to adjust my brain to a world without her, fabricating reasons why it wasn't even that good to begin with, I'm frightened that another rewiring would prove to be too much for me to handle. I feel I've already revealed too much, given too much away, rendered myself too vulnerable.

I turn down her offer to meet up, don't see her despite the fact she's barely six blocks away, and by the time I'm at the gate waiting to board my flight, I redownload the dating app. It was too good, too great, I feel, so it's best to head out before it's no longer good, no longer great—an outcome I think certain. The prank, I figure, is over.

I get on my plane to go home-home, let my friends scroll through my dating app profile, scour and scout what's out there, and ask me some form of *Why don't you settle down?* question as I stare with adulation at their unadulterated, adulthood joy. I adjust back to the safe, riskless, unfulfilling life I've had, and figure the process of moving on from L can be accomplished by adopting a hyperbolic and reductive slogan—by just doing it. The dating apps will present an abundance of choice I'll be able to distract myself with, and I persuade myself just enough to believe that all the trouble occupying my mind means I'm not "in the right state of mind to get into a relationship," anyway, which a part of me will end up regarding as a weak excuse. The hopeless romantic part will think this, since it believes there is no right state of mind. There is—and please pardon the cliché—no right time to meet the right person. Whenever it happens, you just go for it, and figure everything else out as it comes.

Except, of course, I'm choosing to not believe that yet.

Why, I'll end up asking myself in the not-so-distant future, in the moments I feel worthless, uncertain about the future, or am dealing with grief, wouldn't I want some*one*—not some*thing*—next to me, resting in my hand, appeasing my mind? But right now, the instability feels like a stable enough excuse to lean on, to tell L I'd like to retract my bet from the table, which I do after I get back to the city and we see each other one last time.

Step Three

Knead

(2)

Dani is about four inches taller than me. Whenever we hug, I turn my
face 90° and my cheekbone gently clanks into his collarbone. Our hugs
have never been proverbial man-hugs—dap, back-pat, 'Sup—but more of
a bear hug. We let out a big smile, spread our arms wide, let mine circum-
vent his midriff, his landing somewhere atop my shoulder blades, and hold
each other just long enough for one of us to come up with something both
of us—and probably only both of us—find funny. We've perfected this
Long time no see hug as we've lived in the same area code for only two of the
last dozen years of our friendship. His soccer career took him from Israel
to high school in Switzerland, then college in Pennsylvania; mine had me
recruited from the Holy Land to an undergraduate stint in Florida. By the
time he moved to the Sunshine State post-grad, I was already in New York,
chasing a new dream—no longer a dream we shared.

At the beginning of our U14s season, the director of our soccer club
picked five players from our team to be bumped to help the not-very-
good U15s team. Dani and I—good players, but never labeled as child
prodigies—weren't moved up, but were named co-captains of the leftover
squad. With five big egos removed and a chip placed on our conjoined
shoulder, Dani and I ascended as leaders, so by the time the five phenoms
were moved back down to play with us, the team was no longer theirs.

One Saturday morning, our original team restored, we mustered a
hard-fought 2-0 win. Dani scored; I played really well. I'm not one to
boast about has-been athletic performances like some balding, middle-
aged man caressing his beer gut. I'm only comfortable admitting to having played well that day since after the game ended, a man named Henri
approached our parents—and not, may I add, the parents of any of the
five prodigies—to discuss the prospect of sending us to play for a professional club in Switzerland. Dani and I did our best to remain poised
at the idea of being shipped to Europe as two budding talents, and the
massive middle finger this would flip to those who didn't recognize our

potential. We allowed ourselves—when it was just the two of us—to day-dream of a new life, the validation this would bring for the hard work we'd put in, and, most importantly, the exciting paths that would unveil them-selves after boarding this train. First stop, Bern. Second, who knows?

Much of what tethered Dani and I, early on, was our cultural sim-ilarities. We grew up in the same town, played the same sport, and came from a somewhat similar Anglo-Saxon culture—he British, me South African—meaning we both spoke English with ridicule-worthy accents. We felt as if we were ingrained with a mentality different from that of the stereotypically lazy, slacking, corner-cutting Israeli one. Not that native Sabras didn't go all the way around the cone, stay to stretch after training, or run as hard as their lungs allowed. Many did. Dani and I just shared a certain wavelength, believing our drive and perseverance would eventually triumph. The common ground we shared, we assumed, meant that whenever the chips would end up falling our way, they'd be collectible by both of us.

Some weeks and coffees and meetings and phone calls and highlight tapes after that 2-0 win, Henri informed us that the Swiss club was only in the market for a center-back, not a forward. Given that Dani played the former position and I the latter, the process proceeded solely for him.

When Dani flew to Switzerland for tryouts, Henri said he was still working on setting something up for me.

When Dani impressed and was offered a contract, I was combusting with pride and envy.

By the time Henri called my dad to say hopes for me were all but gone, Dani was packing his bags and researching online about his new team and school and city.

As he was falling asleep giddy and zealous, I was lying awake resentful and despairing.

At Dani's goodbye party, a dad of a blue-eyed friend handed him a present: a gag T-shirt of the Google home page with "Where to find friends?" in the search bar, the result being, "Fuck Google, Ask Me." The floor was then opened to anyone willing, and with the proverbial captain's armband, I ambled to the front and mumbled some cliché or another. We—Dani and I—had kept it a secret that I was a part of the initial process, so when at the closing of my speech I choked up a bit, people must've assumed I was saddened by the imminent departure of my dear friend. But I—and maybe Dani, though we never really discussed it until I wrote an essay about us and sent it to him—knew there was an additional layer at hand. I swallowed the lump and wrapped up my speech with some version of *Good luck and we'll be cheering you on from afar*, then he and I met at center stage for an embrace: a non-proverbial man-hug.

On his final night, when a group of us went over to say our goodbyes, I snuck into Dani's bedroom to leave a letter I'd typed out for him. I knew, even at that young age, that there are certain words I can't speak, but can write. I penned sentimental words, but demanding ones, too. The essence of the letter was a plea and a push, a reminder for him, just in case he needed one, of the opportunity that lay ahead, the mandate placed on him, both by himself and by me, to capitalize on the golden ticket he'd been awarded. I wrote words of affirmation and validation, at an age I didn't quite know what those concepts are, indicating my faith in his individual ability to pursue our shared dream. At the bottom, I pasted a candid photo of us, captured by his father, at the end of our 2-0 win that Saturday morning. There's no one in the frame apart from us two, moments after the referee blew the final whistle, in our sapphire blue kits with the thick crimson stripe across the chest, a fraction of a second before embracing.

In hindsight, that moment of me leaving the letter in Dani's bedroom was a perfect reenactment of the photo. It's like both moments are identical snapshots, except in the photo Dani and I are heading towards each other, and in his room we're drifting apart. Or, more accurately put, he's drifting away, untethering himself.

Perhaps that's dramatic to say. But, standing in his bedroom, young and naïve and susceptible, I was saying goodbye to my closest ally. The loss of love is often thought of as the romantic kind, but love is love. My person, my best friend, was not only leaving, but he was leaving to live out what was our dream.

Despite the envy and dejection, I still found it in me to fold the letter like a fourteen-year-old boy would, then squeeze it into the box of Oreos—his favorite at the time—he'd packed in his bag. So, if anyone wants to know how to be a good and supportive friend, even when they really, really don't want to be one, fuck Google. Ask me.

(3)

On May 7th, 2019, Trent Alexander-Arnold took a corner quickly, caught Barcelona napping, and Divock Origi side-footed the ball into the top right corner. It doesn't matter if you understand any of the words I just said. I watched this Champions League Semi-Final standing, alone, in my living room. I was wearing my teacher attire after rushing home from work, having completely disregarded the principal's instructions to stay and monitor student dismissal. The attire comprised a single pair of black dress pants I wore every single day, along with one of an alternating array of long sleeve shirts. Being enveloped in fabric under the Florida sun was far from ideal, but was needed for the purpose of hiding my tattoos. I much preferred sweating my life away while monitoring recess over having to deal with questions about the apple on my calf or the DOn't quIT on my left forearm.

On that May 7th, I wore a cashmere American Eagle shirt that used to be creamy white and soft on the skin, but, over the course of the year, sprouted prominent yellow pit stains. I haven't worn this once-lovely shirt in years, yet it still hangs in my wardrobe. It's sentimental, dare I say.

As soon as Origi's shot hit the net, I sprinted past the kitchen island and instinctively did a belly slide on the hardwood floor—the soft cashmere and polished wood optimizing the friction. If I could only choose one feeling I've ever felt to relive, this precise moment, that I still recall as vividly as anything, would be my second choice.

When the game ended and all the players and coaches linked up arm-in-arm in front of the Kop to sing "You'll Never Walk Alone" with the fans, I stood alone in front of the TV, chanted the lyrics I'd had memorized for as long as I could speak, and cried tears of joy.

Three and a half weeks later, in a packed Liverpool fan bar in downtown Orlando, I watched the legend that is Divock Origi score to seal a 2-0 win in the final. I fell to my knees as soon as the ball went in, living that feeling—the one that would be my second choice to relive—one more time.

When the final whistle blew, I put my arms around an overweight, bald, 50-something-year-old man from Liverpool who'd gone to every final the team has played in during his lifetime, but whose wife booked a non-refundable family trip to Universal Studios without consideration for the date of the Champions League Final, and we cried together. He and I and all the other drunken, sweaty men wearing red shirts jeered and cheered and hugged and chugged as we watched the confetti be shot and the Hendo Shuffle be born and the trophy be lifted, through glossy eyes.

(1)

A couple of months go by. I saunter through life, graduate, renew my lease, vaguely figure out what I want to do next, and my mother's health takes a turn for the better. I feel a little more grounded, a little less fragile. I go on first and second dates—some better, some worse. I make jokes and share kisses—some better, some worse. I assume the way to move on is to replace and recreate, for better or worse. The problem lies in the prefix "re." No one brings out the same degree of casualness and certainty. Nothing starts the way L and I started, which makes me feel it's impossible to reach the same feelings or exist within the same love I felt towards her. I find myself sitting with someone new, drifting away mid-conversation, wondering what L's response would've been to whatever I just asked, squinting my eyes to focus on the face across from me, when a lucid image of a different face registers in my mind. I feel bad about wasting a date's time, but I'm not sure how else I can try to move on.

I slowly come to my senses, and wind up lying in bed one night typing out a message to L. I write about the circumstances that troubled me, and how I'd conditioned myself to not want to share my troubles. I admit to how large a part of my brain she still occupies and acknowledge how my guardedness messed things up the first time around. I promise my best effort to do away with my reluctance to communicate and share and ask her for another shot. I presume that a text, out of nowhere, in the middle of the night, may not be the best course of action. I save the message in my notes app and go to bed, thinking I'll send it at some point the following day. The next morning, while doing some work at the coffee shop underneath my apartment, I hear the door open, look up from my laptop, and my eyes register a familiar, elucidated face.

We hug, she jests at the book on my table (Jia Tolentino's *Trick Mirror*), I irresistibly and comfortably smirk, as does she before walking to the back garden to meet a colleague. I sit down and laugh at the world, for its ironic timing, and at myself, for the incomprehensible ways this woman makes me feel.

We text later that day, the conversation rolls on, and I eventually tell her of the text I drafted, and send it to her. She, in turn, reveals that she's moved away since I last saw her. She's no longer six blocks away, but, in fact, in a completely different borough. More than thinking about how many subway stops are now between us, I think about how it wasn't only my lease that was coming to an end.

The next Saturday night, we meet, late, Sunday morning basically, at Union Square. I'll tell you about that later, I promise.

Three days after Union Square, she tells me she'll be near my neighborhood to have dinner with family, and we decide to meet up again.

(2)

Dani and I remained close after he moved to Switzerland, but reliance on Skype (talk about a throwback) and different demanding schedules resulted in a natural distancing, during which he expeditiously grew closer with someone else in our friend group who had more time on his hands. I was upset (I'm refraining from using the phrase "pissed the fuck off") by Dani's demotion of me as his closest ally, but it'd happened to me before. It happened with a different friend, one I've had since the age of four, whom everyone—teachers, coaches, parents—aside from his array of girlfriends over the years, has always called by his last name. My dad can, to this day, impersonate to perfection my friend's young Ukrainian accent asking to speak to me on the phone on a Saturday morning, when his dad would, routinely, drive us to the park to kick a ball around, after which we'd both go back to my house to have lunch with my family (we lived a three-minute walk from each other).

We were inseparable as kindergartners and throughout elementary school, where we were clearly the two best soccer players, evident by the fact we were barred from ever being on the same team. My friend, especially, since he was an early physical bloomer—taller and faster and bigger than the rest of us—was considered the Child Prodigy. In those early years, whenever a coach would ask all the players to pair up, there was a mute understanding—not just between he and I, but across the team— that we were an inseparable duo.

While we remained classmates, teammates, and quasi-neighbors, in middle school a new facet of my friend burgeoned, molded by his immersion into a new social circle. He began wearing bling-bedazzled Billabong hats and Nike Shox shoes, neither of which, to this day, have ever made their way onto my head or feet. Don't get me wrong, I wanted to fit in with the fashion, be one of the cool kids, but never even dreamed of asking my parents for such extravagant commodities. By the time I was able to afford them for myself, not only were they no longer within the realms of coolness, but the notion of wearing something merely since everyone else is, quite aptly, wore off.

My friend is not, nor was he ever, overly superficial. He's one of the most genuinely kind people I know, and my dear friend to this day. But as he began spending lunches and evenings with the other cool kids, talking and hanging out with girls, and amassing admirable levels of jargon and street cred (his one-nameness aiding his ascension into local stardom, sort of like Oprah or Prince or Cher), I was, as they say, pissed the fuck off. He spent his time with guys on a similar social pedestal, one I didn't have the necessary shoes to try to mount. We were nowhere near the best friends we once were, and his decision to sit and share jokes with other guys irritated me far more than envying his new wardrobe. It was a different feeling of loss from the one I'd have when Dani left. One that had more to do with my self-consciousness in not being up to social pace, while seeing my brother seamlessly succeed. I wasn't able to comprehend (let alone articulate) these feelings at the time, but I could feel them fester, overpower my ego.

In *The Man They Wanted Me to Be*, Jared Yates Sexton traces how toxic masculinity came to manifest itself in Western culture. Sexton dissects how race, sex, war, and politics have led men into the catch-22 of seeing anyone who challenges us as our enemy, and how our narrow-mindedness and lack of introspection causes us the most harm. "The programs we consume, the advertisements we're fed, the entire mythical life of the United States of America," Sexton writes, "is premised on the falsehood that if anyone else succeeds they're doing so at your expense." This means that seeing others—even loved ones—succeed or progress has become an ingrained source of envy.

And it was impossible for me not to be envious of him. "Him" being, of course, all of them. Of Dani for the way people admired his abilities on the field; of the friend Dani demoted me for; of people whose names were known; of those who owned branded clothes or shoes; of friends who had girlfriends at a time I couldn't look a person from the opposite sex in the eye; of guys whom people wanted to share jokes with; of anyone taller or faster or stronger or better looking or trendier or richer or more of a prodigy or who had a defter accent or who simply played the position that a team in fucking Switzerland had an opening for.

(1)

It is the evening of Game 4 of the 2021 NBA Finals. She played varsity basketball in high school, L did. It was on her profile as a fact that would surprise people. She always refers to it as "bball," so I've started doing so as well. All those men who philosophize and theorize about love don't tell you that's a part of love, too. How you'll subconsciously and happily adopt the way they use em dashes in texts, ironically start using terms like "sus" and for long enough that they become part of your lexicon; how one specific color of heart emoji (orange) becomes a synonym for love, forever associated with one person; how a synonym for love will one day become a synonym for pain, forever associated with your mistakes.

Once, as we walked towards the Hudson, we passed by some kids hooping at the Ten Mile River Playground. She was wearing her cozy red sweatshirt—the kind your dad owned in the 80s and you stole from his closet and that exudes Sunday morning coffee on the couch vibes. *You should call "next,"* I told her, *go embarrass them.* I don't remember what she said in return, but if I had to guess it was probably something about not having the right shoes on. She has a knack of replying to my sarcasm seriously, or with sarcasm even more sarcastic than mine. She somehow acknowledges I'm joking yet still ignores my joke. It pisses me off, in the best way possible. It makes me try harder, want to be wittier, smarter— not than her, but simply as a person. The sweet spots are when I get her to crack and laugh—reach the standard she deserves.

She didn't call "next" that day. Instead, we plopped down on a bench overlooking the water, she threw both her legs over my thighs, faced me, and strung her arm over my shoulders.

I want to watch Game 4 tonight, and as we try—in helter-skelter fashion—to make plans, L brings up the game. She says she low key wants to see it, so we decide to go to a bar around the corner from my apartment.

I walk west out of my building towards Broadway. I see L crossing the street, wearing light blue jeans and a white tube top. It's golden hour of a summer's evening and she's illuminated by the sun peeking between buildings, beginning to set behind her. I'm wearing a cornflower blue T-shirt from Zara that used to belong to my friend's brother. It's oversized with a waning neckline, but the bagginess feels perfect for a warm night that forecasts pit stains. L doesn't see me and starts walking towards the bar. I pick up my pace. I round the corner just in time to see three guys perched on a staircase looking at her, because of course they are. Everyone should be looking at her. I catch up to her, tap her shoulder, she swivels, and it's clear, from our hug, that she's mine. As we amble to the bar, I glance towards the guys, and their look is some concoction of props and jealousy and how in the fuck did you get her. I try to get my eyes to utter the phrase, *I have no fucking clue either.*

The bar is packed, so after one beer standing up, we close out and seek somewhere else to watch. We stop at the corner where I first saw her tonight, next to a still lit but now closed Dunkin' Donuts. As we try to figure out where to go, she steps forward, grabs my face, and kisses me. Her soft lips meeting me firmly catch me by surprise, and my eyes stay open for a moment. I see, behind her, a guy walking past, noticing us, and he throws two thumbs up my way. I close my eyes and see that I am, once again, in blissed existence.

We walk south and pass by the bar/café where we had our first date. It still hasn't gone through its total renovation and rebranding, so it's empty. *That place looks cool,* I tell her, and I win, because she laughs. *I can't believe we went there,* she tells me, and I agree with her, even though of course I believe that's where we started. Nothing between us, it seems, was ever meant to work out smoothly. We walk another block then decide to turn around and go back to my apartment because I have a TV and a best friend who has an ESPN account.

The elevator in my building is, for lack of a better term, sketchy (the fact I even have one and don't live in a walk-up is a privilege in and of itself, I know). I refer to it as the McDonald's ice cream machine because of how frequently it's out of order. Much like human beings, even when the elevator seems functional on the surface, it shows concerning signs. Pressing buttons is akin to pulling last year's Christmas lights out of the shed: you're in the dark as to which will turn on. Sometimes, the elevator stops an inch or so below a floor, prompting incautious tenants to trip on the way out. And, every now and again, the elevator reaches the right floor, but the doors decide to dress up as an archetypal man and refuse to open up.

Whenever I ride this low cost theme park ride, I wonder at what point I'm definitely safe. As in, should some cable rip and the box go tumbling down, how high a fall could I survive. I find myself making mental calculations, considering at which precise moment I'm in the clear. There's a part of me—either the hopeless romantic one or the stereotypical masculine one—that thinks that even if the elevator does tumble with me in it, I could jump my way into safety. That part naively and mildly believes that if I jump when the elevator is about a foot or so from impact, the velocity of my body's plunge would reset to zero, despite the chamber's accelerating nosedive. That part idealistically believes that the elevator won't be squeezed like the subject of one of those hydraulic press videos. That part presumes that the house may crash but so long as the self-asserted masculine scholar inside it sticks the landing, he'll survive. I know physics or gravity or reason all contradict me, but the thought process gives me some peace of mind whenever I'm on this scary ride, and, sometimes, that's all we can hope for.

The building's leasing company knows the elevator's perils. The company can't put up a sign that says, "RIDE THIS DEATH TRAP AT YOUR OWN WILL," or one that says, "take the stairs you lazy fuck." Instead, they've taped up at every corner of the building—including inside the elevator—a notice with the contact information for the people who run the elevator company. A deflection of responsibility, perhaps. The contacts' emails all have the company domain but different usernames.

Which is to say, their first name is the username. Which is to say, the first name of the final contact listed, the Service and Operations Manager, is L.

When L and I enter the elevator on our way to watch Game 4 in my room, she leans against the wall on which the notice is taped. *Is this one of your side hustles?* I throw her way and nod my head towards the wall behind her. She turns, sees her name, chuckles, and I win again. We make it safely onto the fourth floor then take a right then a left then a right. I twist a key then we go right then left then through a short hallway and a door then lay down on a bed and watch a game and everything points in the direction of a picturesque, heavenly, lazy morning.

With a minute to go and the game in the balance, Giannis blocks Ayton at the rim. If you're into basketball, you know the play. I turn to face L on the bed, the second it happens, and—doing my best to not mansplain or be hyperbolic—tell her how decades from now people will look back at this play as one of the most iconic ones in the history of the game. The look she gives me makes me think she gets what I'm saying.

Months from now, on a Saturday night, I'll sit, alone, drunk, with an open laptop and a pint of Guinness, at the darkened end of the bar L and I started our evening at. I'll drunkenly write about these moments of peak joy in the present tense: a Guinness Record. I'll feel like I'm living through this personally iconic evening again. I'll see her denim and the sunset again; I'll feel my T-shirt loose around my collarbones; I'll see the smile she can't contain when I make a joke that's so bad that it's good; I'll search my lips for a trace of hers; I'll feel warm and full until I'll start feeling cold and empty. I'll close the screen, take a big sip, look up, see that Giannis and the Warriors are on TV, and hope the pint will do the blocking.

(2)

I don't know the backstory and nuances of the couples at the Rosh Hashanah dinner party. I don't know the struggles they went through, what they fought over, and how many times, if at all, they were close to blowing the whole thing up. I don't know when the initial thrill wore off, how they resolve their conflicts, and at what point they discovered they'd settled into each other's lives. I don't know what it was like when love became stagnant, date nights a hazy memory, and effort a chore instead of a privilege. I don't know how each member of the pair, individually, got over their own anxieties, when they chose to commit to this person, or what made them do so. I don't know what it was like for Mr. 2-Chapters's mother to cope, at a relatively young age, with the loss of the person she chose to build a life with. I can't imagine how many nights, perhaps even to this day, she spends tortured, craving an insatiable desire's fulfillment—one no longer a part of her world. Only they know that about themselves.

The middle-aged couples at the dinner party didn't remind me, despite the logical connection, of my parents. They're of similar age and culture, and one of the men even had my father's balding head and sun-kissed, beige skin. But I've never thought of love—the romantic kind, at least—when looking at my parents.

When I was ten, my sister and I came home from judo training on a Friday afternoon. Our parents sat us down, told us they're getting a divorce, and hugged us. An hour later, instead of a traditional Shabbat dinner, we ordered in Nando's. It was a treat. I wished my parents would get divorced every night. That's how peri-peri happy I was.

The phrase *My parents are divorced,* even with hindsight, carries the same emotional resonance for me as saying, *I had chicken for dinner.* There's nothing unique about it anyway. Everyone's parents get divorced (and if they haven't, maybe they should give it a try, see what happens). But perhaps the event had a bigger impact on me than I'm willing to admit, as I grew up to have a string of relationships I couldn't devote to as well as two tattoos of my favorite team, never considering whether my behavior is a byproduct of having a father who committed to Liverpool Football Club but not to his wife.

If I had to place moments of my life on a scale of emotion, one through ten, Liverpool winning a Champions League final would rank at a far farther extreme than my parents' separation. Everything in my sober life, frankly, would fluctuate between three and eight, with the only facet of life pushing me to either emotional extreme being eleven men in red jerseys (the keeper wears a different color, I know) kicking a ball across some field more than 3,000 miles away.

I've no recollection of growing up in a home with, as hooks would call it, two deeply loving grown folk. They must have shared love at some point in their two-decade long relationship, but I was either nonexistent or not coherent enough to witness its manifestation. Had I been able to learn from them, maybe I'd have been better equipped to deal with my one long-term relationship, which took place when I was 23 with a girl I met in undergrad. She was—and still is, presumably—a wonderful human. She was kind and intelligent and caring and had the capacity to accommodate me. I loved her romantically, but in hindsight that feeling wasn't all that rendered me so happy over the course of that year. Much of my pleasure in the relationship was the idea of being in one.

After going through high school witnessing my taller and blue-eyed friends talk to girls (their height and irises presumably enabling them to reach and see confidence I was unable to); after going through three years of college without going on a single date; after never having engaged, tried, or failed at love while growing up, this relationship was my fulfillment of love. I became infatuated with the thrill of being within love, of sharing my day and life with a person, of being seen as someone who is possessed by and in possession of love. I relished the self-affirmation in my capacity to encompass, listen to, and be a source of stability and grounding for another, and prove I am trustworthy and able to share love.

I was being selfish in a way—maybe every bestowing and receiving of love is, on some level. I spent so many years seeing my friends find, own, and give love. I just wanted to have my chance. I was on the bench, seeing the people closest to me feel unadulterated joy, partaking in the game, which further brewed my self-induced envy and pressure, till I too found someone. Someone, as I said, who is a wonderful human, and whom I'll forever be grateful to for allowing me this experience. Still, while I did love her, I loved who I was in the relationship more.

My mom remarked during that relationship that I shouldn't marry someone who isn't Jewish—which my girlfriend wasn't—since the cultural disparities would prove too much to overcome. Her sentiment, I think it's safe to say, came from personal experience. I dismissed her comments, and they didn't play a part in my decision to end things, mainly due to the personal detachment I have from religion. When I mentioned my mom's comments to my dad, who's far more aligned with me when it comes to religion and therefore I believed would affirm my dismissal, all he said was that I was far too young to even be thinking about marriage.

My dad was right, but not in the way he intended to be. The roadblock to thinking about marriage was not the age I was in, but the person I was with. There is—cliché alert again—no right time to meet the right person. I may be slightly older now (evident by the fact I've sprouted a singular, closely monitored gray hair), but I idealize love in the same way as at that still fully-black-haired age. I romanticize the here and now to the point where the only envisaged future is just as romantic, ideal, and rosy as the present. I've learned, though, that I'm better off not looking too far down the aisle. I should simply embrace love as it comes, continue to aspire to an ideal future but enjoy love in the present tense. Even if it no longer is.

I broke my first relationship up just short of our twelve-month mark, mainly because I began to realize it was more the idea of the person, not the actual person, that I was in love with. I'd be remiss if I didn't add, though, that the separation process, in my head, was sparked by my mistake. A few months into our relationship, I kissed another girl on a drunken night out. I confessed, there were lots of tears and apologies, but eventually she forgave me. We seemed to move past it, and spent several more happy months together, but in my mind, I blemished us for good. When I came to terms with going through with the breakup, a significant part of the reasoning was my mistake on that drunken night, and how it tarnished the unimpeachable ideal of love I've always believed in. I realize, now, that me justifying going through with the breakup, as if I was doing my former girlfriend a favor, is doubly wicked. She was kind enough to award me another chance, our love another opportunity at being unblemished, and I was foolish enough to think I was doing the right thing.

Since that relationship I'd not felt something close to true love—if we were to exclude watching Liverpool Football Club play—until I sat at the foot of a bed in a room dimly lit by streetlights, a smirk smeared across my face, wildly underrepresenting how truly happy I was, there, an arm's length away.

(3)

Men's stereotypical relationship with sports is a tad ironic, or perhaps has oxymoronic tendencies. Reductively, it's men being obsessed and enamored with other men, exhibiting erratic emotional behavior, and showing unwavering commitment (excluding bandwagoners). The world of sports fandom is one of the few that welcomes behaviors in men customarily ridiculed and discouraged. Behaviors considered, dare I say, female.

In *Females*, writer and critic Andrea Long Chu argues that everyone is female, and everyone hates it. Chu defines *female* as "any psychic operation in which the self is sacrificed to make room for the desires of another." She then creates a clear distinction between being a woman and being female (adding that most females are, in fact, not women), and argues that human civilization has a long and diverse history of suppressing and mitigating femaleness. Not too dissimilar, I'll boldly add, from how I spoke about weaklings earlier. However, when it comes to being a sports fan, while there may be an embracing of "feminine" tendencies, a man is not required to make any sacrifices of the self. Quite the contrary. What is sacrificed is often the time, space, and emotional capacity that could be allocated to another. Moreover, men can exhibit femininity in this realm due to its stereotypical masculine elements: defeating another, an association with violence, striving to be an alpha. This, of course, is somewhat predicated on the kind of sport (football: great; figure skating: yuck). The feelings' origin in a hyper-masculine realm widens the range of emotions both accessible and acceptable.

Men have been known to form similar emotional attachments and identities in the realms of guns, hunting, war, or fighting. In an environment where participants impose their power and will over others, there is, perhaps ironically, more leeway to relinquish the masculine façade. Remembering hooks's claim about the one-up-one-down dynamics mistakenly attributed to relationships, perhaps that's why men can let go of that façade with the person they love. Perhaps the very same flawed perception that we can win or lose in relationships is what allows us to be submissive. The acceptance of the rules of the game (be it sports or a relationship) is what allows us to embrace a truer self. Even if that self is one that wants to drink wine on the couch and watch *The Bachelor* and be the little spoon. But, like, a manly little spoon. One with superheroes on it and that you grip with your whole fist as you scoop teeny tiny Cheerios into your mouth cause they make you big and strong and brave and manly. That kind of little spoon.

I'm sure there are plenty of studies out there about sport's role in developing, deterring, or expanding the masculine role, but I don't have the time to read them. One does not become a self-asserted masculine studies scholar by reading other studies. All I know is that my love for Liverpool Football Club, along with my comfort in admitting to this love, have never been questioned, but maybe they should. Not in the sense of asking why I feel so strongly about this team (they're the best fucking team in the world, what do you mean why), but why aren't I able to not only feel, but vocalize similar feelings towards others. Feelings similar to the love I have for Liverpool, a love I know I'm committed to forever, a love I've inked into my life.

Every time I take my pants off or bend my knees while wearing short shorts, I see a tattoo of the Champions League trophy along with the date June 1st, 2019 on my left thigh. I got inked immediately after the final, in a downtown Orlando bar that's also a tattoo parlor (a wonderfully dangerous business idea). Drunken tattoos can easily turn regrettable, but despite the fact some of the lines need recoating, I don't regret this one, nor the Liver Bird crest I had tattooed on my shoulder blade at the age of fifteen. They aren't images of silverware or dates of the year or my favorite team's symbol. They're etching arrangements of ink on skin that forever remind me of facets of life that can bring me to tears in the best way possible; of how much love I have to give.

(1)

The morning after Game 4 and Giannis's block, I work in the coffee shop under my apartment while L stays in my room to take a work call. I forget my water bottle—a black, metallic one that has my school's name on it—and ask L to bring it with when she joins. When I tell her where it is—under a black beanie on my white dresser—she says, *Of course it is,* because of course it is. She joins me for a while. She gets a simple coffee with a splash of milk, which, for reasons I cannot explain, surprises me. It's as if everything she does is awesome. As if I can construe all her actions as ones that bring me joy.

She leaves to go see her old roommate from six blocks away while I head back upstairs. When I walk into my room, I see that L made my bed, but put the comforter the wrong side up. I chuckle but won't mention it when she comes to say goodbye later. I'm flying tonight to help a friend—whose brother's cornflower blue T-shirt from Zara was given to me—move from North Carolina to Chicago. I pack my bag, and L comes over wearing a tight olive-green T-shirt instead of the white tube top from last night. I ask whether she asked her old roommate for a change of shirt. L says she'd packed another one in her bag.

She lies on the upside-down comforter and I ask if she can try not to leave her fucking mess everywhere, pointing to a small gum wrapper she left on the nightstand. *Is this mine?* she asks, then apologizes and puts it in her jean pocket. I lie down next to her and tell her I'm clearly joking, but she already knows that.

Ever since I revealed myself to her—told her about my anxiety, feelings towards her, sense of worthlessness—I've been in physical pain. In moments of mental silence, like when I'm daydreaming or out on a run, when my mind is clear and I'm reminded of how much of myself I gave away and shared, I feel like someone is clamping down on my organs. It's as if my body is informing my mind that I've gone too far. I can physically feel my liver and lungs and kidneys and spleen all clench themselves, signaling to my brain that we aren't yet ready to let go, aren't okay with doing away with two decades worth of conditioning to remain under the blanket, refuse to open up. It feels like I'm in the waning seconds of a ten-minute plank. My body trembles, my core is squeezed like an old rag, sweat gushes from my forehead and the tip of my nose, creating a pool right in front of my eyes, and there's barely enough space between my knees and the floor to swipe a credit card. Everything hurts.

I'm not able to articulate this feeling yet, so when I turn to face L atop the upside-down blanket, I just tell her I've been in physical pain, but I can't quite explain why. The look she gives me, our heads sharing a pillow, her face not even two inches from mine, makes me think she has no idea what I'm trying to say.

(1)   (2)   (3)

I say goodbye to L then board a flight and load a van and carry and build
IKEA furniture and wind up driving an empty minivan alone back to
North Carolina from Chicago.

I get pulled over somewhere in Indiana by a pair of cops: one young,
buff, and tan, the other old, pale, and overweight. I assume the younger
one is still in training, as the older one supervises how he leads the in-
quiry. They say I'm driving recklessly, which they deduce from the fact I
don't keep my turn signal on for long enough *after* switching lanes. The
younger one asks to see the car's insurance, and as soon as I pull it up on
my phone, I notice it expired two weeks ago. As the young one examines
the insurance, the older cop notices my water bottle—a black, metallic
one that has my school's name on it—in the cup holder and asks what
I study. He's overly impressed by the fact I (allegedly) write, saying he
wishes that he could but knows that he can't. I make a joke about how it's
just like writing traffic tickets, only more therapeutic. He laughs, which
catches the young one's attention, and he hands me my phone back, never
mentioning the expired insurance. They take my license and run a check
and everything is clear so they let me go with a warning. *Keep writing,* the
older one says. *Start writing,* I reply, he chuckles, and I keep my turn signal
on long after I merge back into traffic.

With my mind clear on the road, I'm reminded of the internal pain I
still can't articulate. I told L truths about me no one else has ever heard,
and now she knows a version of me that no one else has ever met. I'm not
sure if she understands the decades of guardedness that preceded her, but
I'm also timid about emphasizing my exposure. Knowing that someone
out there, even someone who is compassionate and caring and kind, is
holding an exposed and honest version of me in their hands is, I think,
the essence of what's paining me. Having grown up in an environment
where vulnerabilities tend to be exploited, I can't forget that the potential to be labeled a weakling is always there. There's not a single ounce of

me that thinks L would use what I told her against me. Still, the lack of control over who I am in the world, in other people's minds, is taking its toll. I can't reel my words back in, but I wonder whether I can assuage the pain by distancing myself from the only other person in the world who knows them. Maybe, I hope, I'll be able to render myself unexposed by simply going back into hiding underneath the blanket—a logic that I'll later find to be upside-down.

If only I could hold on to this plank just a fraction longer. If only I had the experience of trying and failing while growing up, the wherewithal to ask someone caring and compassionate and kind to wrap their arms around my chest, trust they will hold me up until the timer goes off, the pain becomes a thing of the past, and their arms around my chest become a gift, a thing of the present.

"Since true love sheds light on those aspects of ourselves we may wish to deny or hide, enabling us to see ourselves clearly and without shame," hooks does her best to find logic for me, "it is not surprising that so many individuals who say they want to know love turn away when such love beckons." With more than a borough between me and L, I decide to give into the pain before the timer goes off. I let my knees hit the floor, drown my face in the pool of sweat, and, once again, retract my bet. This time, though, fully aware of how much I'll lose. I know, as I cancel our plans to meet downtown, as I articulate a long-winded apology for my inability to be what I told her I thought I could be, that this is going to be it. With a certainty like the one before our first date, I know I've already pushed my luck far beyond what should've been allowed, and another sudden, steep slope on the roller coaster I've put L through will be the last. It won't be fair of me to ever ask her for another chance, and even if I did, she will have no reason to believe next time will be different.

I rationalized the first time I ended things by faulting life's wretched timing and circumstances, though it largely had to do with the condition-ing I'd undergone and had imposed on myself over the course of my life.

This second time, I have no upcoming graduation or winding down lease. The reasoning, decision, and repercussions are all mine.

I try to find solace in thinking it was so unlikely, in my mind, that I'd ever find anyone like L, anything like this, on a stupid, superficial, frivolous app, that it's just as likely to happen again. An impossible lightning that strikes once can surely strike again. Maybe it'll even strike with someone who's not a borough away, I attempt to further fortify myself with little-to-no logic.

I go over my apology one more time, come to terms with my decision to commit to a riskless, blissless life, hit send, put my phone away, and crash into bed.

When I eventually pick my phone up, I see her response about how foolish she feels for having believed anything had actually changed.

I accept my own pain, but no matter how much of it I'm willing to carry, I can't take on any of the pain I'm inflicting on her, and that renders my organs more clamped than ever before. I made her question herself again, I failed her, and my role as an imposer of pain, a mistake in her eyes, feels more than just permanent. It feels justified.

I throw my phone across the room, take a big swig of gin, and hope I don't crash even harder.

Step Four

Let The Dough Rise

(1)

My bear hug with Dani comes to full effect when I land in Coral Springs to spend Rosh Hashanah of 2021 with him. We embrace when he gets home from work and finds me in the living room that I let myself into using the key he left for me under the mat. The hug is short lived, though, as we quickly change into our running gear, hoping to beat the inevitable afternoon Florida downpour.

Both he and I hate running in a group, but our status as best friends, seemingly, renders the ordeal tolerable. I cannot speak for him, but reasons why I hate running with other people mostly boil down to feeling self-conscious about not being up to pace or restrained by fear of moving too quickly. Not to mention my immaculate diaphragm-appeasing rhythm getting confused by others' huffs and puffs and shoes on pavement.

We turn left out of Dani's apartment complex and embark on three laps of the 1.67-mile loop surrounding it. I'm on his left, and the exterior lane means that over the course of the five-mile run, I'm forced to cover a slightly larger distance than him. Not to mention, of course, his longer limbs, forcing me to take more steps just to be able to keep up. (We'll test the specifics post-run, out of my curiosity, and for every ten steps I take, he only needs to muster, roughly, nine-and-a-third.) We don't speak throughout the run, so I spend the time wondering whether Dani realizes that however much effort he's putting in, I'm having to strain myself that little bit more. Just so that I can stay parallel to him, so that when I glance down to look at my progress, then ogle sideways to see his, I'd be crossing the same exact line of the pavement he is at the exact same time. The thought festers in my mind, but never enough to overpower my ego, which would not permit me to vocalize anything that could potentially be perceived as a struggle or an excuse. The only words uttered over the course of our run are Dani's ascending tally of fractions of 1/6s, at the midway and ending points of each of our three loops. The distance elapsed growing, seemingly, at a rate similar to how much his declaration of the distance elapsed irritates me.

Dani and I haven't run together in years, so as we huff and puff on the Florida pavement, I think about the separate paths we've been on. How he and I haven't been like horses in a race: blinders on, plowing ahead one foot after the other, eyes solely on the finish line. We've been human: looking sideways, assessing ourselves in comparison to one another. I've molded everything I know about drive, hard work, and motivation alongside this person who, in a way, is my barometer. *Accountability partners,* he calls us. It's natural to think about, but the main reason I spend the run obsessed with this idea of progress and the motivation behind it is a debate I've been having for the last few days with someone. Someone intelligent, caring, compassionate, and kind, whose opinions I crave.

I've left L alone for the couple months since the Bucks secured their NBA title. She's been living her life, I've been doing my best to live mine, our canvases wholly detached. For some reason, completely absentmindedly, I texted her a few days ago wishing her a happy upcoming new year. She's not technically Jewish (father is, mother isn't, another stupid rule), but we've jested in the past about our lack of religious identity. Maybe I just felt like sending a tongue-in-cheek message. Maybe it was just my subconscious gauging whether my liver and lungs and spleen had loosened, even slightly. She replied, to my surprise, returning the wishes, and that was that.

The next day, she texted me to say how many times she'd been stopped on the street—people inquiring whether she's Jewish and interested in attending services. I asked her if she'd been wearing her Star of David shirt, and she replied that she wasn't, and that they were stopping anyone who could potentially be Jewish. It was the day Drake's new album *Certified Lover Boy* dropped, which our conversation rolled towards rather seamlessly. She told me kids in her high school loved sad boy music, which led me to say I recall one specific night where she played The Weeknd for us. *I definitely did,* she replied, *I needed to not hear Adele.*

With one serious reply to my sarcasm; with the fact she, too, remembers; with a jab at my love for Adele that makes me laugh out loud, it's back to being then.

Her disappointment with Drake's album triggered me to say that artists' older work is always better, which led us to a debate that we'll be having for my entire time in Florida. I told her a quote I heard Colin Cowherd use just the other day: "It's hard to get out of bed when you're sleeping in silk pajamas." *People lose their drive*, I added. She brought up a Kiese Laymon quote about how his brilliant grandmother would never be mediocre enough to run for politics, and how the notion of drive is deeply rooted in an individualist and potentially militant mentality. I considered the fact that I quoted a Fox Sports 1 talk show host while she brought up a writer (whom she loves) and the tales of his Black grandmother in the South. A part of me felt at an intellectual disadvantage, as if the database of my knowledge isn't worthy enough to challenge her, which, I think, on some level, we're both hoping to do. Another part of me felt like there's value in my ability to draw arguments from spheres of life completely distinct from the ones she exists in. But I was keen on finding a chance to prove that I can play on her field too, spar with her, prove that I'm some man of literature, some hot dude who reads.

When she asked me how it feels being back in Florida, I asked if she's read the famous David Foster Wallace Florida cruise essay. She said her high school English teacher made her read it, and I said it's a good depiction of this place as some faux vacation heaven, which is how I felt landing in Fort Lauderdale airport. I told her I just finished reading DFW's book after a friend recommended it to me, as he knew I've been writing an essay collection about masculinity, which I envision titling, *Somewhere Between a Dude and a Little Bitch*.

His stuff is okay, was my erudite review of DFW's work, *but his vocabulary is insane*. L said she's not a fan of his because of the way he iconizes himself, and the fact we punched at the same bag for a moment felt like progress. I followed up on my hyper-masculine reference with one from the "Commitment" chapter of another book I'd recently finished: bell hooks's *all about love*. Our conversation drifted to Kobe Bryant—whom we've argued about as much as anything over our time in each other's lives—and Cristiano Ronaldo. Examples of self-drive at its best, to me; of mythology and unfeasibility, to her (she added Kanye West to the list).

The earlier Sexton quote I used, about how the entire mythical life of the West is premised on the falsehood that if anyone else succeeds they're doing so at your expense, would have been great to bring up in my debate with L. But I won't start reading Sexton's book for another month or so. The book I brought with me to Florida, instead, is an essay collection written by Sarah Gerard, aptly called *Sunshine State*. I finished it on the plane and as I skimmed through the raving reviews at its beginning, I saw one particularly flattering one written by Kiese Laymon. I took a picture of his review and eagerly anticipated landing so that I could share it with someone I know loves him. *Damn, he really loves it,* L replied to the picture I sent, and I told her I can lend her my copy if she wants. Next Friday, when I'm back from Florida, I'll take the book with me as I board a local, weekend A train to a neighborhood Brooklyn bar, where I'll see L for the first time for the third time, and give her my copy, unaware that I won't get it back.

As Dani and I approach the lamppost that signifies the end of our third and final 1.67-mile lap, he informs me, in one exhale, that we'll immediately transition into a light jog until the following post. We do, then turn and walk back to his apartment, restoring our breath. We splay ourselves on a little patch of grass to stretch and cool down, where I make a sly remark, with a wry smile, about my having the exterior lane. Dani says he'll take the left side next time.

This inequality of the distance each of us had to cover could have been avoided, of course, had we not run in loops, but, as I do back in New York, in there-and-back straight lines.

(2)

Perhaps the reason I'm a there-and-back runner is because there's no viable loop surrounding the Hudson. My preference, then, is more circumstantial than voluntary. Maybe my mind will change if/when I leave New York. Maybe not. Either way, the river is just a two-minute walk from my apartment, and running up from Riverbank State Park to the Little Red Lighthouse, around the small roundabout that has a circumference of roughly 16π feet, then back down is wildly convenient and soothing.

I went on my run, once, a couple hours after it had rained. It was late spring, nearly summer, so the remnants of rain kept the evening warm, yet not humid. For someone who grew up where it never rains in summer, the concept is still so foreign and detestable to me, even after seven years of the phenomenon in Florida and New York. After it rains in summer, when I come to my halt and stretch out on the grass, the bugs and flies come swarming. The heat exuding from my body invites the salivating pests to come feast on my blood. But in late spring, when the bugs still hibernate or cluster round the warm confines of NYC garbage (and I don't mean FiDi Finance Bros), my pest-less post-run stretch and decompression, in which I bask in the breeze of open air and an occasional whiff of salt and sewer from the Hudson, is delightful.

On that late spring run, I was enamored with my body's gliding (yeah, I said gliding) past fishermen resting atop the Hudson's breakwater, people hammocking by Fort Washington's Sisyphus Stones, and shirtless heads of families grilling meats, free of humidity to overheat me or cold air to refrigerate my trachea. With the evening's serenity, obviously, not going unnoticed or underappreciated by the rest of upper Manhattan's residents, the trail was overly populated. A point of emphasis for me when I run, much like in real life, is to not be a nuisance in anyone else's journey. I constantly check my shoulders for approaching cyclists, go the long way round walkers so not to creep up on them, and plan well, well in advance for potential children chasing balls or each other across the trail. On my way back down that evening, as I neared the asphalt courts under the W 158th bridge, I saw a cluster of people slowly trudging in both directions, occupying the paved path. The path's girth thins and thickens throughout my route, and at this particular point, it narrows to be about six feet, which, even during non-Covid times, isn't a space for many people to occupy at once. Confidently approaching the cluster, and without breaking stride, I veered right to overtake them through the patch of grass and mud separating the trail from the water. I forgot, of course, about the rain's remnants on the ground, and as soon as my left sneaker stepped right onto the mud, it skidded, sending me tumbling down.

I couldn't see the tumble myself, but I'm sure that if anyone saw it in its entirety, they would have thought I'd rehearsed the fall. As soon as my body hit the floor—which parts of it precisely made impact first I couldn't tell you—I was, quite literally, up and running again. The thud of the impact and the flapping body in their peripheral vision caught the attention of the pedestrians around me, who—though I cannot wholly confirm this and it may be a figment of my imagination—gasped. Running away, I extended a backwards thumbs up into the air to affirm everything is fine to the woman—bless her soul—who shrieked an *Are you okay?!* at my rapidly fleeting figure.

My pace hastened once I returned to two feet, hoping that distancing myself from those who'd seen me fall would help assuage—or at least make me forget—the pain. The adrenaline of the run played its part in my disregarding the pain of the fall, of course, but in the grand scheme of things the epinephrine was a minor contributor in comparison to my engulfing sense of embarrassment. Only when I reached my finish line, after Ten Mile River playground and the two conjoined baseball fields, did I look down to see the damage.

There's a video of a soccer player from a few years ago who suffers a horrific leg break on the field. What stands out in this squeamish video is the player seeming completely fine for a couple of seconds as he lays on the ground, until he looks down at the state of his leg, at which point a mix of panic and horror takes over his face. Pain, sometimes, is only felt when seen.

By no means did I break my leg on that tumble, but I was surprised to see my self-inflicted damage. Both my knees were somehow bleeding and muddy, the left side of my shorts begrimed. My left palm, in which I hold my keyring when I run, stung, too. Of the three keys (mailbox, intercom, front door), two must've gashed me, as a pair of parallel red lines decorated the inside of my hand. What really, truly stung, though, as I imagine you can already guess, was not my knee or shin or paw, but, of course, my ego.

There's a part of me that believes, or perhaps even hopes, that all those people I glide past (yeah, I said glide again) take note of me, too. As if they check their watch as I pass them the first time, then glance at the time when I pass them again, and share, in awe, with all around them, the impressive progress I'm making. As if they know precisely where I started, where I turned, or where I'm going.

I've been doing this route north and south for north of two years. Never once has anyone awarded me a(n) (un)warranted round of applause for trying so hard, posted about *The really fast dude in the really sweaty gray shirt* on Missed Connections NYC, or approached me when I finally come to a halt, to ask how I reached this ending point, which, lest we forget, is also my starting point, so swiftly.

I'm doing my best to stop hoping for that. To stop assessing myself based on who I am, in comparison to others, when I head towards the lighthouse; who am I, in comparison to them, when I head away from it. To believe my self-affirmation is sufficient; to believe the gratification I get, personally, from making it back past some shirtless griller with my lungs still full of air and my legs still devoid of lactic acid is enough. I really am. But I know that my need to be recognized by others, have them deem me impressive or successful or, at least, on pace, will never fade. It's not just about my constant need to check my shoulder and look sideways, but it's about my innate yearn to not only be seen, but be seen progressing, not tumbling down.

(1)

The real reason I'm down in Coral Springs, other than just to visit a friend and indulge in some Jewish camaraderie on the first of the Three Pilgrimage Festivals of the calendar year, is to help Dani pack. A few months ago, he decided to return to Israel permanently. He has his reasons: perhaps professional, perhaps personal, perhaps he's simply had enough of living somewhere where it rains in June. When he told our friend group from home-home that he's returning, a blue-eyed friend made the comment that I won't be too far behind, as if I'm obsessed with staying on the same path as Dani. I joke with Dani, over the course of the weekend, about how the number one reason I won't be following him is I can't give our friend the satisfaction of being right. (This, obviously, is a very serious joke.)

When I told my mom that Dani is moving back to Israel, she responded—in spectacularly rapid fashion—with, *Hm, must be nice for his parents.* A mistake on my part, really, not anticipating the Jewish mother induction of guilt from 6,000 miles away. But I'm content staying put for now. I'm chasing a new dream in New York City, one that has less to do with kicking a ball around and more with putting words on paper. This new dream would have never materialized, though, had it not been for my relative adequacy at kicking the aforementioned ball. The route has changed, without my knowing, and I'm glad that it has.

He's never written about our friendship, but, if I had to presume what his unheard voice would say about us, maybe I'd guess that he'd talk about how his bigger body means that every one of his steps requires him to exert more energy because of the larger weight he has to carry (Dani, these are simply facts). Maybe he'd tell you how on gray and gloomy evenings in Bern, all he could think about was how lucky the hive of us friends back home-home was for having each other. Perhaps he'd even relay how every time he sits down on a plane and his knees ram into the seat in front of him, he wishes he could be a perfectly average 5'10".

Maybe instead of likening us to horses with blinders on, he'd equate us to chameleons, conjure up some metaphor about how their 180° vision enables them to look sideways, and how they can so seamlessly fit in anywhere. I'll leave those decisions up to him.

Ironically, it's Dani who's doing the there-and-back. I've yet to figure out whether my path ends up being a loop, a there-and-back, or a squiggle like the one you do on the side of the page to check whether the pen is still working. I'm in no rush to figure that out, mostly since I'm not done growing and changing, and I don't yet feel comfortable doing so in front of those who think they know me best.

After our run and stretch and (separate) showers, we go pick up our beloved Indian food. We share spicy lamb vindaloo and chicken tikka masala and meat samosas and garlic naan, and sit down to watch a 9/11 documentary. We get through about half the movie before we pause for what we call a "dopamine break." Dani rolls a joint, and we each check our phones for any doses of attention. Dope and Dopamine. I see a text from L asking what my buddy and I have been up to, I tell her, and terms like US propaganda and war on terror and post-9/11 all swiftly appear. Dani grinds his weed and I share some of L's thoughts with him, saying they come from this girl I've sort of been seeing but also haven't, describing her as annoying in how smart and unsettling and curious and relentless and cerebral she is. This conversation between my best friend and me, a few brief, off-hand sentences spewed into a room scented by terrorism and curry and weed, nearly half a year since our first date, is the most I've talked to anyone about L, or the way she makes me feel, since a text I sent to a three-man group chat that read, *She's the one, boys.*

If I don't let people see me run, they won't see me tumbling down.

Back when The Cool Kids started smoking in middle school, they handed me a cigarette and told me I gotta take it *to the lungs*. I tried. I coughed. They laughed. On the rare occasions my younger self confidently and drunkenly accepted a cigarette since, I remembered my lesson. Inhale, swirl the smoke in my mouth for just long enough so it seems like

I'm taking it *to the lungs*, exhale. It wasn't about smoking. It was about being—briefly, disingenuously, illogically—not a weakling, but The Guy Who Smokes.

I've never really found value or merit in smoking weed, so don't do so very often, but I can smoke when called upon. Dani hands me the joint and I have a puff or two, careful not to take up too much time or substance. I stare down at it, take a breath—a deep one; one that makes the tip crackle. I consider asking Dani for advice about this girl I've sort of been seeing but also haven't, maybe just unload or vent some of the story onto his collarbone. I keep my eyes lowered as my cheek muscles give their final purse, then swirl the toxins in my mouth for a moment, decide against saying anything, and, instead, produce a cloud of smoke. I love the man sitting next to me, and he knows me better than nearly anyone in this world. He'd say there's nothing I can't talk to him about, and I know that. A part of me is desperate to do so. But another, a stronger one, is still struggling with the question of why. What's the point.

We decide we've consumed enough early 00s talking head content for one evening, then start watching YouTube clips of live performances of classic songs that crowds sing along to and will always be safe bets on karaoke night. We sit in silence and listen to The Killers and Oasis and Snow Patrol and Coldplay and, eventually, Adele at the Royal Albert Hall.

We had this family tradition on Friday nights at my mom's place, where Adele's show would be the soundtrack as the scent of Shabbat dinner would permeate through the apartment. I can monotonously recite the Kiddush off the top of my head and can sprinkle thyme over a lemon-stuffed bird any day of the week, but the spiritual connection I feel towards a family being a family or Friday nights carrying any sentiment stem from Adele's lyric mezzo-soprano dedicating "Make You Feel My Love" to Amy Winehouse. So, as Dani and I alternate song choices, permeating the room with more emotional resonance, I resort to, just as I have with an unfunny number of jokes with L, Adele.

We sit on this crummy couch, a couple of guys being dudes, passing around a joint in silence, watching Adele ask the hall's lights to be dimmed then for each audience member to turn on their phone's flashlight. There's a cacophony of light and the arena's upper terrace looks like a star-filled night. An elongated B flat along with repeating D and F notes emit from a piano, before being quickly overpowered by the voice of a 23-year-old from Tottenham belting a ballad about the offering of love when everything seems to be going wrong. And they, her voice and the notes and the lights and the lyrics, are beautiful. They really are. But what I think about, as I listen to it all, is how even the most tender and genuine offerings of love, even ones organically built over the course of a dozen years, can be hard to accept.

Sometimes, it's hard for us to understand that there are people in our lives whom we can wholly trust. People who've tumbled in front of us and whom we've helped up before. People who would do everything in their powers to prevent us from tumbling down, wouldn't think any less of us even if we do, and would always be there to get us back up and running. But, again, sometimes, it's hard for me to accept that.

It's hard to understand that I can render myself exposed without being vulnerable; accept that I can unload my problems without them being a burden; show someone where I'm hurting without worrying that I'll be hit in that exact spot—perhaps a byproduct of growing up in a social environment where any weakness, identified and created by others, is exploited.

The admission of weakness to the wrong ears results in mockery, but the admission of weakness to the right ears, ears that have been there for me for over a dozen years, can grow to be just as onerous. Giving doctors and nurses as examples, bell hooks tells us that she's "always amazed by how much courageous trust we offer strangers." Simultaneously, we "fear placing our emotional trust in caring individuals who may have been faithful friends all our lives." It's a bit paradoxical, for me, because this faithfulness I have in my best friend is the precise reason why I don't want to put my trust in him. I know he'll always be there for me, and so long as he will be, this imperfect, problematic, weak version of myself that I've manifested, this version of myself that I hate, will continue to exist.

Admitting to Dani I'm wildly in love with L would invite past tense questions that would force me to vocalize my flaws and mistakes, present tense ones that would force me to come out from under the blankets, and genuinely caring, future questions such as, *How are things with L*. And in the case that I'm not with her, should I find myself still tumbled down, begrimed and gashed, I'll be forced to make a choice. I'd have to either lie to my best friend, or speak my failure, externalize my tumbled self, into existence.

To accept an offering of love mandates a recognition and admission that even the parts of me that are flawed are worthy of loving. But when I look at those parts, I cannot fathom how they can be loved, so I keep them hidden from others. The irony of it all is that this concealment of my "unlovable" parts is what ends up preventing me feeling love.

I'll tell Dani about L, eventually, in written form for him to read on his plane ride home-home. In a few months, he'll ask me questions, over a breakfast of shakshuka and salad and Turkish coffee by the Mediterranean sea, and I'll reply relatively honestly, as honest as I can allow myself to be, and it'll be uncomfortable, and I'll clench for a bit, and I'll break up my answers with whatever is left of the meal, but it'll feel like progress. It'll be a small step in a new direction towards a new path, one I'm not sure whether will be muddy and slippery, or paved and stable. Until that time comes, we just remain on the couch, two guys being dudes, as I hear Adele tell us how she's—much like me, I guess—*chasing pavements*.

On the Sunday morning of our weekend together, Rosh Hashanah eve of 2021, Dani and I go running again. I'm on his right this time, but when we reach the exit of the apartment complex, Dani absentmindedly suggests we go the other way around the loop this time; switch things up. We do, and I'm allocated the exterior lane again. Dani's favorite thing about our relationship, undoubtedly, is watching me be irritated. Something about me losing my temper makes him laugh more than anything, which is rather beneficial, as him laughing, without fail, makes me laugh, too. But I'm not irritated as I'm forced to amass a slightly larger distance again; as beads of sweat hit the pavement, it's indiscernible which of the parallel, proximate bodies they're falling from. I chuckle to myself, filled with gratitude that I have someone to look sideways at, considering how much of myself I want to show in return.

Dani and I wrap up our loops, lie in the late morning sun, stretch, shower, eat an acai bowl, relax for the afternoon, drive to his boss's friend's house, park outside, chug one and a half airplane whiskey bottles each, then walk inside, where I accept a bottle of Heineken and am promptly escorted into the host's bedroom to see and hold an authentic ivory sculpture. We sit down at a dinner table where there are nine of us, and just as proceedings begin, Dani halts the evening, walks outside, and returns with his girlfriend, whom I'm meeting for the very first time. Proceedings, conducted by Mr. 2-Chapters, resume, and soon enough we're all eating and drinking and listening to the couples at the table profess their three favorite things about each other. I look sideways at my curly-haired, tall brother, and listen to him speak his love into existence. My mind swiftly drifts elsewhere, to think about what I would have said about L had she been next to me, and maybe even what three things she would have said about me, despite the fact we haven't seen each other in months. Had she been there for my best friend to meet for the very first time. Had she been there doing what the bottle of Heineken was. Had I been asked to do what I so desperately want to: speak my love into existence.

(3)

I've taken the GRE standardized test five times in my life. Only one of those was when I was applying for grad school, before I realized MFA programs don't require the test since there's absolutely no correlation between quantitative reasoning and the ability to make ~art~ (though the lowest common multiple tangent I went on earlier would beg to differ, then again, I'm not sure we can consider that to be art). Three of the other four times were for friends who wanted to go to grad school but didn't want to spend months creating and studying vocabulary flash cards. If you run the ETS (the company that offers the test) and are reading this, just know that A) Requiring standardized testing is an incredibly obsolete practice, and B) It's relatively easy to cheat when you offer it online.

The secret to learning the vocab words, for me, was practicalizing their usage.

> **hel·ter-skel·ter**
> *adjective*
> involving disorderly haste or confusion.

Friday, the first one of the
Jewish New Year, 2021, 12:00 p.m.

Do you have a busy weekend coming up? /would you
wanna get coffee or a drink at some point?

L:
lol I have a kind of busy weekend but
I'm not opposed to coffee or a drink
Only because I might still need u to take
the GRE for me
But what's your weekend like idk

You do wanna meet up tho?
We rly can just be pan pals

> Yeah we can be pen pals, just give me your address and I'll
> ship this essay collection and some Israeli chocolate your
> way

Lmao
But for real like
You know what I'm saying

> I just think it would be nice to see you, I'd like to
> Not trying to really think of anything that's happened. Not
> in the sense that I'm disregarding it or anything, I just feel
> like I want to see you
> Idk how you feel

I feel okay
I don't feel like I'm thinking about what happened either
I think it'd be nice to see you
Tonight honestly I might be around like later for a drink or
something
Tomorrow I'm gonna be in LES for this day party and
could sneak out at some point to see you for a bit

The hopeful, hopeless romantic in me was desperate to see L as soon as I got back from Florida. The logical side of me, though, knew I'd need to be patient. I figured I'm best off surfacing the prospect then being as logistically flexible as possible without coming across as trying too hard. I could say yes to more social events in Brooklyn with friends, just so I could have the chance to tell L I'm actually in the neighborhood; tell her that yeah, of course I'm free, then cancel whatever work shift I had scheduled. I wanted to make sure I'd be available for whenever she initiates a step, make my presence felt without coming across as overbearing, put on a happy face, take whatever I'm given, and make sure it doesn't seem like I'm asking for anything at all.

Friday, 3:00 p.m.

I'm not doing anything tonight, so yeah a drink could work.
Do you have anything? Or like what does being around
mean

I'm prob gonna free up around 9:30,
idk if that's too late

Are you gonna be in Bk?

Yes
But tomorrow I will be in manhattan
most of the day

Lol don't want to whip you out of your fancy LES party
But if that makes more sense for you, or if sometime next
week is better/less convoluted then that's fine too

It's just a riverside bbq lol
I can text you when I'm done later
and if you're up for the train ride
then come down?

Isn't riverside on the opposite side of the east side?

Sounds good
Like FDR drive, east

Where does he rank on your favorite presidents list?

Lol he's the best
Number one

He served 4 terms!
High key sus
Such a driven individual, he was

Very sus
I am very behind tbh re: tonight
Do you think you're up for a late
late night or should I just see you
another time maybe

Lol all good
How late do you think? But also just text me,
can figure something out. Worst case
tomorrow or next week
Go have fun! Whatever the thing is lol

Back when L and I first met, I went through a phase of waking up at 6 a.m.. Perhaps as remnants of the pandemic and an adamant desire to try to make the most out of the day, I thought I'd enjoy becoming this early riser who reads and has his coffee and catches up on news before the day even starts. I fucking hated it. I'd feel forced to go to bed at 9 p.m., and L would make fun of me for being an 80-year-old man. I eventually grew tired of feeling like I need a nap by 9 a.m., so I gave up the idea. I was trying to be someone I wasn't, and, in hindsight, my insistent attempt at maintaining this disingenuous façade that really wasn't for me is a micro-cosm of why things went wrong with L the first time around. I had less time to give to her, and less of my true self to hand over, too.

Friday, 8:30 p.m.

I think it'll be more like 10:30
So if there are other things you
wanna do then def do them
Or if you wanna just chill

> Oh that's not late late, we're night owls these days
> I don't mind coming down at 10:30 or 11 or whenever
> you're done, so no rush
> Unless you think you'll be super tired lol

Can I let you know in like an
hour ish
We could go to this place called
lunático in bk

> Sure, sounds good
> To both of those haha

I get my best reading done on the subway. In bed makes me sleepy, in the coffee shop I get distracted. I think it's because of the duality of productivity—I both accumulate pages and get to where I need to go. Plus, you know, the whole Hot Dudes Reading Instagram account dream thing. I have, in the past, unabashedly, boarded the 1 train downtown on a Friday night just to do some reading on the train, walk around West

Village for a while, then return home. Once, specifically, I did that with Hanya Yanagihara's *A Little Life* as I went to 57 Lispenard St. to see where Willem and Jude lived.

So, around 10:30 p.m. on the first Friday night of the Jewish New Year, knowing the prospect of meeting L is there, knowing how long the train ride will be, I figured I'd get a head start. Just in case. I walk to the A train station, board the express that heads to Brooklyn, and dive into Paul Beatty's *White Boy Shuffle*. If we don't end up meeting, I'll at least get some reading done.

Friday, 10:50 p.m.

Hey
I'm going home now
You sleepy?

Lol I am not
Are you?

No?
Should we just meet tm
It's late

If you wanna meet at lunacita I'm in, unless you really prefer going to bed which is also totally fair

You really wanna make the trip? both
ways
I could do it if they're open for a bit
Tm I can meet at like5 or 6
Up to you

L it's really up to you, i can be there/somewhere else near
you, or we can do tomorrow if you're tired/prefer an early
night

It just closes at one
that's the only thing
But if you want to come down and
don't mind the ride then come
I just honestly don't know what's up
after 1 am

I can be at lunacita in like 25 mins lol
Or whatever the name is
I just feel like I've misspelled it this
whole time

How would u be there so soon
I need to take a shower
I can try for 25
We could go to the crown inn
It's a very chill place

I don't know which is more pretentious: moving to Brooklyn, or purposefully not moving to Brooklyn because everyone is moving to Brooklyn. I prefer the latter.

Saturday, 12:05 a.m.

So the crown inn?

Lol we really don't communicate
That's fine with me

The fact that we don't communicate or that we're going to
the crown inn

But where should I walk

Haha the crown inn
!

Okay
Wild Bird has music I think
But that's all I'll say

Lol where are you

Walking towards franklin
On Dean St
Just stay at the crown inn if you're there

I am indeed there

(1)   (2)   (3)

It's past midnight, and I'm leaning against the street sign pole on the corner of Park Pl. and Franklin St., holding Paul Beatty's *Tuff* and Sarah Gerard's *Sunshine State*. I'm wearing a soft, thin sweater that looks like TV static noise, and my phone is on Do Not Disturb in my jean pocket. I swivel my neck like an oscillating fan, trying to suss out from which direction a breath of air I haven't inhaled in months is going to come back into my life.

L shows up from the diagonal corner wearing a tight dress with a jacket in her hand. I'd have never guessed that she was sweating and playing bball just an hour ago, which she tells me about after we hug and I hand over the book. I say I'm surprised she didn't need another hour to pick out an outfit and do her hair and makeup, and having to explain that I'm being sarcastic makes me feel like I'm dusting off a book I haven't touched in an eon. The image I've always had of her face, lucidly registered, has always been swiftly and effortlessly assembled. Strands of hair seamlessly in place even when they're not.

The Crown Inn is loud and packed and rambunctious and anything but a very chill place, because of course it is. It surprises L, who says it's a bar she tends to come to with a book for some rest and relaxation. It's impossible to talk as we squeeze through people at the bar, and there's a certain first date awkwardness feeling where silence is acknowledged and felt. I've never felt this way with L before, not even at the impromptu yet planned actual first date on April Fools'. We make our way to the back garden, where there's a vacant, small, circular table on which we place my books and her jacket, and settle in. There are two women sitting at a table parallel to ours, and for some reason I feel like they're judging us. Maybe it's for our outfit choices, maybe because we've brought books to a bar, or maybe it's the fact that we're actually giving this—whatever this is—another shot. Whatever that is.

I walk inside and stand at the bar for what feels like forever then return to the table with two beers, which we have about three sips of before the back garden's lights are shut off ahead of its closure. I realize that those two women at the parallel table, who much like all the other outdoor patrons have already left, were giving us that condescending stare because they were privy to information we weren't. They could see the unavoidable destined outcome that L's and mine settling in won't last very long.

We pick up our beers and books and walk to the outdoor seating at the front, then we're told that's closing, too, so we traverse back inside and nestle into a corner high top table. L insists on getting the next round (which she, not surprisingly, gets in next-to-no-time). While she's gone, some guy at a table next to us starts talking to me about the book I brought to the bar. L comes back. He turns away. I ask her if she could please stop cock-blocking me, and her laugh brushes a bit more dust off the book.

It feels like more and more dust is swiped away as jokes about me taking the GRE for her transition into a candid conversation about the prospect of grad school, old professors that have left a mark on her, and what she wants to do with her future. It reassures me to know I still have this space in her life, one where my ears and existence and advice carry value. I tell her about my time in Coral Springs, and how I have this idea for an essay about how us men evaluate ourselves in comparison to our friends, which I began thinking about as Dani and I huffed and puffed on the Florida pavement. She doesn't seem particularly impressed at how I plan to structure the essay like the run—six sixths, just like Dani's tallying—and is more concerned with whether he'd mind that I'm writing about him, and whether I plan on showing it to him. I exonerate myself by saying that he's my boy, that of course I'll send it to him, and that I'm sure he wouldn't mind. (I will send it to him, and he won't mind, and we'll end up having a long conversation about things we'd never talked about, like what it was like when he left for Switzerland, and it'll bring us even closer together.) I tell L that as a writer I have to value my art, my writing, above people sometimes. It may be the most pretentious thing I've ever said, but it's something I have to believe. Write, make sure it's valuable, and deal with the repercussions later. *Everyone in my life should just assume I'm writing about them,* I tell her, and her eyes ask the next question, but her mouth doesn't, so I don't answer it.

When we close out, we see that the bartender charged me for two beers but L only for one, because of course he did. She tells me about another bartender in circulation who's hit on her, because of course he has. We carry our literature and head south on Franklin, walking past a group of people standing outside a dive bar, and I feel like they're all staring at us. Feels like every dude is wondering how in the world did this brown, bearded, book-bearing bro wind up with her, and every chick is questioning whether she needs to start looking for men who carry books instead of those who go to dive bars. The latter, perhaps, a bit of a stretch on my part, and the new most pretentious thing I've ever said.

When L and I turn the corner, we walk near a woman squatted down behind a restaurant's entrance. Her black tights are rolled around her ankles and a stream of pee drizzles down the pavement. L is in the middle of telling me a story and somehow doesn't notice the river of urine trickling its way towards us. I don't interrupt either of these women. As we try to decide where to go next, L says Wild Birds has live music so she looks up the hours and sees they're open till 4 a.m., which is still a couple of hours away. The bar is north on Franklin, so we turn around and walk past the same people at the dive bar, the pisser nowhere to be seen.

Wild Birds is empty and whoever was playing live music tonight is packing up their equipment off stage, because of course they are. L takes out her phone to scan the QR code and we scan the menu together. *Do you think this drink blows your brains out?* I ask her and point to a cocktail named "Kurt Cobain," but don't get much of a reaction. She's tired and doesn't really feel like drinking, so we end up getting waters and sitting perpendicular to one another on a cornered cushioned bench with thrift store pillows where L rests her head against the wall and hugs a pillow and sporadically closes her eyes or just takes lengthy blinks and we hushedly chat in this warehouse till we're asked to settle our tabs because the bar is closing so we just get up and leave. We'll learn, later, when L gets home, that she forgot her phone at that perpendicular cushioned corner. I'll feel somehow affirmed and flattered for being distracting enough for that to happen, then instantly guilty for making her stay out till she was tired enough for that to happen.

I have no expectation to be invited into L's apartment when we arrive at her building. She did, after all, ask whether I have the energy to take the train "both ways." Even in the unexpected case that I am, though, there's a part of me that wants to decline the invite. Maybe even say I can just crash on the couch for an hour, just to restore my bearings, and leave before the break of dawn. But the invite never surfaces.

We lean against the railing outside her building, parallel to one another, her on my left, barely enough room to swipe a credit card between us. She thanks me for the book, I tell her it was really nice to see her, and she concurs. I don't need to look down to see how close her hand is to mine. I can feel how small the space is, and all I want is to fill it with us from six months ago.

No part of me wants to leave this moment, and later—much, much later, in bars that have Guinness on tap; in crevices between beds and nightstands—my insistence on fixing myself into this moment will prove to be a problem. But I don't know that it's a problem yet, and for now, I'm here, and so is she.

I reach out my index finger and brush the back of her palm, and she reciprocates. Soon enough, my left arm wraps around her shoulders, and she rests her head against my chest that's under a soft, thin sweater that looks like TV static noise. Her eyes face downwards, presumably looking at where her and I are standing. I place an open right hand, an offer, in her sight, and she places her right palm inside it so that our thumbs interlock in a way that mine can stroke the crook of her hand. The books balance on the railing next to us, and we stay, completely silent, in this moment, for what feels like longer than the amount of time it takes to get two beers at a Brooklyn bar that isn't very chill at all.

Eventually, L breaks the silence by saying she has to go to sleep. I say that I know. Our hands let go and we shift our bodies to face each other the same way we would, months ago, in her bed, except we're standing now, and the ruffling sound of her duvet—the one that sounds like love—doesn't reverberate. She puts both her arms around my waist, I string mine around her shoulders, and our bodies mesh into one. Her face is buried somewhere in my chest, and I turn my head down so that my lips can feel her hair and the top of her head. It's not a kiss. My cheek muscles never contract, my lips never purse, and it's as if I'm restraining myself from actively exhibiting affection out of fear of scaring her away. Much like the books on the railings next to us, it's simply a placement of one thing on another with the hope of maintaining balance.

This night would've been a bittersweet and somber and perfect way to end our story, but we still have a chapter or two to live through. There's still going to be a little while longer that'll prove to be confusing and detrimental and enlightening and beneficial. A little while that I'll wish would've never happened but be begrudgingly grateful that it had. And this, this barely balanced moment at the end of a helter-skelter night, would've been the perfect bow to place on this gift that I'll eventually learn how to unwrap.

All the moments L and I have shared in the past have engraved themselves into my mind naturally, but this one outside her apartment feels like I'm intentionally etching it. I never made the active choice to absorb her outfits or words or expressions into my mind—it just sort of happened. But now, after the turmoil and the bell hooks and the dinner party, I'm finding myself actively cherishing the hug, a conscious decision to remember how her body feels when it's pressed against mine. Where exactly her palms are grabbing the lower back of my sweater, the way the top phalanx of each of my fingers can feel her, how warm my hand gets when it's tucked inside the collar of her jacket, and what the inside of my thumb traces as I brush it across her trapezius muscle and the strap of her dress. I wrap my arms tighter around L, continuing to squeeze every ounce of this moment for as long as I can. She's tired, and she needs to go to bed. I am, too; I do, too. But it's around 5 a.m. in a pitch black and dead silent street in Brooklyn in which two people are holding on to the faint residue of a soul connection in its truest and purest meaning, despite the inevitability of its demise. I love her. I love her for everything she is, everything I know she'll be, and, perhaps most importantly, everything she's making me become. But I'll slowly have to come to terms with the fact that no matter how long I hold on to this hug, I can't keep holding on to her. All I can do is hold on to the warmth, the idea of it, while letting the remnants of the twilight's cold air begin to come between us. In some universe, my arms will always hold on to L, but in the world we're in, the one it's my fault we wound up in, they have to let go.

She leaves my chest, lifts her palm that's tucked under the sleeve of her jacket up towards her face, wipes the top of her cheekbone, just underneath her eye, where a tear would be. I can't quite make out if she's wiped away a tear or if she's just tired. I'm not sure there's much of a difference.

She opens a door then disappears into a brightly lit lobby, while I turn and walk down a pitch black and dead silent street in Brooklyn, towards a station in which I board a Manhattan-bound local A train, on which I'm too tired to do any reading, and where I do my best to keep my eyes open as, one stop at a time, I'm taken away.

Step Five

Braid

(2)

Max is annoying in how well he gets along with everyone. What ampli-
fies the annoyance is that I love the fact that I get along with him too. It'd
have been great if I could've made him earn my affection; stared into his
big brown eyes and not instantaneously melt. But from the very second
I walked into Dani's living room and saw him napping in his doggy bed,
I was in love. He's like a puppet, Max, in how easy is it to just pick him
up and plunk him next to you and love on him without any resistance.
On the one hand, the fact that even if Hitler himself had walked through
the door, he'd have been allowed to hug and pet and cuddle with Max
should undervalue the love bestowed by this puppet. On the other, the
unconditional and open-armed approach to love Max has towards any
and everyone is beyond heart melting.

Whenever Dani's girlfriend would leave town, she would leave Max
with her trustworthy partner. Since she was gone and Dani was at work
when I arrived at Coral Springs, Max was my greeting party of one. Max
(who according to his owner's uncertain but best educated guess is a mix
between a pug, Min Pin, beagle, and angel) cuddled with us on the couch
as we passed along joints, splayed with us in the sun after our runs, and
placed his chin on my forehead as I was lying down, in what was the most
wholesome and affection-filled moment to ever happen in this world and
I have the photos to prove.

On Sunday night, after we wrapped up Rosh Hashanah dessert and
debriefed in the car about how eccentric the hosting family was, I and my
best friend and the woman he loves went back to his place, where Max
greeted us in the most adorable fashion. I parked on the couch as the
three of them sat on the floor, bundled up, and leaned against the side
of a staircase. I stared at their unadulterated, adulthood joy, then took
my phone—that was on Do Not Disturb in my pocket—and snapped
about twenty pictures of this makeshift and beautiful family. Dani in his
light pink dress shirt with the rolled-up sleeves, Max resting on his back

between Dani's straightened legs like the goddamn cutest fucking toy in the world, and Dani's girlfriend, in a cream-colored matching strapless top and long skirt, by their side, alternating her love-filled stare between the two men in her life.

Looming in the air of the evening's festivities was Dani's imminent departure to Israel. The feeling that love in its tangible form will soon cease to be an option between these two truly beautiful people loomed over my makeshift photoshoot of them, too. Had I looked at this man I grew up alongside through the eyes of a pent-up testosteroned teen, I'd have been envious of him, perhaps even carry some resentment. As if he were holding a free plane ticket to chase his dream in Switzerland but was declining the offer. His dream ticket this time around is the privilege of existing within the love of *the* person that makes him the best version of himself. His decision to walk away from this spoke volumes, but my no-longer teenaged ears heard nothing. I just looked at him proudly, not necessarily for the decision he chose to make, but for the act of making one, for deciding to follow whatever his heart and head were telling him, for emboldening himself to take risks, try and fail.

There's a "falsehood that if anyone else succeeds they're doing so at your expense," Sexton told us, but I'm not envious of Dani's love, which was put to the test after his relocation, and which passed with flying colors. His girlfriend is no longer his girlfriend, but his wife. And Max is no longer the only bundle of joy in their lives, as they've welcomed a beautiful baby boy into their home. They did it, the pair of them. They moved past the initial thrill, the early days where each one presented their best self, and, layer by layer, revealed who resided deep in their core. They handed one another what they consider the raw and flawed versions of themselves, trusted that their person will handle that version with care, and promised to do the same in return. They chose to commit not just to each other, but to whom they've become under each other's influence, which, and I say this confidently, is the most beautiful, very best version of them both.

And being by Dani's side through it all, the ups and downs and distance and expansion, something became elucidated for me. There's at least one facet of life in which Dani has unequivocally bested me. (I'm not counting his genetic height superiority, which is totally unfair and I will attribute to our progenitors.) He has the ability to talk, to look at the people alongside him and tell them what he's thinking and feeling, vocalize the problems he has, and ask for advice on how to solve them. It'll become so glaringly obvious, as he'll do so with me, how far I am from being able to do the same.

(1)

This third stint of L and me being in each other's lives was sparked by my random "Happy New Year" text. I soon thereafter reverted my tone, mannerisms, and mind to how they once were—I just didn't know any other way of being myself around her. But trying to immediately take us back to months ago was unfair to her. So, we spoke, to a small extent, about everything that's transpired and where we've ended up, which is when we agreed to just let things be for now; simply exist in each other's lives. I've toned myself down, and despite how unclear our location is, it is certainly very far from where we were in the spring. We've been chatting, sporadically, with messages that are neither a continuous conversation nor a surprise when they arrive. The seamless flirtations and deep conversations are emblematic of what still exists, but her prolonged silences in between—minutes and hours and days of me imagining what her reply may be, failed attempts at thinking her name into appearing on the screen of my phone—indicate, to me, an active and conscious decision to not let me near. I've been timid, when her name shows up, to reply promptly, despite wanting to do so. I sometimes feel as if my messages are like a pesky email in her inbox folder that she holds off on taking care of. By the time she finally gets around to doing so, I don't want to make it immediately reappear. So, I hold off on responding, take my time, act casual, all the while detesting myself for partaking in this absurd, juvenile texting game. I don't know what an adequate response time is. Half the time I feel the need to reciprocate whatever she's giving, and the other half I feel like I just need to be myself and constantly remind and show L that I'm here; that I want to be here, whenever she has the time and space for me.

I don't think L concerns herself with who texted what, when, and where. She's not that kind of person. I try to not be that person either. But I'm confused. I just don't know why sometimes we enter these hour-long discussions where no topic is off the table, where I feel open and honest and close to this woman again, and then she just vanishes, which,

I know, is a taste of my own medicine—one I must take. I don't know exactly where she is, but I regretfully understand and accept it. I'm choosing to believe that my existence in her life as someone who's at arm's length, and not an arm's length away, is temporary. Maybe I'm foolishly choosing to keep hoping.

I try to distract myself by watching *When Harry Met Sally* but wonder whether I can surprise her at a New Year's Eve party. I try to forget the way she mumbles into a pillowcase but lay my head on one and still hear hushed mumbles echoing. I listen to acoustic covers of love songs, but also to angsty emo songs from the 2000s. I hold my planks for as long as I possibly can but also let my pain crash onto the page. I imagine conversations with her in my head but go out and talk to other people. I come up with punch lines only she will get but write jokes I hope everyone will enjoy.

We fluctuate, float—I flare, flatter, flicker; she flees.

I'm assuming much of her gravitating to and fro stems from her simply not knowing how near, if at all, she wants me. The fact we still chat means there still is a part for me to play, and the fact we've met means that maybe I could still be cast in the lead. Or maybe she knows how desperate I am, and, out of pity, she feels bad cutting me out completely.

I know exactly how near I want her and what part of my life I want her to occupy. I also know that the main reason I know this now is because I didn't know it before. I understand what I've put L through, and how that renders my hopes unlikely for the time being, but that can't stop me from wanting. I'm in a battle between maintaining a shred of hope, while recognizing the ship may have sailed and will not return. It's ironic, I guess, and fitting, that now that I'm ready to talk, I missed my chance at having her listen.

If that is the case, and the prospect of love is gone for good, I still care about her greatly and want to be there for her. Be a solace and an escape and someone she can lean on, vent to about her family or future or lease or the person in front of her in line to get empanadas. Be a person in her life, even if it's not the person I'm desperate to be. I try to do my best to ensure she knows my presence is within reach, should she want it, while giving her the space and time she needs to figure out what it is exactly that she wants. I try to express cathecting without overwhelming, live with her silence without making a fuss. Each of us is brushing their respective canvas, and I just try to make sure that whenever she does open the door, I'll be there, ready to look up, so that our eyes can briefly lock. Despite how confusing this situation is, it's been such an intense whirlwind up to this point, that perhaps this platonic, somewhat chilled existence in each other's lives is what's best for both of us.

That's, at least, the lie I'm trying to convince myself of. Maybe as a means of obtaining some power.

(3)

I think it was the first night we met, but it could have been a different one of those very early ones. I don't remember the before or the after, the context, or the reason. Just the scene itself. As we were bundled together in her bed, I opened the YouTube app on my phone and made us watch my favorite *Britain's Got Talent* audition.

It's Ryan O'Shaughnessy's performance of his original song, "No Name." He walks out with his skinny body and acoustic guitar, wearing a T-shirt with thick horizontal stripes and a sagging neckline weighted by his lapel microphone. He tells the judges that the inspiration behind the song is a friend of his he's liked for a few years. Simon Cowell asks if it's like a love letter, and O'Shaughnessy says it's close to it. When asked what her response to the song was, he tells the judges she's never heard it before. He stumbles over himself when he's asked for her name, and when David Walliams presses him for it and Cowell tells him he may as well reveal since he's already in with two feet, you can see O'Shaughnessy squirm.

Eh, her name is—eh, her name is, he says, and I swear you can see the first syllable about to come out of his mouth, but then he stops himself. *It won't come out, it won't come out,* he punctuates, as if saying this woman's name would make her presence too real for him to handle. With one final attempt, just before O'Shaughnessy delivers truly magnificent lyrics and vocals, Simon Cowell asks him for just the first letter.

Ugh. It's—it's. Ugh. No, I— I— I really can't say it.

In hindsight, I'm not sure cheesy stories and Simon Cowell and that song are L's taste, and, if I recall correctly, the clip drew not much more than a polite reaction and cute smile.

But she was in my arms seeing something I wanted to share with her. I think she liked that part of it. I know I did.

(1)

A week goes by after our Brooklyn bar helter-skelter night. She tells me about her fancy Lower East Side party and this eccentric friend of hers that has a funny social media presence. I tell her I finally accomplished my goal of doing the splits. *Splits of what?* she asks, and I'm perplexed at having to explain myself. *My legs,* I say, and it takes us an irrational length of time to understand I'm talking about being able to create a 180° angle (kind of) with my legs when she thought I was talking about an interval-based workout.

The following Sunday, an almost wintery one but not quite, I come home from an afternoon run, planning to order food and watch the Bucs at Rams game. I wind up having an unfulfilling, solitary scoop of peanut butter out of the jar and hastily turning the game off midway through the first quarter. She's around, having early dinner with some family, and asks if I want to meet her by the river she's dearly missed since moving to Brooklyn. I head out wearing a salmon-colored long sleeve shirt that I've owned for over a decade. It's a favorite of mine for how soft the cotton feels, how well the fabric knows my skin, as if it wears me just as much as I wear it. The shirt has three gray buttons just under the collar, the top one permanently undone, so I often find the right side of the collar folded inwards in a way that renders my right collarbone—the one I cracked two decades ago—exposed.

We initially say we'll get a beer at this god-awful American sports bar by West Harlem Piers, but decide to go to the water first before the sun goes down. I arrive at the piers before L and lean against the railing overlooking the water. There's a party boat docked and blaring music at the pier, and small groups of people are holding solo cups and clustering around benches and patches of grass. L messages me that she's here, and I look south and see her at the pier's opposite entrance, wearing jeans and a white tank top with a jacket in hand. She asks where I am, and I tell her, but she can't see me with all the commotion, so she asks if she can call, and I turn off Do Not Disturb.

It's funny, talking to someone on the phone when you can see them but they can't see you. A microcosm of us, perhaps.

L can't see me, so it's on me to make the move. A microcosm of us, perhaps.

We get together.

We sit on the bench for a while and she tells me she's so full from splitting this huge pasta dish with her cousin, which reminds me how hungry I am. The sun goes down and we both get a little chilly from being stationary, so we walk south along the water for a mile or so until we end up parked on another bench, by the clay tennis courts. Tomorrow, she'll tell me she wound up walking more than ten miles over the course of this day, and I'll feel so bad for having made us not take an earlier exit off the trail. We sit, overlook the water, and talk about tobacco and the river. L tells me how much she misses it, and I genuinely suggest we can go buy cigarettes if she wants. She says she was talking about living by the water, and we laugh at our misunderstanding of each other.

Let's go get some food, I hear her say, and we look up places nearby then walk east to a Peruvian-Chinese restaurant—a fusion that catches us both off guard. We sit and scan the menu for a while, asking the waiter for another minute multiple times, and I can't quite make out what she wants. If only I was Mel Gibson. I'm not sure if the mood is a full dinner or apps to share or what, and as we discuss we slowly decipher that she never wanted to eat to begin with. I misheard her, and she actually said, *Let's go get you fed,* and the miscommunication makes us both laugh, again. The sugar momma vibe the phrase emits instantaneously renders it an inside joke catchphrase.

We decide to leave and go to a bar instead, and since I know there are a few one avenue over, I say I'll lead the way. As we walk out of the restaurant, with waiters running in and out around us, music emanating from inside, and the commotion of people pacing on Broadway, L, walking ahead of me, walks in the wrong direction.

Lucy, I call out, then reach my arm out to grab her. She swivels, and I realize how long it's been since I've said her name out loud. The way the jaw has to clench for the first syllable, shaping the lips as if they're about to whistle; how swiftly the chin has to unclench for the second half to come out, to hear the second syllable, *see* the whistle complete.

Everyone must be numb to the sound of their own name, and this instant probably carries no meaning or uniqueness for L. But after having her name ring in my head for so long, after seeing it appear on the screen of my phone, yearning for it to happen more frequently, the act of my vocalizing it in full makes her presence even more real. Saying her name feels like the shutter of a camera for the speed in which the moment snaps, and for the ensuing permanence of its snapping.

As we walk east, we laugh at the fact I never questioned L wanting to eat a second dinner, and how half a pasta dish could've been only a starter. We sit down at an empty dive bar where the Red Sox and Yankees game is on and get beers and chips and salsa. L sips on a pint, glances up towards one of the TVs, and exhales, with true disdain, the words, *Fuck the Yankees.*

There's a bit of narration in the movie *Gone Girl* (I haven't read the book, sorry, cover isn't bright enough), where Amy Dunne talks about the appeal of the cool-girl trope: something about never getting angry at men and chowing down burgers and hot dogs while maintaining a size two. I remember a blue-eyed brother I grew up with saying, when we were in our early teens, how he wants to marry a chick who would *crush a steak with him.* That's always stuck with me for some reason and feels related here (he's now married to a wonderful vegetarian dietitian, by the way). I don't know how much of the cool-girl trope subconsciously exists in my mind. I also don't know, and, frankly, couldn't care less, what L's jeans size is. But what I do find appealing is how all-encompassing she is, how many boxes, absentmindedly, she ticks.

The fact she drinks beer in sips just as big as mine while cussing out a rival. The fact she's ready to debate post-9/11 US propaganda or the Israeli-Palestinian conflict at a moment's notice. The fact I can learn so much from her bookcase. The fact it never fails to surprise me how firm a kisser she is. The fact she feels comfortable enough to make fun of me. The fact I'm beyond comfortable when I'm made fun of by her. The fact she reads my essay about Kobe Bryant and it pisses me off that she says she wished I spoke more about the unheard voices of the women in his life, because I honestly don't know what that even means. The fact that I read Hilton Als's *White Girls* and I understand what that means. The fact she makes a good point. The fact I still disagree with her. The fact that just when I think I've painted the precise point I wanted to make— be it about bball players or political issues or the angle I can create using my legs—she points to an entire expanse of canvas I didn't even realize was there.

We each have two beers and L asks if we can just get one more to share between us. As we do so, she looks at the half-eaten plate of chips and salsa and asks why I even ordered it. *I was fucking starving*, I defend myself, and for a moment I'm confused as to how she wasn't aware of that, but then I realize I never really said anything. Like the rest of the evening: miscommunication, missed communication. A microcosm.

I feel like I had more than you, L says when there's one large sip left in the pint and tells me to finish it. Much like with a salted pretzel months and months ago, I haven't cared enough to keep track of who had how much, but I gladly swig the beer. L insists we split the check, and it'll dawn on me, when I'll retell this anecdote, that I could've made some joke to her, now, about splitting the check or splitting my legs, but it doesn't come to mind in the moment.

I live between the 1 and the A/C train lines, so could take either home. I know L will take the C then switch to the A, so I tell her I will take the 1. She doesn't ask why, and I wouldn't have told her the real reason even if she had, but it's because I don't want to say goodbye to her at the train platform, the length of our goodbye subjected to the ding of a bell and a conductor's *Stand clear of the closing doors.* I tell her I'll walk her to her station then head to mine, and we soon find ourselves under the scaffolding on the SW corner of Central Park West and 96th street.

We hug goodbye, then our heads—and only our heads—pull back, and our foreheads press against each other, followed by our noses. No matter how much I think it would be smart to restrain myself from actively exhibiting affection, not scare her away, I truly have no option other than kissing her. I simply don't. I close my eyes and press my lips against hers, she presses back, firmly, and it's like a romantic version of Anton Ego taking the first bite of his ratatouille.

The last time we kissed, there were still questions about whether Giannis's game translates well to the post-season; it was still, according to some, the year 5,781; my friend had yet to fully move to Chicago; Dani hadn't decided to move home-home yet; I didn't know there was someone in the world who reads the same two chapters every morning of his life; I didn't know what authentic Ivory feels like; Max hadn't put his chin on my forehead; I wasn't aware of the length of time you're supposed to keep your turn signal on after switching lanes; bell hooks was still a distant, undergrad memory; I didn't know all about love.

The kiss ends but the embrace doesn't, and L raises her arm to press her finger against my collarbone, exposed by an undone button.

We linger in this moment for another beat, then she leaves to catch her train. I take about twelve steps west towards the 1 train, then wonder why in the world I'm making life complicated, change my mind, and decide to take the C uptown. When I finish descending the stairs into the station, I see L in conversation with the MTA worker, who tells her the next downtown C isn't for another 20-odd minutes. She's dismayed, and I tell her I'll wait with her, then the worker says there's actually a train arriving at the bottom platform right now. It's all helter-skelter as we hear the train arriving on the tracks, so we quickly hug again, then I have to rush her down the stairs. Halfway down the staircase she turns to look at me and says, *I'll see you soon*, in what feels like part-question, part-statement, full-on movie scene. I don't know if she's looking for affirmation from me, given the history of my fickleness, or whether she herself is uncertain about it all. Either way, I tell her she will, then add to get her ass to the train, which she does. I take my uptown train and get home and wait for her to reply that she made it back safely, before closing my eyes and feeling some concoction of affirmation, appeasement, serenity, and eagerness.

Her taste still on my lips, filled with, more than anything, hope, I fall into sleep without even having to try.

(3)

The Chair of my MFA program once reached out to me to inquire whether I'd be interested in helping her host the "Nonfiction Dialogues" series. We met over a glass of wine to discuss, and she told me that my name was recommended to her because people in the program saw me as, and I quote, "a strong reader." I briefly imagined I was coming across as someone who can understand Paul Beatty's satire but can also bicep curl 40s like they're nothing more than a pair of chicken wings, which is, frankly, the nicest thing anyone could ever say about me. In reality, I found her reaching out to be, at the very least, amusing, and more realistically, dubious.

I was grateful for the opportunity to rub Zoom shoulders with some prestigious nonfiction literati, but I had the sense my selection had little to do with intellectual prowess in the classroom, given that I allowed myself to speak no more than once per semester. The program's pat on my back had more to do with, I think, and pardon the cynicism, the fact I complained to the school a week or so prior about their handling of the pandemic. *This'll keep him quiet,* I imagined them saying. Perhaps a lesson to be learned here, for everyone: just complain. You may not get a reduction in tuition, but you may get two free glasses of wine.

For one of the dialogues, I had to introduce Lewis Hyde, who came to speak not long after the publication of his latest book. I wrote an introduction that opened with, "In the preface of his most recent book, *A Primer for Forgetting,*" had it approved, and was ready to go.

It's important we craft a side note, here, for a moment. I grew up in an English-speaking house but in a Hebrew-speaking country, so while I've been fluent in English my entire life, the spelling or pronunciation of certain words has occasionally flabbergasted me. *No fucking way,* has definitely come out of my mouth about the spelling of words like *phlegm* or *per se.* That's what you get for having your English depend mostly on hear se. Anyway, I'd never seen or given any thought to the word *primer* before

Hyde's book, and, frankly, didn't even consider its pronunciation. So, when introducing him, I pronounced it as *primer*, which I guess doesn't really make sense to you, reading this. Essentially, I likened it to Amazon Prime instead of a prim and proper lady. Primer, like, more prime. You get my point.

I could see on Hyde's face, from the second I mispronounced the name of his book (which I take full blame for, by the way), that something went awry, though I didn't realize why till about two minutes later, when a professor said the book's name correctly. My ensuing words, in which I raved about Hyde's body of work and glorification of creativity, were rendered pointless. Once you mistakenly read something—no matter if it's the mispronunciation of a book, or a kiss on the second time of seeing someone in your third stint in each other's lives—it becomes near impossible to amend.

(1)

It worked last time, getting a head start towards L when the prospect of meeting up was in the air. It's even easier this time since I'm already in Brooklyn, so when she asks if I want to come say hi, five days after we kissed, I say of course, because of course I do.

I've been in Brooklyn since the late afternoon—met a good friend by Jane's Carousel where I watched him propose to his then girlfriend and now fiancé, before heading to a Brooklyn Heights bar to celebrate my friends then lie to them. I say my goodbyes, saying I'm tired and going home, when in fact I become the sole passenger on a 1 a.m. Brooklyn bus that takes me 26 stops and drops me off by the Williamsburg Bridge.

I'm carrying a maroon tote bag from Book Culture and wearing a long-sleeved, thin, baby blue sweater. It's the same sweater I wore a few weeks ago, on my first Saturday night back from Coral Springs. I spent that evening walking south on the Hudson Trail by myself, AirPods shuffling my 1000 songs, phone on Do Not Disturb in my pocket as I made it all the way down to Christopher Street Pier, spending the 7.9 mile walk along the water deciding what three things I would have said about L had she been at the Rosh Hashanah dinner party with me. I came up pretty instantly with three of her idiosyncrasies, allocating the rest of the serene and breezy and darkened walk to figure out how I'd articulate them, which I will, here, eventually.

I wait for L outside a live music venue where some DJ she knows is playing. She walks out in double black denim, jeans and jacket, with her hair up in a ponytail. I don't think I've ever seen her in this look. We chat outside for a bit, and I briefly meet her friend and his friend. I've no clue how L prefaced my arrival, and if she did, how she described me to her friend. Maybe I was labeled as this guy she's sort of seen but also hasn't. Probably not. Probably just as a friend. Or maybe she didn't describe me at all. L didn't describe who this DJ friend of hers is, and I don't know if he has his own romantic intentions with her. I feel like he does, and there's this unspoken tension when we stand outside the bar.

I don't mean to irk this man; I'm just here to see her. As we chat outside, I find myself being nothing more than a spectator of a conversation between them that I'm not quite privy to, never considering taking the risk of imposing myself onto or into it. I just stand there feeling like a fool with a tote bag, considering whether I feel at a disadvantage in comparison to this man who can get on stage and align beats and get the crowd going or whatever the fuck DJs do, but deciding that there really is no contest between us. Interpret that sentence as you please.

I couldn't tell you what L makes of this moment. If I had to guess, from the outside, it looks as if she's trying to make a Venn diagram out of two separate circles of her life, but they wind up as, at the very most, tangential.

Her friend and his friend go back inside, and L tells them she'll see them in a bit. I notice a couple of guys smoking nearby staring at me and her, though probably mostly at her. L suggests we go sit by the East River, and as we walk away, one of the smokers says, *Can I just say, you're really pretty*, because of course he does. After we walk away, I turn to L and ask her if she thinks he was talking to her or to me. I love that she laughs at my silly joke, but also hate that I couldn't come up with it in the moment, so that he could hear me, too.

On my bus ride over, all I could think about was how it's six months to the day since L and I first bumped into each other. In nine days, I'll complete my 27th trip around the sun, and the (almost) $1/54^{th}$ of my life that's had L in it is proving to be an illuminating ray over the preceding fraction that is much larger numerically, but much smaller in value. I made a note to myself, on the bus, to bring up the semi-anniversary anecdote, but as we sit on a bench in Domino Park I forget to do so. I'm too busy making sarcastic comments about her denim-on-denim look and noticing how many crevices I can see in her face thanks to the ponytail. The distance between us, on this bench, is just as it was six months ago, at the foot of her bed. Except that back then, we were both moving towards each other, and this time, I'll learn, we're drifting apart. Or, more accurately put, she's drifting away. It's like both these moments are two identical snapshots of a singular domino rally piece, except one is about to tip forward a long line of pieces, and the other is destined to fall flat on the ground.

Unlike that first night, this time, I am anxious. Despite how satisfying it is to simply be in her presence, even if an arm's length away, and despite the fact physical contact isn't some highly valuable, be-all and end-all commodity, there's a part of me that's desperate for us to meet in the short distance between us. Not because I want a kiss, but because I need some affirmation. I need her to nod her head, tell me not to worry, invite me over.

We sit there, and I'll learn later that she was starving, though she never says anything. If I'd known, I would have suggested we go get something to eat. Instead, all I do is reach into my maroon tote bag and offer her water from my black, metallic bottle. I just didn't know. She never said anything. I never asked.

We chat for a while, then she says she should probably go back to her friends, and we say goodbye outside of the venue. We hug, I make a silly joke reminding her to not lose her phone, then she hugs me for a second time, stringing her arms around my neck in a way that feels romantic or, at least, affectionate, but the smile she gives me to dismiss my joke, as if it's beneath her somehow, or she's grown so accustomed to my sense of humor that it's become banal in a way, feels, somehow, platonic.

The station is the other way, she tells me as I turn to walk away, but I don't want to acknowledge that I miscalculated my route, recognize I'm heading in the wrong direction, be seen by L and her friends at the door admitting to making a mistake. *I'll figure it out,* I hurl back with a wry smile, and walk away with my tote bag, but without a beaming smile, since my lips never found a new occupation. I go the long way round towards the train station, knowing I'll eventually get to where I need to go, even if it'll take me a little while longer.

I let L know I made it back safely, saying I hope the same for her, and allow myself to add, *Good night, pretty girl*. I'm uncertain whether I'm complimenting her for her or for myself. L won't reply till the next day, something about how late and starving she got home. My compliment—which is more a fact—unaddressed.

There's this meme (memes, by the way, the most indicative and revealing insight into any culture) about how a compliment from someone you find attractive is a compliment, and a compliment from someone you don't find attractive is creepy. The meme isn't revelatory. But when you aren't certain if someone finds you attractive or not, in whichever form of attraction, the only way to find out whether you're creepy or complimentary is by just going for it.

I have no idea whether L finds me attractive or not. One would assume that to an extent she does, or at least did at some point, but far be it from me to know or proclaim. I'm not sure "attractive," in its physical sense, is what I'm aiming for anyway. I mean, don't get me wrong, it'd be nice to be tall or blue-eyed or a hot dude who reads, but that's not the main point. I'm digressing. What I really want to say is that after seeing each other three times in a span of two weeks, after standing in each other's arms for god knows how long at 5 a.m. in a darkened Brooklyn street, after kissing on top of the 96th St. station, after an awkward and makeshift and forced meetup outside a live music venue by the Williamsburg Bridge, I'm not sure how L feels. And it's her feelings that dictate whether me taking a 1 a.m. bus for 26 stops is me making an effort and showing my presence, or me aggressively imposing myself into her space and her life.

I could just ask L, but we sort of agreed to just let things happen for the time being. I'm wary that resurfacing the conversation so soon may make it seem like the only thing on my mind is us giving it one more shot, which, frankly, deep down, is all I want. But L doesn't need to know that yet, so I suppress and bury the urge to spark that conversation for the time being. If we never reach our happy ending, maybe I'll look back at this night at Domino Park and consider it an emblem of how my attempt at keeping us alive was aggressive and naive and stupid and embarrassing. Maybe I'll regret every bit of it, at least till I'll understand what I learned from it.

But in the moment, at the end of this night, as I fall asleep long before L's response comes, as I drift into a dream with some part of me wishing that she lost her phone again and that's why I haven't heard back yet, I just keep, as I have for the last few weeks, hoping.

(2)

It's not that I hate my birthday. Birthdays are great. Other than having
no bread, they are the number one excuse for eating cake. And I mean
proper cake, one oozing with icing and cavities. Not some carrot cake
faux shit. But whenever my day rolls around, I always feel an impending
doom hovering. I think, for instance, about someone born in the 1980s,
enamored with having a day of the year to call their own, counting the
days for its annual arrival, only for that date to be September 11th. I'm
sure that somewhere out there are millennial Virgos thinking to themselves, *Like, yeah, sure, it's sad and all, but why'd it have to happen on my
day?* So, whenever my day rolls around, I just hope world leaders keep
their fingers off red buttons, Mother Nature chills out with a drink, and
my grandma doesn't kick the bucket.

Birthdays are funny with how random their specialness is. July 4th, for
example, draws an *Oh!* that July 14th can only dream of. I get those awed
responses often since my birthday is on the tenth day of October. Awe
quickly turns into disbelief when I share my time of birth: ten minutes
past ten in the morning.

People rarely believe the 10/10 10:10 thing, but it is true. The factoid's
most beneficial use—other than sparing me from having to contrive a
fun fact for some first day of class—came to full effect when I filled out
college forms ahead of my move to the US. My birthdate meant that
being accustomed to Israel's DD/MM formatting wasn't as problematic
as it would be for most other international students. If Jesus were to ever
return to a third stint on this earth and attempt to immigrate to this
country, he'd probably have to explain that he wasn't, in fact, born on the
twelfth day of the 25th month. Much like Jesus, I'm a hairy Middle East-
erner with a predilection for wine, but luckily for me, my DD and MM
are the same, so the form-filling process proved seamless.

I was recruited to an unfamiliar university named Stetson. The school
was in DeLand, which I used to describe as a small, redneck, Florida

town, but subsequently learned that's a derogatory term, so now I just say small, redneck town.

I went to Chili's, my first week in DeLand, with three new teammates. After I ordered, one of them had to chime in and explain to a bemused waitress that I wanted no *tuh-MAY-toes* with my pasta (this was when I was still a picky eater). My accent proved too much for the waitress, and this interaction was, perhaps, emblematic of the two choices that awaited me in the US: be myself or be understood. My time at Stetson could be encompassed by that one Chili's anecdote, but basing an entire experience on an interaction with one person would be unfair, which, actually, brings us back to the topic of birthdays.

The issue started on my twelfth birthday. There was this tradition, in my middle school, where people would meet early in the morning at a corner shop to buy balloons for whoever's birthday it was. With a proverbial captain's armband around my twiggy bicep, I was often the one facilitating and organizing. When the eve of my birthday came along, I was so concerned that no one would step up for me, that I messaged a friend to make sure they made plans to meet at the shop. He said they'd already planned to do so, and instead of feeling relieved, I went to bed feeling pathetic for how anxious the craving for attention had made me. Walking home from school the next day, the bundle of balloons tied to my backpack served as an indicator for passersby who hurled *Happy Birthday* wishes my way. I thanked them in phlegm-filled Hebrew, cleared my throat, and wished, in a language only I can understand, only I can hear, that the helium would lift me up, up high, high enough, enough for me to never be seen again.

Each passerby had only meant to share some kindness, but all they did was remind me of how pathetic I was, how desperately I wanted others to recognize me. From that moment, I swore to suppress any craving for attention that ever creeps up.

Everyone knows how to get attention when they want it. Some people rev a rusty engine at a red light, some go vegan, some wear shorts in winter, and some share their opinion about the Middle Eastern conflict on social media. But on birthdays, attention just floods in, and its inevitable and sudden influx is what not only reminded me of my pitiful pining but destabilized me. So, I began spending most of the day hidden in my room, mostly subsisting on vague and virtual social media regards, begrudgingly surfacing to cut cakes (never carrot) or unwrap gifts, being someone who is best described as a Negative Nancy. My dad called me out, eventually, when I turned 18, and told me the day isn't just about me. It's a day for those who care about me to celebrate me, so I should just let them. Instead of trying to block the flood of festivities, I should just let the stream flow.

So, I learned to tolerate the day, which came in handy, a year later, on my 19th birthday, when I was at Stetson, and ever since, as the tolerating period was prolonged to 31 hours, because 5 p.m. of October 9th on the East Coast is already the 10th in Israel, so while it isn't my date yet, it is for those who care about me, so I let the attention flood, though, fortunately, my family being halfway across the world means that all I've had to tolerate, even if for a lengthier period of time, are virtual regards, which, by this point, after twenty-seven birthdays, nineteen in Israel, eight in the US, many of them angsty, one of them with too many balloons, absolutely none of them with carrot cake, I'm an expert at, but, that's never been the issue, has it, because, like I said: it's not. that I hate. my birthday.

Birthdays are great because they give a chance for those who love you, to love you. My dad told me that. But the way I see what he says, the way my brain works, on birthdays, those who don't love you, don't love you. And it's that yearly social marker that tells me who is and isn't a part of my life, and the extent to which they are or aren't, that scares me. Being unable to avoid this demarcating line is the problem. That's what I'm trying to say. When this day comes, all I can think of is how those who care about you show it, and if she won't, that means she doesn't. And it's that exact thought process, this inevitable litmus test with every trip around the sun, the fact that an entire experience can be based on one interaction with one person, that reminds me, once again, how much I fucking hate my birthday.

(1)

An Irish buddy of mine, one I once went on a double date with to watch *Kingsman: The Golden Circle*, taught me a game they play with pints of Guinness back home: Splitting The G. Order one, and with one sip, try to get the line where the stout and foam converge to perfectly bisect the first letter of the printed "Guinness" in Unified Hobbsian font on the glass. Succeed, and you're free to leisurely drink (whatever that means) for the rest of the time. Fail, and you must order another, then finish the existing pint before the next one arrives. Rinse, repeat.

The first time I ever try this game is on Saturday night, October 9th, 2021. It's still just about warm enough to exist outside in New York without your ugly winter jacket (one I don't own since the warmth of the coolness of my leather jacket has yet to fail me). I sit down at a high-top table in my downstairs bar's outdoor seating. Order, sip, examine, repeat. It's trickier than perceived. If you were to try the game, I'd guess that, most likely, you'd undershoot it. I think it has something to do with the glass's deceptive wider girth at the top. Much like before going to a social event you're not keen on, you need to drink more than you think you do. Then again, now that I've said this, if you ever give it a shot, you'll probably overshoot it. Either way, it's very much trial and error, and heavily depends on individual sip size or gulp girth or swig scale.

I fail on my first try and begin what will wind up being an elongated chain of texts with my Irish buddy where I send him pictures of my pint post-one sip, and he waves a metaphorical green or red flag. After three or four failed attempts and successful inception of inebriation, I begin propping my phone against a mason jar of water for every attempt, to record videos of my sipping, then await being graded by the Irish law of the land.

Me, alone, on my birthday eve, glugging Guinness like a giddy Gaelic goon, having the time of my life, mostly, I should say, because at some point between Guinness number one and six, L texted me.

I've barely heard from her since seeing her at Domino Park. Our communication has become even more scarce and sporadic, and I can't help but think that my going to see her late at night, taking her away from what she was doing and who she was with, has something to do with it. As if she's reluctant to reciprocate anything she's not sure she wants to receive, timid about sending the wrong signal, and I, in a way, forced her to be so. But earlier tonight she texted, unprompted, asking if I'm excited about tomorrow. I dismissed the importance of my birthday, then told her I'm at this American bar/restaurant underneath my apartment, the one we once went to together, and added for her to not worry as this time I didn't bring my own beer here. The fact she laughed without my having to explain signifies she also remembers. Over the course of the conversation, boosted by the booze, I mentioned how that Friday at Domino Park was six months to the day since we first met. *Wait is that true*, she replied, followed by, *No way*, followed by, *No*, followed by asking if it feels that way to me, at which point I said it feels like eight lives ago.

I know that what I'm about to say is silly, but L and I don't follow each other on any social media, so the fact that she just knows when my birthday is gives me the slightest of affirmation that I'm still awarded a small patch of land in her mind. The fact it's actively on her mind, even if passively, before it's even here, means something in my book. In fairness, I have an incredibly easy date to remember. Even more so, the date is probably etched in her memory because our birthdays were the subject of the best joke I ever made with her.

We were bundled up under the covers in that bright bedroom of hers. It was morning, and I told her when my birthday was, then she told me hers is on May 5th. I assume most people's immediate connotation would be to reference Cinco de Mayo, but I didn't. *You're 5/5 and I'm 10/10*, I said before I could even think about what I was saying, then added, *That's because I'm twice as good as you.*

It's not up for debate, the fact this is the best joke we've ever shared. Maybe you want to disagree, say you don't get what about it is funny at all. But humor is subjective, and jokes are assessed by how they're received, and when I tell you that no joke has ever signified, in my mind, how perfectly we fit together, you're just going to have to take my word for it. You'll have to believe that as I couldn't contain my own laughter, giggling before I even finished the sentence, she semi rolled her eyes and quasi pushed herself away from me, despite the fact she couldn't hold back her own laughter either. You'll have to imagine how I wrapped my arms around her, didn't let her get away, and pulled her face back into my chest. You'll have to hear her laughter muffled by my embrace, and my simultaneous uncontrollable chuckling at this silly, self-aggrandizing mathematical joke that is so clearly the exact opposite of the truth. You'll have to picture how just when one of us thought their laugh was finally subsiding, they noticed the other one still giggling, setting us off again. You'll have to estimate how long it took for both of us to finally move on from this joke, and emit a big, long sigh into the air. It could've been five seconds; it could've been ten days. You'll just have to imagine how her lips moved to mouth the words, *You're so dumb*, and how mine reciprocated by kissing her, admitting that I know I am. You can philosophize or theorize for yourself whether this moment signifies love. Whether inordinate levels of comfort, the ability to laugh at each other, the existence in a state where even performative attempts to push away are met with a showering of recognition and affection, the adamant decision that no matter what happens you remain one, are emblems of love.

This moment was plenty of months and failures and ups and down before my birthday eve, and when I sit at my bar's outdoor seating, clutching at any hopeful straw I can, the fact she remembers the date makes me feel like she may also be holding on to this memory of us in her bed. Maybe it's the alcohol that's deceiving me, but I begin to think that maybe, on some level, my outfits and expressions and words have absorbed themselves into her brain; that my brush has stroked the fabric of her canvas; that there's a part of me she's still unable—and maybe unwilling—to get rid of.

I love how I'm drunker in every video, I text my Irish friend, then request a judge's verdict at my latest attempt, and he says that that's it. I got it. I win. I'm done. I tell him how the waiters must think I'm an absolute maniac, he says this was one of the funniest evenings he's had in a while, and we exchange *Love yous.*

After I told her it feels like it was eight lives ago that we first met, L said: *Idk part of me feels like I was supposed to meet you somewhere else or another time or I don't know,* and, L, me too.

But with every attempt to land my dark Guinness precisely across the G, my belief that maybe this could still be the right place, that maybe this could still be the right time, grew more and more *stout.*

(3)

In writing about her novel, *Mercy,* Andrea Dworkin says, "My narrator, who is a character in my book, knows less than I do."

This quote comes in Dworkin's essay "My Life as a Writer," which I read—along with Chapter 6 of *Mercy*—in a collection of her radical feminist writing edited by Johanna Fateman and Amy Scholder. I picked the book up partially because it has a bright red and pink cover (of course it does), but mostly because I understood that my attempt at exploring and understanding and conceptualizing masculinity is futile without an attempt at exploring and understanding and conceptualizing feminin- ity, and by extension, feminism. The two carry more overlap on a Venn diagram than two distinct circles of L's life outside a live music venue in Williamsburg.

This isn't some groundbreaking revelation, nor am I intending to pat myself on the back for reading something that isn't Hemingway or DFW or Jordan Peterson. But if you'd told 14-year-old me, as he and his friends were mastering baiting the family room's computer into going on incog- nito mode, that he'd read 400 pages written by this woman who's re- nowned for her antipornography stances, and somehow totally get her labeling porn as the symbol of everything that's wrong in our culture, he'd laugh in your face. Or, more likely, he'd roll his eyes and laugh at you with his friends behind your back.

But as I trudged (and I don't mean to conjure a negative connotation by using "trudged," but it's just, like, heavy shit to read) through Dworkin's work about the genocidal character of sexual violence, the devastating nihilism of white male supremacy, and the toll it takes, her writing about writing felt most palpable. It's no surprise, really. I cannot relate to so much of the suffering and pain Dworkin talks about; all I can do is try to understand and learn and see. But when it came to her understanding of herself through writing—her usage of an "I" character to dissect what she wants to say—every single word resonated.

Mercy is a work of fiction, and people tended to assume that Dworkin was hiding behind a character to write about her own life (no comment from me about any auto-fictioners out there). Her quote above about writing is meant to dissociate her as a person from the "I" character in the novel who goes through horrific abuse. She is not her. Dworkin tells us that she is not an exhibitionist and does not want to confess. She is using the character's life to show what she believes needs to be shown.

This, that you have been reading (thank you for doing that, btw), is a work of nonfiction. If you don't know the difference between fiction and nonfiction, google it. Or just apply to Writing MFA programs and pretend that you do. Despite the fact that the person telling you this story and the person whom this story is about are one in the same, there is a distance between them. It is only in my dissociation from myself, the distance I've created between the "me" that is now and the "me" that was then—the time that's expanded between us, the differences I've found between the two, the lessons one has learned from the other— that I was able to use my life to show what I believe needs to be shown. "Hindsight" is what people usually call this. And while being smarter in hindsight isn't ideal, it's better than staying dumb.

I said earlier that social constructs have historically empowered men and enabled them to avoid confronting personal flaws. A Hot Take. Power and money and superior social status have always trumped any potential emotional or intellectual inferiority. I cannot be wrong if I can punch you in the face. I cannot be vulnerable if my shirt sleeves hug my biceps. I don't owe you shit if I can pay for dinner. I cannot be held accountable for how fucked up I am, because that's just who I am. Take it or leave it.

This is my attempt at self-reflection, which cannot happen without attempting to wrap my head around the masculine culture I grew up in. This culture that stereotypically refuses to look inwards has made a huge impact on who I am—for better or worse. This perceived unwillingness or inability men have to self-reflect comes, in part, from a reluctance to consider and admit to our culpability in the creation of a poisonous pie. The mere existence of this pie is sometimes questioned, particularly as we go through life thinking everything is fine, not being served a slice, and not having to clean up any of the crumbs. (This pie metaphor is, aptly, half baked.)

In *I Hate Men*, Pauline Harmange says that the root of women's loathing and distrust of men stems from violence inflicted onto them by men, but the problem "also lies with all the men who don't rape, and all the other things they don't do either." Harmange was deemed radical in her thoughts, government officials tried to ban her book, and she was severely attacked in real life and online. It'd be easy, especially for Men, to be reductive of her book. Claim that the book's "radical" stance—even just the title itself—negates the possibility of a coherent and logic-based discussion about gendered relationships and power dynamics. To that I ask, is her book title less coherent and logic-based than a testosterone-scented room? To that I suggest, read the book; to that I say, grow up.

Many arguments attempting to alter men's violent behavior towards women are centered around familial relationships. *Would you want that to happen to your mother/sister* type of thing. Some people push back on this argument, saying it devalues women's basic humanity, as if some preconceived relationship has to exist to warrant respect and decency. I once had the chance to speak to Brenda Tracy, founder of the "Set the Expectation" nonprofit organization dedicated to ending sexual and interpersonal violence. I asked Tracy for her thoughts on this, and she told me that until we learn to value people based on their humanity, women will never be safe. However, she said that the family argument is a fine starting point, so long as it develops and progresses from there. She correlated it to teaching advanced calculus to a basic math student. *It's okay if all you can do right now is addition and subtraction, I just need you to show me you want to know more.* There's an effort that's needed, since "for men, it's the simplest thing in the world to sit back and watch the patriarchy work in your favor." You can thank Jared Yates Sexton for that last quote.

(These parentheses are dedicated to the genuinely sincere acknowledgement that: A. Despite how lopsided the numbers are, plenty of men are also the victims of domestic violence, and they deserve the exact same respect and treatment as any other victim does; B. I'm a man, so there's a decent chance that you want to say I shouldn't be the one to make this argument. There's also a chance you're thinking, *Dude we know we're not supposed to rape,* or perhaps you think that I'm just doing this to pander. Sure. Whatever helps you sleep at night.)

In *The Right to Sex*, which is depressingly magnificent, Amia Srinivasan writes about the alleged "conspiracy against men." She ends her opening essay by discarding any hope that "these disgraced but loved, ruined but rich, never to be employed again until they are employed again" men will ever change. "Why should they?" she asks, "Don't you know who the fuck they are?"

It is far beyond the capabilities of yours truly to understand and discuss the legal, social, and political layers that compound not only the enabling of monstrous men (shoutout to Claire Dederer), but the inability of the current legislative, carceral, or educational systems to solve the issue of sexual violence without turning a blind eye or ineffectively trying to hide it in a cell. Srinivasan does a phenomenal job of laying these issues out in her essay, as does Jia Tolentino in "We Come from Old Virginia" in *Trick Mirror*.

There's an expectation, Srinivasan argues, that "a feminism worth having" is one in which women, once again, must be better than men have been, "but it is not up to women alone." It is imperative, she says, that men are asked to be better. Yes, even those who are already *good*.

A lot of men are good, and a lot of men are aware of the violence imposed on women, and a lot of men don't think it's fair to carry the blame for other men's heinousness. This is where we go back to Harmange's "and all the other things they don't do either." She illustrates this as, "When they don't assume their share of the mental load, meaning that in the twenty-first century [women are] still overwhelmingly the ones responsible for the shopping, the kids and the emotional labour in our re-lationships." We'll see how this next sentence lands, but just because you don't rape, doesn't mean you're a good guy. So, what does it mean to be a good guy? Haramange would say it entails assuming your share of the mental load, going to the grocery store, picking up the kids on your way home, and initiating conversations about the state of the relationship. Or maybe that's not the definition of a "good guy," but just that of a "decent human." Maybe being a good guy includes looking at how conditioning can perpetuate violence, feeling accountable for those in the room with us, and even talking to them about advanced calculus.

Before I ask why feminism is worth having to begin with, it's import-ant to acknowledge that the concept, because of its prominence and ma-nipulation in discourse, these days more than ever, is incredibly loaded. One of the core aspects of feminism is the advocacy for women's right to equality with men. The importance of this "equality," the definition of it, and the means through which it can or can't be achieved are questions I have no business or credentials to try to answer. Plenty of others, many of whom are mentioned at some point in this book, do a much better job than I ever could. Bearing all this in mind, however, as I said in the open-ing of this section, it is impossible for me to understand whatever it is I'm trying to understand without considering my definition of and the value I see in feminism and femininity; without answering the question of why feminism is important *to me*. My instinctual answer is, presumably, the same as most other men's: because we want the best for the women in our lives. Pushed beyond that, perhaps we'd say because we believe equality is the right thing to aspire for, or because we want to be kind human beings. All three of those reasons, as I bring them up now, make me feel like I'm coming across as disingenuous.

Because it's nearly impossible. It's nearly impossible to identify as a feminist or argue that you support women without being questioned for the manner and extent through which you do, the motive behind the identification. I know, I know, I know what you're thinking: "Poor Man, he's being questioned, and it makes him uncomfortable." But that's not what I mean. It seems, to me, that every conversation has become impossible to partake in. You can't support A without being asked why you don't care about B. You can't say you disagree with C without coming across as a D-hater (no jokes here, please). There seems to be a deeply embedded, never-ending, systemic cycle of oppression in the world we live in—a cycle that's inherently intertwined. It seems that it's easier for people to attack you for caring about one part of it and not another, than it is for people to see how the fact that everything is connected means that everything needs to be looked at and cared for. That's, at least, how it seems *to me*. Again, I don't think I'm doing anything groundbreaking here. Go look at world system theories, dependency theories, Karl Marx, Pablo Freire's *Pedagogy of the Oppressed*, and, of course, *Kinne Tonight*'s "Say Cheese" sketch. They've all done this before me, yet I still feel the need to acknowledge all of this now, only so I can be able to disregard it completely.

Srinivasan illustrates this sort of hierarchal cycle in her essay "Coda: The Politics of Desire." When it comes to sexual violence, men of color have often been the victims of the carceral system because of their inferior social position in comparison to, say, white women. However, when it comes to their relationship with women of color, the same men who were victims of the legal system just a moment ago, thanks to their "gendered superiority," turn oppressors. Srinivasan then brings up (though she doesn't necessarily agree with it) supposed desire-based discrimination imposed upon men of color *by* women of color, bringing examples of Asian women who have no interest in dating and mating with men from their culture. On the one hand, she asks, "aren't Asian women within their rights to make such choices?" But on the other hand, she questions where those choices stem from: "Why think that white boys and men are raised any better? *Is sophistication to be found only in Caucasia?*"

In *salvation*, the sequel to *all about love*, hooks touches on these distinct yet related obsessions with power. Hand in hand with the rise of Black feminism came the solidification of Black male misogyny. Any advocacy of and for Black women was labeled by their male counterparts as a betrayal of the race. There was a sentiment that Black men's "newly found manhood could only be affirmed when they could subordinate women." While Black men were deprived of political or economic power, she argues, "they could outdo [black women] on the sexual front."

Maybe the crux of my point here is that we—regardless of who we are—have been systemically conditioned to believe that freedom can be fulfilled only when it includes the restriction of another; that power comes not from the self, but from its existence relative to its absence for another. Except, of course, for the fact that you may be yelling at the page right now: not everyone has had the chance to be free; to wield power. And that means that whatever I've been describing as a cycle is not so much a cycle, but a vertically linked chain. The bottom of each link being the top of the one below it, the chain never curving nor encircling. Maybe that's a bit of a reductive image of the system of oppression our society seems to have been in for, say, ever, but it's the image that comes to mind now.

There are all these things to consider: race, sex, heteronormativity, disabilities, class, capital, age, politics, favorite Premier League midfielder of all time. We could probably trace each of these back to the same hierarchical and historical origin, which I'm not saying we shouldn't; we should. Question black and white and small and big and right and left and male and female and Gerrard and Lampard and rich and poor. Question it all, though, in an attempt to find answers, not in an attempt to prove a point. And my point is that I feel like there isn't a crevice of the discourse, a canvas large enough, or a painter woke enough to be immune to whataboutism.

But that's not the point. The point is that it is nearly impossible, I feel, to enter discourses that are so loaded, toxic, and tarnished to begin with. To better understand what I mean, let's look at a brief case study about Dave Chappelle. (We're almost done with this convoluted section, I promise.)

Chappelle's rhetoric about race, gender, and politics, along with his fabled decade hiatus and SNL monologues, have made him one of the most influential social orators of the modern day. He's also fucking hilarious. In his 2021 Netflix special filmed in Detroit, *The Closer*, in the midst of his "feud" with the LGBTQ community, he shared a story of an altercation with a gay white man in a bar in Texas. Just before things turned physical, the man took out his phone and called the police. "And this," Chappelle says, "this thing I'm describing, is a major issue that I have with that community. Gay people are minorities, until they need to be white again."

I'm not sure it's this book's place to try to dissect how anti-LGBTQ rhetoric (which I'm not necessarily arguing Chappelle engages in) leads to de facto violence, nor how progressive liberal movements can impede freedom of speech and come at the expense of other minority advocation (which I'm not necessarily arguing the LGBTQ community, particularly people of color within that community, engages in). What I am sure of is that Chappelle's quote is an extreme microcosm of the linked chain I'm trying to wrap my head around, or I'm trying to wrap around my head. Chappelle, throughout the entirety of his body of work, has been primarily advocating for the Black community in the United States. In his last few specials, this advocating has come hand in hand with, according to some, a dangerous belittling of the LGBTQ movement. This case study, which truly I am ill-equipped to unpack further than its superficial laying out here, is meant to illustrate the question: How do I place myself in a discourse, be it at a bar in Austin or on a stage in Detroit or on this page you're holding, in which I'm higher up on the chain?

I'm on the higher end (if not at the very top) of most of these historical hierarchies. Even my brown skin, attributed to my mother's Yemenite roots, which on its surface should take my privilege down a notch, doesn't count for much, I've been told, as my being Israeli means I'm supposed to check "White" when filling out the race section on forms (I'm "white-passing," I think I've been told). How can I, a man, and a largely privileged one, at that, talk about feminism, or being a feminist, or why one should be a feminist, without being told to shut the fuck up because what the fuck do I know. I know, I know, I know, "We've been silenced for decades, you can't handle it for ten seconds." I know. Anyway. Regardless of how kind I may hope to be or how genuine my intentions are, the person I am, by definition, paints (or even taints) my point of view and opinion in a particular way. But maybe that's *exactly* why I should be the one to answer these questions. I don't know. This isn't the point, anyway.

The real point, which I've labored you towards, is this: I cannot understand who I am without understanding what I grew up thinking it means to "be a man," which inevitably leads to asking what am I if not a "man," which inevitably leads to thinking about femininity, which inevitably leads to thinking about feminism, which inevitably leads me to consider not only how I fit into this chain, but answering, for myself, why feminism is important. If you don't want my answer, please feel free to skip to the next section (this has been a long one, I'm sorry). L is in the next one, I think, if you prefer that thread.

To begin finding my answer, I asked Google, because of course I did. The first result was a website with the URL mentalkfeminism.com, on which I survived precisely 17 seconds before cringing too hard and exiting. Mainly, I should say, because of their choice of Calibri as the website's font, which means it may be a 13-year-old boy's social studies project.

Staying true to my self-asserted scholar status, I'll come up with my own answer. I'll say that, yes, I do want the best for all the women in my life. Yes, I do believe and support gender equality, as well as all other forms of it. Yes, I would love if we could all be judged by the person we are and not the identity we're told to check on a box. Yes, I would like to think I'm more of a kind human and less so kind of human. Yes, I would say I'm a feminist. But all these superficial claims, much like an extremely poorly designed website, aren't where I should be looking for answers.

"I cannot relate to so much of the suffering and pain Dworkin talks about," Eyal Cohen wrote a few pages ago, "all I can do is try to understand and learn and see." All of us who exist in any chain probably should.

Amia Srinivasan ends her book by saying this:

> It is often the case that those with power are the ones least capable of see-
> ing how it should be wielded. But this needn't be, for feminists at least,
> a cause for despair. Feminism is a movement. In it there have always
> been, always are, those for whom power remains elusive—those who
> have still not won, those for whom winning so far means surviving. It is
> these women, at the sharp end of power, to whom the rest of us must
> turn, and then, turning, follow.

I don't think I could ever articulate anything more succinctly to answer
the *what* or, especially, the *why*.

Bearing all that in mind, there's still one more thing that cannot be understated: a lot of people just don't care about any of this. A lot of people
care, primarily, about themselves. They have no interest in turning or in
following. Fair enough. Their body of interest, their choice. Luckily, bell
hooks has us covered there as well: "Feminist thinking is useful to black
males, and all males, who are grappling with the issue of self-love because
it offers strategies that enable them to challenge and change patriarchal
masculinity." Or, in other words, and perhaps in a language better suited
for the audience, I'll say: Ask not what you can do for feminism – ask
what feminism can do for you.

At the end of the day, and to some extent, we're all selfish. Men, women,
bees, birds, whoever. So, it's worth remembering that, often, we get a slice
of the same poisonous patriarchal pie we help bake. In his book, Jared
Yates Sexton shares how he made the mistake of thinking he was okay,
that he "wrapped his head around the dangers of toxic masculinity," but
wound up spiraling out of control, "turning into a miserable person," and
not knowing how to cope with these feelings of sadness.

He talks of a routine that had become "old hat," and which he "carried
out as if it were muscle memory." He'd, in the past, touch his gun, remind

himself of its realness and power, and load it with bullets, but then began "inching up on something else." That something else he started doing was put the barrel into his mouth, bite the metal with his teeth, and trace the trigger with his finger. He'd black out and sleep with his rifle, then wake up and be reminded of his sadness. "Unlike years before," Sexton says, "I wouldn't hurry to hide the gun in shame."

There's a creation of distance that's needed for the purpose of introspection. The "you" that's telling the story has to dissociate from the you that the story is about, in order to be able to tell an honest version of that story. It's a dive inwards, while at the same time a removal of yourself from the scene you're in. A lot of people tend to go through this process in a therapist's office, or perhaps next to their best friend on a weed-scented couch with Adele in the background. Some people find themselves going through it running up and down along the Hudson, reading books with bright covers, or weaving three threads of literary challah together. The key is, I think, to find what works for you before you hit rock bottom.

I'll get to my rock bottom pretty soon here, but in the meantime, here's the one Jared Yates Sexton talks about in his truly phenomenal book: He'd spent an evening drinking, came home, locked the door, poured himself one more drink, and put on Neil Young's record, *Harvest*. He listened to "Old Man," which he describes as "a haunting song about the legacies of fathers and sons and how we learn self-destruction from those who come before us." He was sobbing by the end of the chorus, and as he went to retrieve his gun, thought to himself, "If I was going to end it, and I fully intended to, what better song was there to play when I did it?"

He mused to himself how long it would take for anyone to find him, as he'd distanced everyone away from his life, except for his mother, whom he felt the need to call and say goodbye to.

I feel like there's some subliminal weak attempt here from me to try to get you, whoever you are, Man, to start your introspective and therapeutic process (if you've not done so already), and examine your share of the pie. You know what, maybe I am. But if you don't want to, okay. It's difficult to get someone to admit to the culpability and responsibility they carry when everything seems to be going fine, when they don't care to look at the big picture, when they've not yet tasted the poison for themselves. There's no point in trying to fix something that doesn't seem broken, they could say. I'll just say that it's much better to start the process of thinking about what's wrong before you have a gun's barrel in your mouth. And I say that while being (slightly) smarter in hindsight, after spending a very long time being dumb myself.

Sexton's mom picked up on the first ring, saying she was worried something terrible had happened to her son.

"'I'm fine,'" I told her, the loaded gun resting on my lap," Sexton writes, adding that his mom told him he can talk to her. That he needs to talk to somebody. He does find someone to talk to, and slowly begins his climb back up.

When Harmange says men don't assume their share of the mental load or emotional labor, she discusses the matter as it pertains to the repercussions this behavior has on the women in men's lives. She's right, and at the same time, the same behavior takes its toll on men themselves. The unwillingness to engage with practices that have stereotypically been labeled as feminine is what's holding some of us back. Perhaps I shouldn't say "some of us," and instead talk solely about myself, but I'm content going on a limb and asserting that I'm not the only man who's felt the brunt of this repression for himself.

I've alluded to a conflation in this section between being a feminist and being feminine. While those aren't synonyms, they have historically been thought of as such, or close to, at least. Because of this conflation, I feel, many men (more so in the past, I'd guess) have been hesitant to say they are feminists out of fear of being labeled as feminine, which is the worst label a man can be given. This rejection of behavior associated with introspection and emotional well-being directly correlates, I'd argue, with the deteriorating mental state of men. And this, for a change, isn't just the claim of a self-asserted scholar, but an argument based on skewed suicide rates, substance abuse, and willingness to reach out for help. There's still a discrepancy that favors men's side of the gender spectrum in a variety of realms: from the workforce (pay gap, promotion opportunities, positions of power and leadership), through reproductive rights and birth control onus, all the way through the denial of basic human rights from others. All of this, of course, muddled and conflated with all the other links of our society. At the same time, there's also a lack of attention for the mental well-being of men, particularly teenagers and young men, who are growing ever more anxious, depressed, and prone to committing gun violence and self-harm. Some of this because of the toxicity imposed on men by themselves, but some of it also imposed on men by women, and the society they live in. The ensuing struggles men go through, though, can all be traced back to historical archetypes conditioning men to be a certain way and figure shit out for themselves. Historical archetypes that condition us to not engage in behaviors we're not stereotypically supposed to.

All of these arguments can coexist. Making the argument to change and work on any one of these issues should not detract from another, and the dismissal or diminishing of either helps no one at all. Feminism is the advocacy for an equality of rights, and men's inclination to support that cause can and should be in conjunction (maybe even conflated) with our right to be more feminine. Share the mental load and emotional labor, for our sake and their sake alike.

But again, what do I know or who am I to say any of this. I'm still in the dumb part of my story in which I'm attempting to figure out what's wrong.

The realization that something is wrong will always be dependent on something—an experience. But that experience doesn't need to be hitting rock bottom. That experience, for me, is the process of penning the words you've been reading (thank you again for doing that). An act which, idealistically, hopefully, ironically, could maybe get you to start yours.

"There is always a tension between experience and the thing that finally carries it forward," Andrea Dworkin writes in her essay. "Without that tension, one might as well write a shopping list."

(1)   (2)   (3)

Three (3) stints in each other's lives

Two (2) regrettable decisions to walk away

One (1) reciprocated "Happy New Year" text (Kosher, if they have)

Three (3) meetups in two (2) weeks

One (1) kiss (make sure firm)

Six (6) helter-skelter months

Twenty-seven (27) years of conditioning

Twelve (12) people for a birthday brunch reservation

Bottomless screwdrivers (however many fit)

Fifty (50) dollar McNally Jackson gift card

One (1) text to L telling her about my two (2) sweet writer friends who got me a $50 gift card to this bookstore I've never heard of called McNally Jackson

One (1) pick-up order of lamb vindaloo, garlic naan, and samosas for dinner

One (1) text to L saying I'm drunk and eating Indian food so the birthday is perfect

One (1) Ah Eyal, I'm sorry, I feel like it would have been lovely to see you today

One (1) feeling of affirmation and relief, since while actually seeing her is what we really want, the fact that she wants to see us, or that the idea of seeing us at least crosses her mind in some capacity, is good enough to make us enjoy this birthday

Four (4) McNally Jackson locations, all either downtown or in Brooklyn

One (1) drunken offer to go peruse a bookstore together (accepted, if possible)

Step Six

Brush Egg

(2)

Affirmation is quite a wonderful thing. Only one of the five love languages includes the word "affirmation" explicitly, but all five are centered around the idea, I think. It is only the method in which affirmation is received that varies. Words, acts of service, gifts, quality time, or physical touches are simply different ways to be told, or tell someone, *Hey, I'm here.*

I took the Love Language Quiz once, lord knows how many years ago. The result was that I receive words of affirmation, which makes sense, though I wouldn't be surprised if the result would be different if I retake the test. I wouldn't be surprised if everyone would register different results each time they take the test. Some days we need a hug, some days we need to be told we're pretty or our biceps look bigger, some days we need a surprise Venmo of $12 to go get McDonald's. It's less so, I think, about the manifestation of the affirmation, and more about its consistency and mutuality. And mutuality, I think, is not just two people reciprocating a feeling, but also sharing a clearly defined, intimate space, in which neither person has a defined role, and both are welcomed and encouraged to be themselves. I think.

Given the fact I'm seemingly uncertain about all this, I'll, once more, defer to bell hooks. She dedicates much of *all about love*'s "Mutuality" chapter to detail the problems that arise from men and women's adherence to stereotypical gender roles within a relationship. She talks about males' "Peter Pan Syndrome," which leads to their substitution of the unconditional care and love given from their mother with care and love given by their partner, never requiring them to grow up emotionally. She claims that on the other end of the spectrum, women's obsession with love is a covert way of holding onto power, and any relationship that hinges on a struggle for control is bound to fail. Both men and women, hooks says, "are wounded in the space where they would know love during childhood," and these are often so traumatic that it becomes fearful to attempt to inhabit the space of love again. The case is particularly true for men, she says, as women are far more likely to "receive encouragement both to think about love and to value its meaning," despite the fact women are not necessarily "more emotionally equipped to do the work of love."

As I said earlier, I grew up in a house where romantic love was not there to be felt or seen—perhaps the reason why the depiction of love in corny romcoms and my friends' relationships carries so much weight. While I was—and still am—fortunate to be showered with love and care by family members, the version of me that's received this love has been, in a way, a dishonest version. I've adamantly not wanted to be seen, so have suppressed any urge to be truly encompassed. In *salvation,* bell hooks writes that "many men use withdrawing into silence to express their power over others." As long as I was in my own hands, I held the power, and I loved having the power the same way lactose-intolerant people love ice cream: at my own expense.

Now, as my true self wants to make its way out, he doesn't know how to cope with the feelings he is being offered or the ones he wants to give. I do not mean this as an excuse for my mistakes or a deflection of blame, but just as a recognition of my reality. I hid under blankets, subdued who I was, and presented an exteriority of a persona that I thought would be best accepted and least questioned. As a result, I became overly occupied with how my persona is received by others, regardless of how genuine or indicative of who I really am it is. In other words, having a bright cover that people would want to candidly take a picture of on the subway carried more value than what the pages inside say.

The near-subconscious obsession with other people's idea of me explains why external affirmation plays such a large part in my internal affirmation. I've been provided, over the course of my life, with validation in the form of friendships and acceptance and laughter and—dare I say— relatively genuine female (and occasionally male) interest in me. More importantly, for me, I've found gratification in the form of an avoidance of questions and concerns and ridicule and pity. Few things provide me with more relief than a conversation centered nearly entirely on someone else.

I'd like to add, too, that I feel genuine pride and love in earning another's trust to the point where they confide in and vent to me. I'd even dare to say I consider myself a great active listener, which is why I often find myself in conversations that feel like someone else's therapy session. I feel honored and privileged that there are people in this world that look at me and my role in their lives, and think to themselves, *Yeah, I trust him enough to give myself away.* They fill the conversational and emotional vacuum we share with their feelings, and the fact there's no space left for me makes me feel like I have all the power. Maybe we could argue over who gets the short end of the stick in this kind of relationship, but maybe it's the fact that a short end even exists that's the problem. Even in instances when I'm pressed to fill the space with my words or troubles or feelings, I've mastered the ability of infusing just enough substance for the other side to feel like I've shared, but not enough to reach the point where I feel like I've actually shared anything substantial. So, the validation and affirmation I've received in my life, to a large extent, have always been given to a version of me that I performed, not that I actually was, rendering the affirmation somewhat fake.

Yeah, yeah, high school English teacher, I know. "Show, don't tell." Fine. Here:

Flying to Israel can be, for lack of a better word, a bit of a bitch. This is especially the case when required to subsist on a college student budget, overly valuing a flight's price over its itinerary. A 17-hour layover in Kiev? Easy peasy. A four-legged route that culminates in over 24 hours of travel time? Lemon squeezy. A sketchy third-party booking company that put me on a Rome-Tel Aviv flight that didn't exist, resulting in me being stranded at FCO and forced to book a new flight? Let's not talk about it.

My recent NYC-TLV trek wasn't awful, with only one layover in Toronto (you will not hear a single word from me about the prominent demographic on this flight *ahem orthodox Hassidic Jews ahem* but you better believe I have some words to say about their lack of respect for flight attendants or consideration for personal space and seat belt signs

and basic hygiene and honestly any fucking norm that as a society we embrace as a part of our airplane etiquette. Not a word). So, yeah, it wasn't
awful. Still, taking into account the Downtown 1 from my apartment and
the New Jersey Transit to Newark and the airport queues and the layover
and the two flights and the delay and the commotion and the rude people (*ahem ahem*) as we tried to get off the plane and the long line for
Covid testing upon entrance to Israel, by the time I opened the passenger
seat door to my mom's car at Ben Gurion's curbside pickup, I was pretty
fucking exhausted. I threw my carry-on bag inside, crashed into the seat,
lowered my mask to my chin, and let out a big sigh.

You won't believe the day I've had, were the first words spoken in the
car, by my mother.

Now, I love my mom. Whenever she comes up in conversation, I tell
people she's as good a human as you can hope to meet. People are drawn
to her energy, and I cannot tell you how many people confide in and rely
on her as their therapist and caregiver and most reliable and competent
friend (she likes to say we're similar in this sense). I don't see her in that
role, though. We've reached a point in our family nucleus, and I suspect
this happens in many families, where the children assume some of the
parental role. A natural transition, I think, as the kids begin handling
transportation and restaurant checks and grocery shopping. Specifically,
I'll say, and I don't think my mother would mind me saying, she relies on
me for emotional support. That's fine. I'm happy to oblige, and as I said,
I'm honored that anyone would consider me reliable or wise or empa-
thetic enough to trust, especially someone as strong and impressive as my
mother. I've just never felt the need to lean on my mother—or anyone, for
that matter—to help me stay up.

As I was walking towards my mom's black Seat Ibiza outside the
airport (and I apologize for the forthcoming first world problems in
advance), my shoulder sore from carrying my bag, my feet sore from
traversing through airport queues, my back sore from keeping my seat
in an upright position (side note: people who lean back in airplanes are

at the top of my "inconsiderate pricks" list, tied with people who strangle kittens and those who enter the elevator before you walk out), my brain sore from lack of sleep, I just wanted to vent. I wanted—and dare I say needed—to be the recognized victim of a long, logistical day, the center of attention for just a few moments. As soon as I crashed into the seat, and she said what she said, that need and want completely evaporated. Whatever emotional space I wanted to occupy was completely taken up, I felt, and—despite the fact this isn't true—I felt that there was zero space for me to say a single word. Perhaps you'd say that's brittle-spirited of me. Perhaps you'd say men don't need a second invite to open their goddamn mouth. Either way, that's just how I felt. *It was fine*, I eventually replied when we were well onto the highway, after my mom told me all about her early morning appointment and parking issues and whatever else happened, and she asked how my flight was. And truly, I've grown to believe it was and is fine. It was and is nothing new. It was and is just another instance of ignoring what I want to say and avoiding an expression of a true feeling.

Like a tennis ball being wrapped by rubber bands: each band keeps the ball a little warmer, safer, and better hidden, to the point where it's easy to forget what's at the core, and how much pressure is being put on.

(3)

L's acceptance of my invite to go to McNally Jackson together, on the day I became eligible to join the 27 Club, indicating that she wanted and wants to see me, and the affirmation bestowed by her saying those words and me hearing them, were, unbeknownst to me in the moment, a sort of peak of hope. As more days of her silence and after-the-fact apologies for silence have continued to amass; as more of my, *Lol it's really fine, please don't apologize* lies continued to spew out of the keyboard; as more busy weekends where I could maybe be squeezed in before or after or in between have evaporated nearly as soon as they'd materialized; as I've gone through another handle or two or six of gin and drunkenly set more reminders on my phone telling me that I just have to wait and I have to make this work and I have to hold on; as I've been wondering how much longer I can wait and hold on; as I've continued to leave my therapy application unsubmitted; as I've convinced myself that I can still carry a little bit more, the weight of reality has grown heavier and heavier.

The reality is that there's a void in my life. Voids can be filled in a variety of ways: family, food, friends, sex, religion, drugs, TV, books, a favorite sports team, or, in the latest 21st century development, social media induced dopamine. I promise to not go full Deepak Chopra on you right now, but, without the happiness and fulfillment that comes from within, all of these fillers will be rendered futile. Nothing is sustainable. Nothing is reliable. Nothing is what you'll be left with, and I know that because I am hypocritically preaching this idea of recognizing self-worth while in the midst of being unable to see my own. Easier said than done, I guess.

And it's all L's fault. Well, sort of. She's not the void's genesis, but she is making everything else frail in comparison. Even if kind family and friends, feel-good romcoms, Liverpool winning, or laughing crying emojis replied to my—objectively—hilarious Instagram stories would've been sustainable fillers to whatever this thing is that I'm defining as a "void," they would've been nulled and voided by this woman. It's a dumb and dangerous way to go about life, having your entire sense of worth and emotional well-being in the hands of one person (that isn't you your-self or Steven Gerrard), but that's just where I wound up. I've grown so in love with this woman, idealized and iconized who she is, that her affirmation is not only the only one I crave, but the only one that means anything. Again, I know, it's a stupid thought process that's bound to fail, but, man. When I get her to giggle.

Two things are exacerbating this situation. The first is the unavoidable hopeless romantic's deluded belief that eventually she'll allow herself to let me near again because she'll understand that she won't find this with anyone else. All logical signs, though, are indicating that she's moved on. The second is that the scarcity of her existence in my life not only sucks for the de facto scarcity, but also because it serves as a constant reminder about how it's all my fucking fault to begin with.

But we kissed, man. Not that long ago. We still talk and she still con-fides in me from time to time in a way that you don't do with just anyone. Surely that means something. Surely what I did wrong couldn't have ru-ined things forever. I don't know.

It's fitting, I guess, that I'm toiling and addled because of mixed sig-nals. A taste of my own medicine sort of thing—an idea of what it was like to be on the receiving end of my fickle and nebulous behavior over the course of our knowing each other. But she's not doing it on purpose, I don't think. I don't know.

I don't fully know what I do know and what I don't know, but I do know that what I do know, I do know, and what I don't know, I don't know, you know? "There is always a tension between experience and the thing that finally carries it forward," Dworkin said, and more often than not, time is what carries us forward from experience to knowledge. To knowing. But the ignorance of being inside the here and now can never be understated. Heck, even bell hooks admits to it: "In my twenties and early thirties," she opens her "Mutuality" chapter with, "I was confident I knew what love was all about. Yet every time I 'fell in love' I found myself in pain." First of all, same. Second of all, and far be it from me to critique or question or edit hooks, but I don't get her use of the word 'yet'. The contrasting conjunction makes no sense, because, as many men have philosophized and theorized before me, there is no contrast between love and pain. They exist in each other.

One day, after I've tallied more years of experience and snippets of knowledge about both the world around me and the one within me, I may look back at my feelings towards L without considering them to be true love. But my naïve and inexperienced mind that's still here and now in its twenties is telling me that this is what love is all about. Because alongside all the bliss, I'm finding myself feeling the polar opposite. Somehow, as many have said before me, love can lead you to a dark, painful place. Love doesn't leave you there alone. It's still in the darkness with you, and that's exactly the problem. You wind up hating that you ever found it. Rather, I should say, I hate that I ever found her. Because had I never met her, I'd have never prevented her from getting closer to me, never pushed her away, and never would've been left agonizing over how far she now is.

It's my fault that it's her fault, you could say, but if I tried to convince myself of that, I'd hate myself. Then again, I'm feeling that way anyway, since—and to paraphrase Louis CK—love + mistakes + time + distance = self-hate.

I'm not sure there's a big market for self-hate books (unless we were to count books about how to trade cryptocurrency), even if they're designed to have extremely bright and appealing covers. I don't have any literary backdrop, nor an anecdotal dinner party in which I listened to people relay the three things they hate most about themselves (maybe that happens unprompted in every dinner party). All I have to rely on to comprehend the disgust I have for my former self and the decisions he's made, which by virtue has led me to loathe my current self, too, is my personal experience. Had I ever met bell hooks, became one of the men in her life, perhaps she'd have said she's despaired by how easy it is for me talk about or admit to hate. Maybe she'd have said I'm being unnecessarily harsh and am making too much of the feeling of self-detesting I'm carrying, which, if I had to describe it, feels like you want to give someone directions.

It's late. It's night. You're lying in bed. There's a person out in a car somewhere, and all you want is to guide them in the right direction. Your direction. But you have no idea where they are, which is ironic, since you're the one who sent them away. You sent them away, turned your back, and by the time you came to your senses and turned back around, they were gone. You have no idea how to guide them back, despite how badly you want to do so. Now, not only do you not know where they are, but you don't know if they can—or want to—hear you anymore. It feels like your only option is to stay in this helpless, powerless, silent bed, resign to the fact that sleep has been deemed a sober impossibility, and stuff your face into the pillow to eclipse streetlights that peer through curtains, reminding you of brighter nights. It feels like you're desperate to call or text or get into a car yourself, set out onto the dark road and hope that by some miracle you bump into them, that your paths somehow cross again. It feels like you know you have to suppress that urge. You have to withhold the feelings till you think they're ready to be received. You cannot guide them. All you can do is try to survive as you wait, hope they know you're here, waiting for them, hope they decide to make their way back to you.

It feels like you physically cannot lie still, so you jolt up in bed, bend your knees, and ram them into the mattress. You clench your body as hard as you possibly can, stuff your face into the pillow, silently scream into the pillowcase, and nearly gash through the mattress pad with your kneecaps. You grip and twist and clutch the bedsheet with your palms till the corners come loose. You try to exert every dying ounce of energy in your body without your own corners coming loose. You hold still and hope to release into the bed any inclination to move or do or act or say or, most importantly, feel. You hope this silent, inert outburst will somehow condense the pain into a tiny ball you'll be able to suppress and hide in some place deep, deep inside you, where, if worse comes to worst and the feeling begins to fester and rot, you'll just cut it out. You hope that this motionless manifestation of a combustion will award you some respite without waking up your neighbors, without mangling your knuckles or the wall. It feels like you know this unhealthy coping mechanism won't work long term, but maybe it'll buy you just enough time for them to come back to you, because you feel like that'll solve everything. Maybe if you grip and twist and clutch hard enough, you'll be able to banish, if only for one fucking night, this concoction of regret, affliction, useless-ness, and gloom.

This, I guess, is where hooks would say I'm making too much of the feeling. Dare I say that I, a cisgender, straight man, am being dramatic. But this is how I feel—in a sadomasochistic struggle with myself. Not wanting to move on, unable to move on, yet knowing moving on would be the healthy thing to do.

In her "Commitment" chapter, hooks claims that before loving anyone, we must first of all commit to loving ourselves. Learning how we have acquired feelings of worthlessness and low self-esteem, she says, "is usu-ally only one stage in the process" of building self-love. And these nega-tive feelings, for me, derive *from* love. From holding it in my hand like a delicately wrapped present adorned with a bow, being unable to gift it, incapable of putting it down, and forcing myself to hold on to it as the weight continues to amass.

The second part of the process, according to hooks, is "actively intro-ducing into our lives constructive, life-affirming thought patterns and behavior." Maybe I'll be able to do that one day. Time, I know—and I apologize for the cliché—is the only thing that will get me past this feel-ing. Because L is in her own car somewhere, too far for me to string my arm and touch her, unable to hear my voice, the one that's yearning to croon but knows that it shouldn't, too perfect for me to have anything other than her fill the void.

I'm left to lie in bed, regret the past, learn from the present, and hope to bump into some solace in the future. For now, I vent and clench and drink and grip and twist and clutch and breathe, hope the corners stay attached, and wait. I lie in the darkness, move my hands from the neck of the bottle to the back of my own, feel my fingers run atop my spine, trying my best to simulate what hers felt like, and wait.

I'm frightened, because much like what bell hooks says about embarking on a relationship you believe to be true love, as I wait, there is nowhere for me to hide from the fact that these feelings of regret and pain all trace back to my own mistakes.

(1)

There's no point in heading home uptown just to head back down later, so I go to The Flame Diner on 58th and 9th instead. The Farmer's Omelette and refillable black coffee should do wonders for my hangover, particularly after it was exacerbated by my having to tutor math to a 12-year-old boy who, presumably, had just as little interest as I did in us meeting up today. Alas, his mother's autocratic ways and my need to pay for rent and pints of Guinness has led the both of us to spend our Sunday going over exponent rules in the lobby of their midtown high-rise apartment building.

I was out last night in Brooklyn. A friend who lives there invited me to this warehouse club in Gowanus to celebrate her sister's birthday. Over the course of the next week, we'll learn that everyone in the group, apart from me and my Bk friend, got Covid.

Nearly two months after L first accepted my drunken offer to go peruse McNally Jackson together, a period during which I gulped down and subdued any frustration or exasperation at tentative plans not panning out, we're going today. I'm excited and nervous, but mostly relieved. The concreteness of this happening today has given me some tangible hope over the last few days, along with affirmation that I do still have space in her life. While I don't expect to walk out of that bookstore with three new novels and an updated relationship status on Facebook, I do think that us spending time together for the first time in more than two months will be like a defibrillation of sorts. What exactly will be electrically shocked back to life—her feelings, our future, my sanity—is yet to be determined. We'll see.

Frankly, it wouldn't be completely illogical for me to go back up to my apartment to drop my bag off before heading down to McNally. In fact, it would probably make a whole lot more sense than simply staying at the Flame Diner for hours. But I want L to see me with my suede bag that was gifted to me on my birthday by my lovely Irish friend. I want her to be reminded, in case she forgot, who she's dealing with, who I am. A man who reads books and wears cardigans and drinks black coffee and stays out till 3 a.m. at warehouse parties in Gowanus and educates the youth and knows exponent rules and carries around a brown suede side bag and expertly lines up his own beard and wants to listen and uses coconut and shea butter lotion and whose laptop screensaver is—and always will be—Steven Gerrard and who, in case she doesn't know or forgot, adores her.

So, since I have plenty of time to kill after devouring the omelet, as the kind waitress continues to refill my porcelain coffee mug, I extract my laptop and read through this essay I started writing, as a form of venting, really, a couple of months ago, and that I sent to Dani two days ago without even proofreading. The essay started as me musing about bell hooks's *all about love*, but I felt like it was missing something, so I added a thread about this Rosh Hashanah dinner party I went to. It still felt unsubstantial, so I started writing about L, and the act of getting the thoughts out of my head has proved to be helpful. Therapeutic. The three threads sort of fit together, in my mind, and I have no idea what I'll end up doing with these words, but I promised my best friend I'd send him something to read on his flight home-home. The flight was yesterday, so I asked him to ignore any potential rushed typos and remained a man of my (hopefully not misspelled) word. I apologized for how long the essay is, but the 40-odd pages I sent him were, more than anything, my way of telling him about this girl I've sort of seen but also haven't, which is progress. I'm not sure whether I'm able to talk about L out loud, but something about the medium of writing, the freedom I have to incorporate masturbation jokes and tangents about Indian food into our story, is making the act of exposing more palatable. Plus, Dani is in the dinner party scene, so maybe he'll find it funny. (He will.)

I read about half the essay before the kind waitress hands me my check and I'm reminded how fucking stupidly expensive things are in Midtown, but I'm seeing L later, so who gives a shit. I close my laptop and pay with cash and sit through the South-Ferry-bound 1's delays and get off by One

World Trade Center and, since I still have time to spare, walk towards the water.

There's an early winter's sunset, and the fact it's already dark and cold means there are almost no people around. It's so quiet that I can hear the Hudson's slow flow, with the water illuminated by a singular sliver of the waning sun's orange that makes its way beneath one massive lead gray cloud. The top of the sky, above that one cloud, is still glaringly bright thanks to the sun's orbit, and this contrast between the immediate darkness resulting from the cloud and the brightness over the horizon is so pretty and perfectly metaphorical for what I hope my life to be. I embrace the cliché and sad girl vibes of it all, and, uncannily, post this view on my Instagram story without a pun or joke to make it more palatable, justifiable, or unique.

I listen to the water flow for a while, and when the meeting time is a half an hour or so away, I start ambling east towards the Seaport McNally Jackson location. I take my sweet time walking from one end of Fulton Street to the other, and L tells me she's running a little late because the trains are messed up, which of course they are. She says that she's supposed to go see her brothers after, but still wants to come if I'm not in a rush, which of course I'm not. I sit for a while on a concrete bench in this cute square outside the bookstore, where there's a little market and a big Christmas tree and a scattering of people.

The combination of the cold weather and the refillable coffee take their toll, and I instantly have to find somewhere to pee. I walk into McNally but don't see a bathroom in my immediate scan. Despite the fact I'm bursting at this point, I'm far too self-conscious to ask if there is a bathroom to use, not wanting to come across as someone who just came in to use this place as a waste disposal location. I decide to walk out and exercise my male privilege of being able to pee pretty much anywhere one can find a tree or two slabs of cement that create a 90° angle. I go around the building towards a construction site, then mark my territory with the boldness of a drunk woman who has her black tights rolled around her ankles outside a restaurant's entrance in Brooklyn at 2 a.m.. Relieved, I walk back into McNally, and there's a part of me that's kind of glad that L is running late, because it gives me a chance to familiarize myself with and properly assess the store.

There's that one *Friends* episode where Joey feels like he needs to intellectually impress his professor girlfriend, Charlie (who, by the way, is the only Black character in the show that's ever had a recurring role[1], which didn't come until season nine, which is worthwhile thinking about from time to time). So, Ross, who's obviously in love with Charlie himself, writes out a script for Joey to regurgitate to Charlie as he takes her to the Met. What a great friend Ross is. Joey ends up leading Charlie right instead of left (or left instead of right, I don't remember) as they enter the museum, so he botches the whole thing, but none of it really matters, anyway. Ross ends up with Rachel, Charlie is quickly pushed towards the outer ether of the show, and Joey winds up the star of a catastrophic and short-lasting spin-off show carrying his name as the title (*Episodes* was pretty good, though). All of this to say, I have time to walk up and down McNally's two floors and come up with a script to regurgitate to L. Identify books I've read that I can impress her with, where the fiction and nonfiction sections are (those are usually distinct), and find covers and titles that I can make puns about. I imagine this is the kind of prep improv performers or Carrot Top do before a show. Just kidding. No way Carrot Top preps. Pure natural raw talent.

After a couple of laps, I feel acquainted enough with this store that I've come to realize is the bookstore equivalent of Jason Mraz. It's bougie and hipstery and there's a café/bar on the first floor. Since the Farmer's Omelette is a hazy memory at this point, I park my hangry buttock on a barstool and order a chocolate croissant (the only pastry left at this hour of the evening) and the hazy IPA the bookstore has on tap (yes,

---

1. There's a LEVEL article published in 2020 that's titled: "The One Best Black Character on 'Friends,' Ranked" which I find to be phenomenal journalistic work.

the bookstore has IPA on tap). I take my hipstery denim laptop case out of my hipstery suede bag and roll up the sleeves of my hipstery cardigan and continue reading this very rough and early version of this piece of writing that I sent to my best friend and that I'll end up describing as an interwoven, three-threaded book-length essay, which is, by far, the most hipstery part about all of this. But I kind of like it.

There are two entrances to the store, and as I bask in reading my own words (someone has to), I try to envision which one she's going to walk in from. Logically, it'd be the one that leads into the bookstore side, since that's the first one en route from the subway station. But if it was in my hands, if I had the power to write the next chapter of our story, she'd enter through the café entrance. It'd be this cute romcom scene where she sneaks up behind me as I read a page that isn't about her, and ask, *What are you working on?* and, startled, I'd shut my laptop screen, and it'd be tender and funny when I give her an answer that's generally true but specifically dishonest—something like, *Oh, it's this essay about how men understand, withhold, and express love*—and she'd do that zooming out thing with her eyes when something piques her interest, and she'd ask if she can read it when I'm done, and I'll pause and give her the confident half smirk I wear when I think of a joke I could say but I'm not sure if I want to say it—something like, *Only if you promise to not say that you wish I spoke more about the unheard voices of the women in my life*—then probably decide against making the joke, and say, *Sure*, instead, but keep the smirk, which will make her say that I look as if I'm being disingenuous or cynically appeasing or deflecting or confident or whatever else her unheard voice that never fails to make me smile wants to say.

I read my words, and she texts me that, *These trains are just like not coming*, and I instantly know what will be coming, and there's this immediate masochistic inclination in me for it to happen just so I can have a valid excuse.

She tells me the trains keep saying five minutes, then twelve, then twenty, then she says she's so *annoying*, then corrects her typo to say she's so *annoyed*, then says both words kind of fit, and I don't tell her this, but I don't disagree.

I'll tell my therapist, in a few months, how sometimes I kind of wish for a loved one to die or for a car to hit me or something like that, just so I can rationalize my sadness, feel like my suffering is substantiated and my victimhood is validated.

That's shitty, I'm sorry, I text back, because it is shitty and I am sorry but mostly I give this banal response since I have no idea what I'm supposed to say. It feels like something that could be said to me as well, though if someone did say that to me, now, as I'm not the real victim in this whole debacle, I'd tell them to fuck right off and save their pity for someone else.

Go ahead, go full Nike. Just do it. Just hit me already.

It finally comes in the form of, *I think I should go straight to my brothers or just go home at this point*, and it really doesn't matter how many open parentheses she adds after a colon to express her sadness in the form of a frowny face (she uses four), there's just no fucking way she's as upset as I am, and, frankly, I'm not going to buy that she's upset at all. I'm far more inclined to believe she's relieved.

It's about her, anyway. She's the one who needs to be recognized as the victim of a long, logistical day. She should be the center of attention. It doesn't matter that I want—or dare I say need—to vent.

She hits me, I sink deeper into my barstool seat, finish the beer, reply, *No worries*, and whatever need or want I have to vent my sadness and frustration completely evaporates.

I'm really sorry, she says, then calls me by my name, which maybe makes my presence even more real for her, but definitely makes her absence more real for me. I reject whatever emotional space she tries to offer, and when she says, *You don't have to say anything*, all I want to shout back is that I fucking know that I don't have to say anything. I've not said anything for twenty-seven years and one month and twenty-five days and— give or take—eight hours, so what's a few more fucking minutes.

But I don't say any of that. Perhaps you'd say that's brittle-spirited of me. Perhaps you'd say men don't need a second invite to open their goddamn mouths. Either way, that's just how I feel. Just another band around the tennis ball.

L it's really okay, I tell her and add that I hope she enjoys candle lighting with her brothers, and I despise how well I can still hear her pronouncing that word. *I assume that's what you'll be doing,* I say, when, in reality, I'm assuming she's hanging out with her new boyfriend or something, because of course that's what she's doing, but of course I can't say that, so instead I make a silly little ironic joke about her having a religious identity because it's Hanukkah and she's quasi Jewish and maybe the fact I can make a joke will make it seem like things are fine on the surface, which, of course, they are.

And, yeah, sure, she says (again) that it's not okay at all, and she didn't communicate well at all on any of this, and I say (again) that it really is okay. She has so much cachet in my book, and no matter how badly she may have communicated today, or any day since the new Jewish year started, it's nothing compared to how badly I messed up back in 5,781. I tell her I don't want to add stress to her life, and she says I'm not at all and she's just bad at these things these days, but I'm just not able to believe her. I know everything she's saying is true, but I need a better reason to be this annoyed and frustrated and upset.

Yeah, sure, it's just a silly little trip to a bookstore that didn't pan out because the New York public transit system is, well, the New York public transit system. Today is not that big a deal, except for me, I guess, it is. Believing that today and the months of our drifting apart that have preceded today are just unfortunate and circumstantial and logistically induced simply isn't a good enough reason, a valid enough excuse. It needs to be her fault. Because while everything she's saying might be true, what's also true is that if you really want to see someone, you get on a train.

I don't know what to reply to, *Wednesday I will be uptown during the day for a meeting and could meet u after,* because of course you will be uptown and of course you could fucking meet me, but what are the odds of that fucking happening. I just put my laptop in its denim case and put it in my suede bag and trudge upstairs and crash into one of the couches (of course the bookstore has fucking couches) and sit there quietly for a while in an attempt to decompress until I decide to fill the silence by scrolling through Instagram and checking who viewed my story, and the tiny dose of fake dopamine is just about enough.

Maybe it's on me to read the signs, though. Maybe my expectations are too high and my hope is too unfounded and naïve. There's a Maya Angelou quote I often give others as advice: When someone shows you who they are, believe them. L has shown me that she doesn't really need to talk to me. Maybe she enjoys chatting to me, sure, but there is no reciprocation of feelings or mutual dependence. If I don't initiate conversations or the idea of us seeing each other, whatever remains of us will evaporate. There is no clearly defined, intimate space in which neither of us has a defined role, nor are we both encouraged to be ourselves. I just take on whatever personality or character that enables me to have a part in her life, just so I could have a part in her life. I had the option of being myself with her, existing in a shared, intimate space, but I messed it up. I just have to accept that and move on. It needs to be my fault, because it is my fault. It's embarrassing, frankly, that I'm still holding onto this hope, and, sitting on this couch, deflated and pissed off, it's time for me to let go. And, honestly, while I'm at it, fuck her for leading me on. For popping up out of the blue once a week and being kind and funny and close and smart and interesting and interested, only to disappear without notice, leaving me confused and frustrated in a silence that can only be filled by her; a silence I've been silencing in ways that do me no good.

But she stared into my eyes, man. Told me she was scared by how much she liked me. Not that long ago. She still keeps me in her life for some reason. It can't all be gone.

I just want you to know that since you're not here there's no one to talk me out of getting this, I send to L along with a picture of Hilton Als's *White*

Girls. I'm getting the book because I'm supposed to meet Als in a few weeks, and I figured I should read something of his beforehand. We're meeting to discuss the thesis I submitted for school, an essay collection about masculinity with a title I've made more concise, *Dude, Little Bitch*. I send a picture of the book to L, specifically, because she's long told me *White Girls* isn't as good as Als's other book, *The Women*, and how she prefers his work on Baldwin anyway. I'm mostly hoping she asks me for the reason I'm getting the book so that I'll be able to impress her by saying I'm meeting him soon. She doesn't ask, but she does laugh at my text, and the tiny dose of fake dopamine is just about enough.

I check out, and despite having a $50 gift card from my two kind writer friends, still end up paying a hefty amount for the five books I got, because it's a bougie and hipstery bookstore on the Lower East Side, so of course I do.

I subway uptown and pick up a burger from the American bar/restaurant underneath my apartment and get home and line up the books on my desk and get the gin out the freezer and turn on Sunday Night Football and shut the lights and it's just me and Gordon's and Cris Collinsworth and Patrick Mahomes and shoestring fries and she's still texting me back and Sunday nights, these days, really don't get any better than this. She tells me she's going to this bday party on Saturday *but before during the day I could say hello.* I think I know whose bday party it is so I make a reference joke about them because I want her to know that I still remember random shit she told me months ago and I want it to impress her and I'm correct with my guess and it makes me happy and, you know what, maybe this time we will say hello. (We won't.)

I set L, a while ago, as a favorite contact on my phone. She's the only one. I was drunk when I did it. I'm not sure why I did that. I mean, I know why. My phone's on Do Not Disturb nearly constantly, so doing this doesn't only enable me to know immediately when she makes herself available, but it also prevents me from having to go through the disappointment of having my phone buzz and light up, only to pick it up and see that it isn't her. If it buzzes, it's her. I spend my time, whenever I'm in this drunken darkness, not wanting to be disturbed, knowing that her words are the only ones that can reach me.

The gin does what it always does and I dare to tell her I'm actually going to be in Brooklyn this Saturday for a friend's wedding, but then I'm flying home-home next week. What she doesn't know, and what I'll never admit, is that I booked my return flight for before New Year's Eve, since there's this wishful thinking part of me that hopes she and I will end up at the same party at 11:59 on December 31st. I know the prospect of us being in the same place to welcome in 2022 is incredibly unlikely, but it'll be even more unlikely if I'm on a different continent. (We won't meet. I'll end up welcoming the new year while in line to the bathroom, bursting to pee, at this club on the LES that the entry ticket for will cost far more than I'll care to admit or be happy about, but there will be an open bar, so I'll recoup my money in alcohol, which is probably why I'll end up counting down from ten while standing on a sticky floor all by myself next to people I don't know, dying to piss, which, honestly, could have been a lot worse, as one of the first things I did in the new year was feel incredible relief from peeing followed soon thereafter by an Irish Goodbye which is, too, an incredible relief.)

She says she's excited for me to be going home-home, and I ask if she has any travel plans. She's debating whether to go to San Francisco for a bit but she's worried it'll screw her up somehow. I tell her that she'll have a lovely time and she really should go, all the while hoping this trip won't fall on the last days of 2021. (She will end up going, and she'll text me after to say that she's very glad she went because she really needed it, and she'll thank me for encouraging and supporting her to go since it helped a lot.)

She asks if I want my Sarah Gerard book back before I leave, despite the fact she hasn't finished it yet, but I say that she should just keep it if she's enjoying it. I bring up the meeting with Hilton Als on my own— or the gin's—accord, and I tell her she can return the book and I'll tell her more about how my meeting went when I see her in 2023. She laughs, and says she'll see me before that. More than the actual words, and even her laugh, what gives me hope that that will actually happen is the fact she still responds to my sarcasm seriously. And, of course, the gin.

I wasn't wrong when I said that that image, the one that's still on my Instagram story for the next twenty hours or so, is perfectly metaphorical. My mistake, or what I hoped would be wrong, is that the brightness over the cloud wasn't approaching, but drifting away.

(3)

A part of my application for my MFA was a critical response to a piece of writing. The pool of literature I'd read by that point was more like a bathroom sink. Luckily, in my senior year of undergrad I took Michele Randall's creative writing class in which I read Kelly Sundberg's essay "It Will Look Like a Sunset." It's brilliant, and still one of my all-time favorites. It's one of the only essays I read in its entirety that semester (sorry, Professor Randall), and I vividly recall sitting on my campus's lawn, under the Florida sun, in awe. I used the one discussion participation I allocated myself per semester on that essay, saying how much I loved it and making an observation about the title. I said something along the lines of how sunsets usually have pretty or positive connotations, yet Sundberg uses the line to describe a bruise placed on her by her then husband. A natural (self-asserted) literary critic I've always been. Sundberg's essay is about the abusive relationship she was in, and it's masterful in how the form and content intertwine. She alternates moments of happiness and sadness, paragraphs of joy and pain, since that's how the relationship developed— it had, for her, both good and bad.

I bring that up now because despite the role that the masculine archaic archetype of invincibility, individualism, and faux heroism played, the fact that things aren't always bad is the main reason why it took me so long to start going to therapy.

(2)

My most played artist on Spotify for three years running has been Vitamin String Quartet, a group that records classical covers of famous pop and rock songs. I love having their music in the background as I work, and their covers are excellent for extra challenging Shazam games. I've always had the dream of being an incredible violin player, and while it may be too late for me (yeah, yeah, it's never too late), I'd love if my future kids would pick up the instrument (and not just to hit each other). I mentioned this hope once to a good friend of mine, a friend whom I helped move from NC to Chicago, and she said, *Your home will sound like it houses a dying cat. For at least six years.*

Yeah, sure, it probably takes a while to get good at playing the violin, but once you are, I bet it's amazing. Plus, it seems kind of easy to do. I mean, not technically. But as long as you make sure the A, D, G, and E strings (in that order) are in tune by adjusting the fine tuners, and, if still out of tune, via carefully twisting the tuning pegs on the pegbox (all the while pressing down on the string because the edge of the peg is tapered and the pressing will stop the peg from slipping) until the desired pitch is reached, then it's easy. All you have to do is just, like, sit there and swipe the blade back and forth (I don't know what they call the stick thingy).

I bet that violinists who've played since childhood can do so absentmindedly—their mind numb, their arms moving independently from their body. It's probably the same as how I feel when I play soccer, having done it for so long, in that I don't have to consciously think about what I'm doing. It's probably the same as how I feel when I drink alcohol, in that I don't have to consciously think.

A day after the dying cat comment, I sent my friend a video that popped up on one of my social medias. It's of this young boy, skinny and shirtless, in what seemed to be a crummy, shabby, dusty living room, playing the fuck out of the violin, his encouraging brother standing behind him. My friend replied, *Yeah that's bearable.* The next day, after sharing VSQ covers, she said, *Okay fine I want four kids and I want a string quartet.* Funny how quickly things escalate sometimes.

(1)

I come to in the morning after the McNally Debacle, sit up on my still made bed, grab the cup of water I left on the nightstand the night before, and chug all sixteen ounces in one gulp. I started doing this thing a few weeks ago where I pass out on top of my blanket without using any of the pillows. It's shades of that viral commencement speech Admiral McRaven gave in the University of Texas at Austin in 2014. He said that excellence starts by making your bed in the morning because it means you start your day with a completed task.

I stand up, glance past the handle of gin in the crevice between my nightstand and bed, and see a perfectly tucked in blanket and four perfectly balanced pillows. Task completed. If someone took a snapshot of me in this moment—one that doesn't include the handle of gin or my bed hair or the paring knife or my bloodshot eyes—and sent it to the Admiral, the "Old Man" would be proud of my undeniably excellent start to the day.

I trudge to the bathroom, brush my teeth, and wash my face till it resembles something, or at least until it doesn't resemble what it is. Back to the bedroom, two Ibuprofens, more water. I check my phone and, as I scroll through notifications, begin to get flashes of conversations from last night. Some are fine, some are bad, some don't really matter. Most don't. Except for the one with her, obviously. I leave my phone to charge, pack my bag, and go get coffee downstairs—always taking the stairs, never my McDonald's ice cream machine of an elevator. The bed is perfectly made, the hair isn't combed but it never is, my sweater's sleeves are down (thankfully it's winter), my leather jacket like a coat of icing, suede bag draped over my shoulder, toothpick dangling on my bottom lip.

The baristas at my coffee shop, all of whom know my regular order (it's not an impressive feat, I just get a large, black coffee), looking at me from the outside, probably think I'm all good, which, on the surface, I am. By the time the coffee hits, and the nutrients from whatever vegetables or fruit I shove in my mouth work their magic, and my brain allows me to read through pages or respond to emails or file reports or whatever else I have to do today, and I rehydrate myself with gallons of water, I'm decently good on the inside, too.

I usually start shaking around lunchtime (could be the caffeine making its way in or the alcohol making its way out), at which point I take the elevator upstairs and eat the same lunch I have every single day (three over-medium eggs on two toasts with a side chopped salad) and drink more water and consume more vitamins, and, on really bad days, take a seven minute nap. This whole process—from the sixteen-ounce cup on the nightstand, through the way I slice, divide, and position the third egg between the two toasts, all the way to the handle of gin in the crevice I wouldn't hurry to hide in shame—is a routine that has become old hat, one that I carry out as if it is muscle memory.

Sometimes, the fact that my daily routine has become a low-cost physical and emotional theme park ride worries me, but not always. I do find myself, usually during the shaky moments of this ordeal in the elevator right before lunch, making mental calculations, trying to figure out if I've sunk too low, whether whatever is holding me has failed, and whether I can still jump my way into safety. I still naively believe that that the elevator may crash and hit rock bottom, but so long as the self-asserted masculine scholar inside it sticks the landing, I'll survive.

By the time I have another coffee and do another shift of work and eat an apple, I'm pretty much as good as new and ready to go on my afternoon run, after which I go educate the youth. By the time I walk back into my room in the evening, it's clear I still don't need to go to therapy, because if I see a made bed and have texts to reply to and am still adhering to my marathon training plan and can teach kids how to use the quadratic formula or MLA citations or twenty-four's factor tree, then things really aren't all bad.

No barrel in my mouth.

(1)   (2)   (3)

I tried writing essays similar in form to Sundberg's, but there was no point. There's no point in mimicking what she did so brilliantly, turning her pain into art. Her bruise into a sunset, if you will. I'm not sure if writing about your suffering is an overused trope by this point, but I'd like to think that there's a difference between writing about pain and writing *from* pain.

I know that it's a character I'm playing: a pained, depressed male writer, in the Bright Lights of the Big City, seeking out comfort in alcohol. I'm not the first, nor even the *second person* to do this. I'm aware of my performance, at least until I'm drunk enough to believe this is actually who I am. That's the thing about alcohol. I said I've always found it magical for the way it reveals versions of a man kept under layers of insecurities and blankets. But alcohol can also embolden us to try being someone we want to be, or think would be cool or provide us with answers. This happened to me in my early days in New York, when I thought I wanted to be this guy who reads at bars. I had to be drunk the first time I walked into a bar with a book, and the second time, and the third, until it slowly became something I felt comfortable enough doing sober. Regardless of where this trope of a character originated from, it's now a part of who I am. I genuinely enjoy being the guy who comes to the bar with a book for some rest and relaxation (one of my all-time favorite NYC moments was sitting at my downstairs bar and finishing, ironically, Ottessa Moshfegh's *My Year of Rest and Relaxation*).

The problem is that I don't always really want to be whatever character comes out when I drink. I don't like some of them, and it's difficult to reseal a Pandora's box once it's opened, which is why, in truth, I worry, sometimes, about drinking.

I worry that one day, I'll drink, and the light coat of water that's keeping my dumpling of a persona together will cease to hold, and all my filling will spill onto a boiling pan, where it will stick and char and burn until it's rendered inconsumable. Until all that's left to do is wash the debris, scrape me off, and cast me down the drain.

Still, I drink. Out of fear, for comfort. The prospect of closing my eyes, sober, trying to fall asleep without even the faintest trace of her on my lips, attempting to shut my mind up, put everything to rest, is terrifying. Like the math problem you look at and immediately dismiss any likelihood of solving, not even bothering wasting your time attempting to. There's no point trying. The moment I close my eyes, I see everything I did wrong, and tossing and turning in bed for hours, physically and mentally, can only lead me to tumble. Alcohol blinds me. Alcohol offers me the comfort of the devil I know. Alcohol ends the day, which sometimes, more and more often lately, is all I want. Sacrificing hours from tomorrow morning to avoid the hours of my brain being aware of and having to confront the sadness tonight is a deal I gladly make. So, before even realizing that I've started, I drink.

I drink, giving my lips a taste, and lie atop the sheets of my darkened bed, keeping the surface perfectly made, intact, presentable, just in case an Old Man comes to take a look at my life. Everything is tuned out, and everything is in tune, and, with my mind numb, I let my arms move independently from my body, in a way that's been romanticized, a way others who seem to be as sad as I am have done before me. I do it halfheartedly, because I don't really want to do it—I just want to reach whatever answers are on the other side of this sadness. This feels like a part of the story my character has to live through, and one in which I have agency over the sadness, the amount of pain I allow myself to feel.

I drink, just enough for the inside to be silenced, then let the violin's bow do nothing more than graze the strings, as others have done before me, in the same vein. Graze, just enough for the music to start playing. Music only I can hear. Music that's not loud enough to wake anyone else, but is loud enough for me to be thankful it's winter.

Legend

I'd say we[2] have three options when we feel lost in life.

(3)

We can read books and watch movies, find characters that go through what we're going through, and try to learn from what they did to reach, or lose, their happy endings. Either by seeing their mistakes, avoiding them, and simply taking the lessons learned, or by deciding to put ourselves through the same ringer, playing their role, living through the same journey. The issue is that these characters aren't real, so they provide us with a false sense of agency. Our story isn't being written by some novelist, nor is it being picked up by some Hollywood production company, which severely diminishes the chances of our story culminating in a happy ending.

(2)

We can look at those around us, our friends and family, see their mistakes and successes, glean from how they've handled life, do our best to follow or avoid. Perhaps even make use of the relationships we've established with them over years of mutual growth, familiarity of each other's selves and tendencies and idiosyncrasies, and the love and care we share. Ask them for help. Approach those who know us best, who've seen us tumble and fall but have also seen us glide through life, those who truly have only our best interests in their mind, and lean on them instead of trying to drink it all up on our own.

(1)

We can try to figure shit out—as it takes place in the present tense— by ourselves.

---

2. By "we" I mean me and my 186 personalities.

That last one is tough. Not impossible, but tough. It can also, if you don't mind me saying, fucking suck, because for it to actually work we have to include every wrong step we've ever taken. So, we may as well make the attempt fun for ourselves by thinking back to things or people or teams or movies or foods or books or Steven Gerrards that make us happy. We can look at the mistakes we've made, embrace our share of the blame, and, instead of rejecting the fact that we're lost, Take the L.

It's about removing ourselves from ourselves, looking at the steps of our story, speaking them into existence, and—and this is the key— telling it to someone. Could be to a Muji notebook, a Word doc, a thera- pist, a subreddit community, an Uber driver, a best friend, a divine entity (good luck with this one), a Writing MFA workshop (even better luck with this one), or, I guess, anyone with time on their hands and an inter- est in reading an interwoven, three-threaded book-length essay written by some dude who played soccer and reads in bars and wears cardigans and is borderline an alcoholic and is borderline a hipster and is not sure which of those last two concerns him more, where he talks about how he thinks men—mostly himself, really—understand, withhold, and ex- press love.

⤜✿⤛

Maybe you, here, now, are thinking about someone in your life whom you wish you could get to talk to you. A friend, partner, sibling, child, parent, cute alcoholic hipster at a coffee shop, whomever. Without try- ing to come across as big-headed or anything, I know for a fact I am that person to a decent number of people (perhaps no longer after they finish this book, or, more likely, they'll have even more questions now). I'm no expert at talking—far from it, probably—but I'm pretty good at having people talk to me. I'll assume that since we're deep into this book by this point, there's a chance you've been reading (thank you for doing that, btw) because you're hoping to find some answers for yourself—whichever side you have in the relationship. I don't necessarily have answers, but I have two truths.

The first truth is that you can't force someone to talk. You can express the fact that you want them to, and that you're here to listen, and you can encourage and support and care and trust and whatever other positively connotated word you want to insert here, but it has to come from them. It's like gaining the trust of an abandoned dog: they need to come to you. All you can do is crouch down and whip out your best doggy voice and ask them who's a good boy, then hope that a good man comes running to you.

The second truth is that Steven Gerrard is the greatest midfielder in the history of the Premier League. I'm joking (I mean, he is, but that's not it). My actual second one is that yes, talking can only happen when it happens on their terms, but the terms upon which we work have to expand. In "The Cult of The Difficult Woman," one of the essays in Jia Tolentino's *Trick Mirror*, she claims, "We are all defined by our historical terms and conditions, and these terms and conditions have mostly been written by and for men." If you want to try to dispute Tolentino's claim, please take it up with her. Just know that *Trick Mirror* has a fantastic cover, so what she's saying must be true (though Lauren Oyler would probably disagree).

We can probably start by acknowledging that we—myself and whoever else may feel like they have stuff they're ignoring and blocking—need to do some introspection, which may not feasibly and beneficially happen on the terms we've been conditioned by. Maybe it's time we start digging on some new grounds, and don't fear sharing whatever it is we might find, in whichever way works. Write it down and show it to someone, count to three and spit it out to break a silence, do it over the phone as you pace around your bedroom, get fast food at the end of a drunken night with your best friend and tell them what's up between bites of a McChicken. I get the feeling these may all be so obvious, but when you spend a lifetime not doing them, or when you don't think there's anything to dig, maybe they're not.

I'll just add, if you don't mind me doing so, and of course you don't because it's my fucking book and I'll say whatever the fuck I want—sorry. That was unnecessary. And mean. And true. Sorry. Anyway. I'll just add, if you don't mind me doing so, that if you're a man who does decide to open his mouth, know that a lot of people are tired of men talking about love, and a lot of people are tired of men talking, and a lot of people are tired of men, and a lot of people are, frankly, just tired. But for us to figure this shit out, men have to talk too. Not always and not always first and not always last and not always louder and not always quieter, but talk, and always think before doing so, and always listen. That's it. I'm done pandering. Almost.

My advice, which you can take at word value (which is prettier than my face value and that's not meant to be a testament to my writing), is that if you want to pique the interest of those who are tired of listening to men, turn your story into something everyone loves. Like some kind of bread or something. People eat that shit up.

Step Seven

Bake

(1)

Your memory really is something, she says, and while nothing affirms me more than her acknowledging and verbalizing how much I'm invested in her and us, I really don't feel as if it's *something*. Our jokes and references and memories are just constantly there. It'd be like saying it's something that every time you open your utensil drawer, the forks are there. Of course they're fucking there.

Five days after the McNally Debacle, we're making plans again. Initially, we discussed going together to an exhibition at the Met, but she told me this morning that her roommate and a friend who's staying with her actually mentioned the exhibit. I chuckled to myself and told her she should just go with them, flushing away any disappointment at another plan going down the drain.

She said maybe we could meet up after since she'll already be in the area. Of course we could, and of course I still believed we could. So, as I was doing my Friday afternoon ab and arm day (using two cans of paint and a backpack filled with books as homemade dumbbells and doing Athlean X's ten-minute ab workout on YouTube), I left my phone off of Do Not Disturb, not trusting that her status as a favorite contact would do its job. Four minutes into Jeff Cavaliere's ab circuit, she told me she was done at the museum. For the only time in my life, I stopped the video halfway through. She said we could go to the river—which she still misses—or a bar or something, and as I raced through showering and shaving my neck and donning my hipster cardigan and leather jacket, we decided to just meet at the river around the 80s/90s, at which point I said I heard there's a really good Peruvian-Chinese spot there, at which point she told me she's laughing her fucking ass off and that my memory really is something.

She's bundled up in layers and a woolen crocheted scarf as she walks west towards me on 86th. The scarf is in different shades of maroon, and the wool and her undone quilted hair mix together in the blowing wind. It's like a scene where she's this mesmerizing main character in a movie. Or book, I guess. I notice her from across the street, but, leaning against the subway entrance on the NW corner, I pretend I don't. We're not at a point where us maintaining eye contact for this long from such a distance wouldn't be awkward in a way, I think. It's been two months and nine days since I walked the wrong way towards the A train from that live music venue by Williamsburg Bridge, not knowing it'd be this long till I'll see L again. There's a certain nervousness in me, probably because of how much I've built up this moment in my head since that night in Domino Park.

I wish I could ironically wave both my arms from the other side of the crosswalk like one of those inflatable tube men outside car dealerships, the way you do when you see someone who knows every intonation of your voice and flail of your arms, the way you do when you see someone who renders the rest of Manhattan nonexistent. But that's not where and who we are, and I'm not allowed to be that, or show that I want to be that, so, as she alternates her steps between black and white on the crosswalk, I swivel my oscillating fan of a neck, ensure my phone is on Do Not Disturb in my pocket, look down at my skinny jeans and worn black sneakers, pretend to ogle north and south, despite the fact that all my focus is on what my eyes pretend they cannot see.

Some hugs are better than others. It's easy to tell when a hug is good, and it's not that this one isn't good, but it's not 5 a.m. outside her building in a pitch black and dead silent street in Brooklyn good. It's not a hug where you feel them in the top phalanx of each of your fingers. It's not a hug where you're surprised by the power—not the force—they're holding you with. It's not the hug we shared two months and fourteen days ago, three avenues east and ten blocks north, on the corner of 96th and Central Park West, right before our lips pressed against each other's, firmly, for the final time. There's too much between us now. Layers, questions, time.

As we amble towards the water and she tightens her coat around herself in an attempt to brace against December winds, she asks me, shiv-
ering, how is it possible that I'm not freezing cold. In some world, I stop
her in her tracks, in the middle of this affluent Upper West Side street
and hide her in my arms. But that's not the world we're in, so I just hope
she doesn't think I'm like one of those teenage boys who wears shorts in
winter, tell her it's really not that cold, and that she shouldn't underesti-
mate my cardigan.

We sit on a bench and stare at the river. We've been here before in so
many different ways—parallel on some levels, straining to face each other
in others, hesitant about what do next in some ways, perfectly comfortable in others. She knows more about me than anyone else does, but she
also has no clue about what's going on. She's still happy to use me to gauge
the value of the birthday gift she got her mother or the price of a flight to
San Francisco, but the value of the *present* is still very much *up in the air*.

She gets too cold, so we head east and park at the far end of a U-
shaped bar. I find out she's started dabbling with meat again, and we share
wings that are truly awful—somehow firm and soft and hot and cold and
dry and wet, except in all the wrong ways. She sips from my Guinness,
and I reference a story she once told me about an evening she spent with
some old British man who drank a bunch of them. She's surprised I remember, but it's a fork.

L has the last barstool at the bar, the one closest to the wall. On my
right is an old lady eating wings and drinking sangria and playing the
NYT Spelling Bee game on her phone. L doesn't know the game, but
I play it regularly. I can't remember the last time something casual dis-
appointed me as much as the fact that today, for the first time in who
knows how long, I haven't played the game and don't know what the
pangram is off the top of my head. We get chatting to this woman about
the game, and L leans over me to look at the woman's phone, perhaps
subconsciously knowing that my space is still hers.

It's funny for a short while, talking to this woman. I don't know any-thing about her, of course, but I can tell the sangria is doing a little num-ber on her, given her verboseness. If there's anyone who knows about alcohol getting you to spill words (be it at a bar or into a Word doc or on a NYT game), it's this self-asserted masculine studies scholar. She starts telling us a story in the fake clandestine, check-your-shoulder manner an old Jewish lady in a Boca Raton deli gossips about Ruth from her retire-ment community. It's about a longtime friend of hers, whose name she can't disclose, but who was the theme of the New York Times crossword the other day. *I had to tell him about it because he had no clue,* she leans in to tell us, as if should anyone around us hear what she was talking about, her famous friend would disown her for life, taking with him the residue of his aura that she's allowed to bask in by proximity. She tells us he lives right around here, this anonymous man, *Well, one of his homes is here, at least.* We try to prod and get some more information out of her as to who this man is, even tease her by saying maybe we don't know who he is, though she assures us that we definitely do. We concede our interroga-tion eventually, though I'm well aware that as soon as this lady leaves, I'll be googling the answer. I think—or assume, at least—that this woman knows we can easily figure out who her friend is, but maybe this is some charade she has to go through in order to flex her friendship with one of New York's elite.

There are moments in the conversation with this old lady where my torso and neck face her directly, my left elbow even set on the bar so that my back is practically turned to L, and it probably seems as if I'm wholly invested in this woman's tale of the Times, when, in actuality, all my focus is on what my eyes pretend they cannot see.

She's here. Her foot is on my barstool. Her eyes, as she peers over my shoulder to look at the woman, surely zoom in on parts of me: the way the line of my beard is stenciled by my jaw bone, the exposed flesh on my cuticles from the skin I've chewed off, and perhaps even the one gray hair

I've been closely monitoring. Our mouths are sipping from the same pint. We're ordering from the same bartender. We're dipping into the same cocotte of ranch. We're listening to the same story that I want to believe is true but there's a decent chance isn't. It's her and I going through our journey, meeting strange people we'll later tell stories about at dinner parties. It's another little patch of a canvas we share, a patch that only she and I will ever paint, and only she and I will ever know how many layers have been ascribed. It's an experience that we're each experiencing differently, but we'll also eternally have together. It's a tiny little anecdote that L may forget about in three days but has already been stowed in the utensil drawer she has in my brain. I'll always be able to access this drawer, close my eyes and see the scene in which the woman I'm in love with sat by me and watched me flirt with a tipsy old lady at a bar. I'll have constant access to our debate about which of us would be more likely to be able to take this woman home in an attempt to figure out who the mystery crossword man is (it's for sure me). I'm living through a glass-of-water-in-the-desert moment where she's here. Her presence could not be more real, and it means everything to me, and it's, frankly, the only thing that means anything.

I guess that, on some level, I'm here, too, and my presence is real, too. I want to say it's impossible for me to know what my presence in L's life means to her, or what drawer it's being stowed in, if it's even being stowed at all. I've spent so long trying to find that precise answer for myself, but maybe I'm making this crossword question more complicated than it should be. All the clues for the answer to who I am in her life are right here, in the form of all the little things that aren't present. She isn't poking her finger into my side as I offer the lady another teasing comment. My left hand isn't dangled backwards, resting against her right leg pressed against the footrest of my barstool, my palm on her knee, pinching the inside of her shin every time the lady returns the flirt.

The lady's blabbering grows as old as she is, and I eventually twist my way back towards L in a way that conflates our spaces—my knee infiltrating her leg room, her forearm on my side of the bar, our presences somehow mutual but exclusive. The bar's name is the first name of who I dressed up as for Halloween, and I spend most of our time at the bar hoping that topic comes up somehow. On Halloween, I went to a house party hosted by my friends in Brooklyn, after which a group of us went to a Brooklyn Heights bar where I celebrated a friend's engagement then bussed to a Williamsburg music venue. Some part of me was hoping that L would bump into me wearing the white tank top and leather jacket and wildly tight light blue jeans I bought from the girls' section of a Harlem boutique. It was an eccentric look, and having to take the subway while dressed up riddled me with self-consciousness (despite the fact absolutely no one cares what you look like on the subway, most of all on Halloween, and no matter how bright the cover of the book you're carrying is). But this costume was strategic. My mask hid my caterpillar moustache and the leather jacket hid my wife-beater tank top, so anyone looking at me just saw a normal dude in maybe slightly too skinny skinny jeans. But at the bar, in full costume with my slicked back gelled hair, the look was eccentric, and I don't think L had ever seen me be that, and there was a sliver of hope in me she'd find herself in this neck of the woods and get to meet another version of me. She didn't, nor does the bar's name or Halloween seamlessly come up as a conversation topic.

We talk about the bar's décor of framed dog photos, and each of our families' troubles, inevitably leading her to tell me again about all the pets her family has failed to keep alive over the years. She tells me about some young guy she works with who requested to follow her on Instagram, which makes me feel at a disadvantage, since I've not breached that social media wall. Later tonight, from the comfort of my bed, I'll request to follow her, she'll text me some sarcastic jab that includes the word "damn," and I'll say that if the 20-year-old was allowed to, I figured I could, too, which is somehow both incredibly jokey but also incredibly true. She'll request to follow me back, and I'll go into the app and approve her request but will leave the notification untouched. Whenever I'll want, for as long as that notification is there, drunk or sober or happy or sad, I'll be able to pick up my phone, swipe down, and see her name not only waiting for me, but still after me.

I pay our tab, which annoys L, but it's not some performative masculinity of picking up the check on a first date. I know that an act like that would do nothing to impress her, and I think she knows me well enough to know that it's not something I'd do in an attempt to impress. It's more like a gesture you do for someone you care about, a token of appreciation for the effort they've made to make time for you.

She goes to the bathroom before we leave, and a cute gay couple show up behind her vacant seat (this is obviously presumptive on my part since I don't know them, but, like, they're a cute gay couple). L's scarf is draped over the barstool, and one of the guys accidentally brushes it and it falls to the ground. He picks it up and says he's so sorry, but I reassure him it's all good, and add that we're about to leave so they can take our seats. L comes back, I tell her we're giving the seats to the couple behind us, and one of them overhears me and tells us there's no rush at all. We chat to them for about twelve seconds as L puts all her layers back on, and the guy who brushed the scarf compliments L on it. She thanks him, then I tell her to be careful because he tried to steal it while she was gone. The two guys laugh, and L does, in a way, too, despite not being there for the context, but she can recognize that a minimal yet perfect form of rapport exists between me and these two guys, and she smiles and looks at me in the same way that I'd like to think a wife looks at her silly husband who just made a silly joke, and, for the rest of time, in the minds of two guys who sat at the edge of the bar at Fred's on the Upper West Side on a cold and windy Friday evening in the middle of December, maybe that's what L and I will be.

We walk out, and L tells me she has some friend in Brooklyn whom she told she may see after she's done here, and I know exactly what that phrase means, and I wonder whether there's more than one of me in her life, and I wonder what kind of friend it is, but I quickly brush the thoughts aside, because there'll be plenty of time for them later, and right now, she's here. We say we'll get food, and my surfacing of Indian food as an idea literally stops her in her tracks, but we think it'll be too much, and keep walking towards a pizza place instead. She insists on paying, then we sit on a Central Park bench and eat slices of pizza and garlic knots that are somehow even more underwhelming than the chicken wings from earlier, but who cares.

She forces me to have the last crust, which is beyond cold and dry by this point. I could very easily metaphorize or analogize the crust to our relationship, but I don't really want to do that. We dust flour off ourselves and I fold the carton box and cram it into the recycling bin and we exit the park and stand atop the 86th street station and that's it.

For the next few months, I'll walk past that pizza place almost every Monday and Thursday as I trudge from one tutoring session to another across UWS streets. I want to say it'll remind me of her every time I see the store's atrocious and massive green, red, and white sign, but to be reminded of something, you first have to forget.

For the next few months, in an attempt to move on, I'll go on dates in this neighborhood. At E's and the Dead Poet and Craft and Carry and Amelie and Owl's Tail and Amsterdam Ale House. I'll never go back to Fred's, but sometimes my date and I would walk by it, and I'll tell them a story about a time I went there and met an old lady at the bar who said her friend was the theme of the New York Times crossword, and my date will never be awed or wowed. They'll never understand how many layers had been ascribed to the story. Because to anyone other than me, maybe even to L, it really is just a silly little anecdote and nothing more. It's New York City, dude. There're famous people and odd tales all the time. My story about meeting not even a super famous actor, but the friend of a super famous actor, really isn't that Big or some Miracle On the Hudson, so perhaps the story is best off just being Cast Away.

We stand atop the 86th street station and that's it. We stand atop the 86th street station, we casually embrace, she says she hopes I enjoy my time in Israel, heads down the stairs, and, despite not knowing it for certain yet, that's it.

I stand atop the 86th street station, and her presence is no longer real, despite the fact it always is, and, in some way, always will be; despite the fact that her presence will never be real again, but I don't know that yet. I walk west, away from her, head home, crawl into bed, request to follow, her name appears on my phone in a way that isn't real, where I'll choose to keep it, until I'll understand that that's it; until I'll understand that it's time to take it, the L, and cast it away.

(3)

I think that's the most perfect metaphor thus far: the backpack filled with books used as a dumbbell. Maybe it's more of a microcosm than a metaphor. Something small that represents something big. Like, how a man's small penis is emblematic of his minuscule masculinity. That's a joke. Relax. Microcosm is like when something miniature encapsulates the characteristic qualities of something much larger. Like, Giannis's block on Ayton is a perfect microcosm of who he is as a player: Willing to sacrifice himself for his team, a dominant physical presence on both ends of the floor, jaw-dropping. Anyway, as I was saying.

The backpack filled with books used as a dumbbell is the most perfect metaphor thus far because it represents my performance of chasing a happy ending in which I am the best version of myself; in which I am who I want to be. I have a backpack stuffed with books and I use it to do biceps and triceps curls. Every time I finish reading a book, I cram it into the bag, incrementally increasing the expanse of my brain by absorbing the books' words, incrementally increasing the girth of my arms by carrying the books' weight.

That's what the bookbag represents: my attempt at continual personal growth and expansion, striving towards the optimal version of myself. The version that can run for a while and lift somewhat heavy items, can recognize how Ottessa Moshfegh uses her narrators to represent nihilism and Jürgen Klopp uses gegenpressing as a de-facto playmaker. It's a metaphor for the development of my physical and intellectual sides, the ones that are tangible and easily assessed. It's my manipulation of an external performance, like a rolled down sleeve, to cover up those internal parts of me that are stagnant, or, dare I say, regressing. As a wise man once said, I cannot be emotionally weak if my shirt sleeves hug my biceps. (It's me. I'm the wise man.)

No matter how dense or heavy the books get, I keep trying to absorb and carry the words and weight, because the performance of knowledge and power is also the assertion of knowledge and power. The performance of improvement, then, even if disingenuous, even if things aren't getting better, even if you're not getting any closer to that happy ending, will surely also be the assertion of such improvement.

Jia Tolentino articulates it much better in "Always Be Optimizing," another essay in *Trick Mirror*. She argues, "Figuring out how to 'get better' at being a woman is a ridiculous and often amoral object." Obviously, I'm no woman (though Andrea Long Chu would say I'm kinda female), and far be it from me to try to make the narrative about myself, but I also feel I have an amoral obsession with coming across as someone who is *getting better*, even if I'm not. "The worse things get," Tolentino adds, "the more a person is compelled to optimize."

Tolentino brings up Matt Buchanan's chopped-salad-economy in the essay, which is a routine engineered to optimize our nutritional intake at lunch while keeping our eyes on a screen. Buchanan's theory kind of fits perfectly with my daily lunch routine that includes a chopped salad, except for the whole alcohol shakes thing. I don't think his theory includes alcohol; I don't remember. It's been a while since I've read the book. Maybe don't take my word for it. Maybe just read it for yourself (doing this marketing for you free of charge, Jia). Maybe I should just read it again. Last time I did that—sat in my coffee shop and read *Trick Mirror*—the world's ironic timing worked in my favor by bringing through the door a familiar and elucidated face, allowing me back into her life, giving me a shot at a happy ending. Until that opportunity comes, no matter how much worse things get, all I can do is continue to do my best; to optimize.

I guess that, in a way, the happy ending I'm hoping for is one more beginning. One more shot to live out the incomprehensible ways that woman makes me feel. The question worth posing, though, is whether it's the feelings, not the woman, that I'm after. They've become conflated, those two. The person I want to be and the feelings I want to feel are the ones that only she ever brought out. My chasing of her, perhaps, is a chasing of the real me. The optimal me.

There's a chance, now that I come to think about it, that the reason I started writing whatever it is you've been reading was because I subconsciously hoped that turning our story into something tangible and consumable would increase the likelihood of it ending the way I want it to. But this is nonfiction we're dealing with. Our story isn't being written by some novelist nor is it being picked up by some Hollywood production company, which severely diminishes the chances of it culminating in a happy ending. It isn't even "our story," frankly. It's mine. Turning the story tangible may, at least, enable me to not only see who I really am, but understand how I can be me without her. Or without anyone, for that matter.

I think that's the most perfect metaphor thus far: the backpack filled with books used as a dumbbell, because I'm just a self-asserted masculine studies scholar who's writing his own story. Absorbing the book's words, carrying the book's weight.

(1)

L? Dani shifts up in his seat to ask, about an hour into our late breakfast.

We still find it impossible to speak in English without laughing at each other's accents, so do so only out of politeness when around English speakers. It's just me and him now, so he actually uses the Hebrew equivalent of the letter L, which has two syllables and I feel like that makes it roll off the tongue a little nicer. We worked out together this morning, and just finished eating at this outdoor café near the Mediterranean Sea, by where his parents live (he's been staying with them since returning, though is moving into his own place soon).

We've not had time alone over the last couple of weeks I've spent in Israel, so we haven't had the chance to talk about the short and early version of the essay he read. When he initially finished reading (took him two stints which I'm not sure whether is a good or bad sign), he messaged me, *I enjoyed reading. I learned quite a lot about you. And the end gave me chills. She sounds perfect and exactly what and who you need.*

I, obviously, ignored the message. But we did plan to have some form of a conversation when I make it across the Atlantic Ocean. This version he read is an iota of the full story, not just L's and mine, but my individual one, so I found it funny that he said he learned a lot. His reading this made him privy to far more than most (if not all) are, but there's still plenty he doesn't know. What he does know, at least, is to not dare say her full name today, make her presence be any more real than I can handle. Him asking this question, which can barely be regarded a question, nor is it even a name, but just a two-syllabled initial, and even that's double what it is in its original language, invites me to fill a certain space.

Somewhere on this wobbly wooden table between us, between the mini cast iron pans the shakshukas were in, the small aluminum bowls that had the chopped salads, the porcelain cocottes for the tahini, my toughened glass cup with the silicone band that's holding the remnants of Turkish coffee grounds in it, his cardboard to-go cup that has one sip of an Americano left in it, and the wicker basket that had my rye bread and his white toast, Dani invites me to place something. I'm not entirely sure what that *something* is, but it's something. More material, more substance, more flaws, more jokes, more truth. More me, I guess.

Once, at a bar, three sweet friends of mine—and I mean really genuinely sweet—emotionally cornered me. The three women weren't all acquainted before that day—I was the hinge around which we wound up encircled. They conjoined forces to interrogate me about my feelings and reluctance to share them, each of the three relaying a similar individual experience of our relationship. A relationship where it is often them who are the ones filling the emotional space between us, me playing the role of the faux therapist. I found the whole thing quite funny. I was somewhat buzzed (I think we all were) and my guard was lowered, so when they asked why I tend to deflect questions, I told them that my instinct is to ignore a question the first time it comes around knocking. *You need to ask me again,* I told my friends, *because I need to really believe you want to know the answer.* A lot of people, I feel, and pardon me for my upcoming cynicism, only ask questions in order to be asked them back. So, I have no interest in partaking in this façade of attentiveness when all you're interested in is one-upping whatever my answer will be. Here you go, have your question back. If you're genuinely interested, if you truly want to make me believe you really fucking care, you'll ask a second time, and even a third if that's what it takes. Even with three genuinely sweet friends, or even the boys with whom a decade ago I conceptualized the world of salacity together, the ones with whom I used to feel a sense of security around our conversations, a sense of security that enabled all of us to openly talk about what our minds and bodies were going through, I need that double affirmation that they care. Really care. The problem, I understood as my friends and I spoke about this, is that people in my life don't know I function this way. For them, asking more than once, particularly when they know I'm reserved to begin with, could be perceived as overstepping boundaries, making me uncomfortable. They don't want to

push, and they don't know that I kind of want—and probably need—
to be pushed or, at least, encouraged to move.

When I do feel that you want to know, when I do have to spit out an
honest answer, I tend to focus only on the first word I have to say. It's usually the lightest word of the sentence: *so, I, what, okay, the;* one of those little guys. I repeat that word over and over in my head, then just spit it out,
which is usually easy, because it's just a simple little silly word. Once it's
out, there's no going back, and the rest of the sentence has to follow. It's a
silly system, maybe, but it helps me provide answers. Not always, though.
Not necessarily, for example, when I'm prompted by a question that can
barely be regarded as a question at a café by the Mediterranean Sea.

What's there to say, achi, things are fine, I cleanse my palate, then tell
Dani that I actually saw her a couple days before my flight, which excites
him as he seems to believe that the prospect of love is still alive. I tell
him that we still talk (which is technically the truth), and that I assume
we'll see each other again at some point when I'm back stateside (which
is hopefully the truth), and that all I can do is wait (which is what I've
been trying to persuade myself is the truth). I don't lie, but I suppose I am
concealing some truth—the alcohol, the extent of the blame I carry, the
unlikelihood of a happy ending, how sad this is making me—from him,
which maybe you could classify as being dishonest. But the fact I'm staring at a person who knows how I feel and how I feel about L, and I don't
want to shrivel into a ball and be thrown into the Mediterranean (I do a
little bit) is progress in my book. Pun, as always, intended.

So, we'll see what happens, I wrap up with one more banal response,
and Dani doesn't push for anything more, perhaps because he believes
that there isn't much more to push for, and perhaps because he believes
that pushing won't get him anywhere, and that, much like me, all he can
do is wait. I'd like to think it's the latter. I'd also like to think that there's
too much on the table for me to place anything else down, though I guess
there is some room in the empty wicker basket which held the bread.
The lack of space on the table is a conveniently pretty metaphor, though,

so I believe in it just enough to whisk the conversation elsewhere, with a rye smile.

He's told me, over the course of our late breakfast, about what it's been like to readjust to a world he's not been a part of for a decade, the missteps and stumbles he's taken as he's been trying to get his feet under him, and what it's like to have his love be an ocean away. It's become so glaringly obvious, as he's done so, how far I am from being able to do the same. Instead of his ability in comparison to my inability being imposing and eliciting envy, I'm grateful. Grateful to have this man, who I've always looked sideways at, to, now, look up to.

He pays (he owes me money after a trip we took to Atlantic City together), then, with my flight back to New York being tonight, we spread our arms wide, bear hug, clank cheek into collarbone, and bid goodbye.

I made a note on my phone, months and months ago, while waiting for a flight at Ben Gurion Airport, where I mused about whether or not I should buy L a gift from Israel. It was during my first stint in her life, and I was—shockingly—romanticizing and aggrandizing my contemplation of whether I should buy some corny snow globe with a camel in it or something. The decision of whether I do or don't was analogized, in my mind, to the decision of whether or not I want to spend the rest of my life with L. The logic behind it, I guess, was that when we'll be in our 70s, sitting with our children and grandchildren and all their spouses, maybe even at a Rosh Hashanah dinner table, I'll be able to put my arm around my long-time love, and tell everyone how no matter where I went in this world, no matter how far away from her I found myself, from the very first day, I never stopped thinking about her, always came back to her, and always had something for her in my hands. It's probably another one of those things I've seen in some show or movie (Marshall and Lily's beer thing rings a bell) that I've learned to associate with the depiction of an unimpeachable form of love, the one I dream to exist in. But the hope would be to not only be within the existence of such love, but also that someone at the table, perhaps a grandchild's friend, some odd, brown, bearded young man who's seated at the corner and is sipping on his Heineken noticeably quickly, would take note, dare I say be inspired, dare I say wish to do the same. The idealistic love my person and I will share would be, I figured, an atheistic self-asserted masculine studies scholar's version of L'dor V'dor.

I'd known L for not much longer than a month by that point, but there was already a part of me that saw a chuppah and a rabbi of sorts and some wine and a glass for me to break, the religious formalities I would have liked to avoid but would probably make an appearance for the sake of appeasing my mother. There was already a part of me that saw our story ending with an *I do*.

There was already a part of me that envisioned a future in which I still make jokes about our birthdays and she still has her smile; a future where she jokingly pushes me off and I never let her drift a single inch away; a future that's perfect. Not flawless, but perfect. I know, I know, it's been exhausted how messy love can be (you should watch *The Half Of It* on Netflix if you haven't already), but it is. It's full of flaws and ebbs and downs and mistakes and stains and whatever else philosophers and Louis CK and Netflix original screenwriters have said before me. But with all that, love can still be perfect, as long as it's one thing: present. That's my philosophy. Take it or leave it.

So, yeah, standing in the airport's overpriced bookstore, mere weeks into this woman's chapter in my life, click-clicking a retractable pen that has a Dead Sea scroll rolled up into it, I floated quixotic thoughts and wrote them down, and I now find myself in that same bookstore, reading the thoughts younger me had in the exact same spot current me is standing, wondering whether I would like to retract my philosophy. Somehow simultaneously thinking younger me is a fucking idiot but also thinking he isn't wrong, which is as good a feeling as you can hope for when reading back your own thoughts.

That last time I was here, I wound up buying some Israeli chocolate on a 4+1 deal the Duty Free Market offered, and gave some to L. It felt like some form of a gesture, but a noncommittal one. If we would end up getting married, it would count at the dinner table, and if we didn't, then whatever, who cares, it was just a part of the deal. Could be the four or the one, I guess. A cop out, maybe. A microcosm, perhaps. I think L liked the chocolate; I don't know. You can get the same one at pretty much any Jewish-run grocery store in New York City, which there is not a scarcity of, anyway, so it's not very unique. Maybe it was just the thought that counted, but I don't know what I was thinking. Fucking idiot.

I drop my phone into my back pocket, walk out of the bookstore, and go buy a single slab of Israeli chocolate which, when I get back to New York, I'll place on the dresser by my bedroom window. Just in case.

As I Promised

I first told her I'm in love with her at around 4 a.m. of July 11th on a bench in Union Square.

I was wearing a light blue buttoned t-shirt with a grandad collar, which is incredibly apt as it belonged to my grandfather and was handed down to me after his passing. The best items in my wardrobe, with no exception, belonged to him. This blue one is my favorite dressy casual shirt (there's a floral T of his that's my favorite *casual* casual one), mostly because there's a button on each of the short sleeves that lines the fabric precisely on the cut of my triceps and biceps, which makes my arms look bigger than they probably are. I feel incredibly confident and unnecessarily boasting and arrogant every time I wear this shirt.

I went to a friend's birthday party on a sunny rooftop in Chelsea on the afternoon of the 10th, where I profusely perspired through my lovely shirt. I was driven to the party by a friend and her husband, and he stared at me on the roof, literally dripping sweat from every gland of my body, and said something along the lines of, *You should be the least sweatiest of all of us.* He reasoned the statement with my having grown up in the Middle East, which should have accustomed my body to handle heat better. No, sir. I'd have pit stains in an igloo. Naked.

People brought all kinds of cans to the party. Beer, seltzers, those margaritas that have more sugar in them than the diet of a privileged and bratty eight-year old child; you know the spiel for a day party. I brought a handle of tequila and tonic and limes. My friend whose birthday it was bought me a tequila shot on my birthday the year prior, so it felt apt, plus it was a party, man. I figured people would do rounds of shots and have a good time and forget the fact that we're all probably developing malignant melanoma while standing on the asphalt of this crammed roof.

I think I was the only person who wound up having any of the handle, which was left more than half full (applaud my effort, at least). The friend who drove me to the party took the glass bottle home in her car, where it remained till she returned it to me, exactly five months and one day later, along with another couple of liquor handles she wanted to offload, all of which I drank by myself in bed as I was working on this book-length essay I was trying to make happen, since writing some sections required me to access places that I could only reach through alcohol, which I hate saying, but is incredibly apt. To paraphrase Adorno, the carefully recorded fizzing of the mineral water types what the sober mind cannot.

Four of us left the party and went to get dinner at this Indian place, which sobered me up some, then a couple other people met us, and I think some of them may have taken edibles or smoked weed or something, but I didn't. I ended up leaving my group to meet a different friend who was in town for the weekend. He wanted me to meet a friend of his who lives in NYC since we both "challenge him, but in different ways." Neither of us knew what that meant, but we presumed it was a compliment. The three of us plus one more person (no idea who he was) all had one drink in this loud ass bar where you're more likely to hold a dodo bird than a conversation. By the grace of god, one of them said they were tired, so we left, at which point I started strolling, at around two o'clock in the morning, in my light blue buttoned shirt, northwest towards Union Square, to meet someone with a familiar and elucidated face, who I'd seen the other day for the first time in a while, at the coffee shop underneath my apartment, where we hugged and she jested at the book I was reading (Jia Tolentino's *Trick Mirror*), in what set in motion my second stint in her life.

I'd said *I love you* in a romantic way to another person before, but not to her. The first time I ever did that was Sunday, September 24th, 2017, a date I know because it was the same day Tom Brady found Brandin Cooks in the endzone with 00:23 left on the clock to give the Pats the win over the Texans. I planned to watch the game, but ended up lying in bed with my girlfriend at the time, who was the recipient and reciprocator of that *I love you* (no regrets about that decision, but it would've been cool to watch the greatest to ever do it do what he does best live). I don't think I ever told anyone that I'm *in love* with them until this night in July in Union Square. There's something different about the admission of being *in love*, rather than just loving, I think. More of an active declaration of sorts; an opening statement; a first swing of the axe.

Union Square, when the market is open, can get as busy and loud and populated as anywhere in the city—hardly a place for an intimate conversation. But it was dark and late and quiet then, and it was just her and me. I reiterated what I'd typed out into a late night note and shared with her, about how large a part of my brain she still occupies, and my acknowledgement of how my guardedness messed things up the first time around, but then I paused. I felt like I wasn't making sense. In our silence, then, as she waited for me to keep going, the only sentence that came to my mind, the only one I wanted to say, was, *I'm in love with you.* As I tried to figure out how to get the sentence out, the word I kept repeating in my mind wasn't that silly little one at the beginning, *I'm*, the one that's easy to say, but the one right in the middle, the one that everything revolves around. *Just do it,* I reductively thought to myself, and I did.

She was caught by surprise when I said it, as if she had absolutely no clue I was anywhere near this feeling. It's hard to phase her, but those words did. Actually, it's not necessarily that she's hard to phase, but that it's hard to tell when she's phased. I think so, at least. There's something eternally composed about her, as if she's so confident in who she is and what she wants and what's around her, that nothing gets her off her spot. That's why it was so memorable when she chuckled into the sleeve of her sweater, all that time ago, when she walked into her room and saw me on her bed, reading her copy of Murakami's book. An unexpected, lovely surprise. Like finding a curly fry.

Her eyes didn't stray from mine when I made my declaration, but they sort of widened, zoomed out in a way so that she could reassess what's around her, regain her composure. I then did my best to try to explain to this woman in front of me the incomprehensible ways she makes me feel. I told her how much I love just existing next to her, tilting my torso forward, landing my forehead on her shoulder, feeling her fingers run along the top of my spine, and breathing her collarbone in. It's not even just a sexual physical thing, I told her on that bench. I just haven't been able to stop thinking about putting my head on her shoulder, have every breath I take be air that trickles off of her, subsist on our blissed existence. I've had this unexplainable desperation to touch her, and be touched by her; to connect our bodies in a way that makes me and her become us, in a way that clears everything up, makes me twice as good, born again, visually acute, 20/20.

I turned to face her, then, and, presumably aided by the confidence of the lingering alcohol or garlic naan or buttoned sleeves of my blue shirt, did just what I'd been wanting to do for so long. We stayed like that for a while, my head resting on her bare shoulder, and spoke, and it was even better than I'd recalled, and her skin was even softer than I'd remembered. If I could only choose one feeling I've ever had to relive, this precise moment, that I still recall as vividly as anything, would be my first choice: The one in which she took her hands, lifted my face off her shoulder, leaned forward, and kissed me. A kiss I could spend a whole book trying to describe but that I would never be able to explain.

We both got home close to 6 a.m., and after a few hours of sleep she told me that she can't believe last night happened. She said she'll need some time to process everything I said, which, of course, I understood. Three days later, I put on a cornflower blue T-shirt from Zara, she wore light blue jeans and a white tube top, she kissed me next to a still-lit but then closed Dunkin' Donuts, and we watched Giannis's iconic block on Ayton before spending the night together in my bed. In hindsight, this night was her affirming the feelings I shared towards her on that Union Square bench; her signaling to me that she processed everything I said and that she's choosing to believe me, give me another shot; her saying, in her own composed way, *You know what, fuck it, maybe I am too.*

A few days later, I drove a minivan from Chicago to North Carolina and tried to do some of my own processing, unnecessarily. My eyes clear on the road, my vision muddled, I lost my composure, panicked, and fucked it all up.

(2)

In his iconic pregame speech in the movie *Any Given Sunday*, Al Pacino as Coach Tony D'Amato says he's made every wrong choice a middle-aged man can make. That he's chased off anyone who's ever loved him, and has reached a point where he can't even stand the face he sees in the mirror. As you get old, Pacino adds, things get taken from you. He tells the men in the locker room with him that their losses, mistakes, and regrets have led them all to hell. They have the option of whether to stay there, or fight their way back into the light—climb out of hell, one inch at a time.

Despite how my portrayal of him may have been perceived, Mr. 2-Chapters was an incredibly kind and gracious host. Proud of his kids, proud of his family, proud of his home. Even his "three things" prompt, which I cynically think he only surfaced in order to have the conversation and compliments rolled back towards him, carries incredible value. I don't know how much time people in relationships spend reminding themselves how much and why they love their person. Reminding themselves first, then each other. If not for the Heinekens, or for having me find out what real Ivory feels like, I'm grateful to Mr. 2-Chapters for bringing this prompt into my life.

Had I sat at the head of the Rosh Hashanah dinner table, though; had I been the one with an aura of effortful nonchalance around him, I'd have asked the middle-aged men at the table to tell me, between bites of challah and pomegranate seeds, about three things they lost. The caveats would have been that the men themselves would have to be the ones at fault for the loss, and they'd have to have come to terms with their loss—accept it, move on from regretting it. I'd have asked the men whether there was someone before the someone they have now, and if there was, whether they still think about the one that was. I'd have asked how they were able to stare at a new face and not see the one they spent so long elucidating, one hair strand at a time. I'd have asked how they made peace with hearing the same words pronounced differently. I'd have asked how they were able to vacate room in their mind, start absorbing from scratch. I'd have asked how—if at all—did their new love surpass a love they deemed unsurpassable. I'd have asked, expanding upon the great Cher, not only *if* there's life after love, but *how*. (I recommend finding Ella Henderson's cover of the song.)

Despite not being a middle-aged man, despite sitting silently in the corner of the table, observing and judging them, presuming this or that about their hairline, posture, and capacity to express their emotions, situating myself as if I'm better, more emotionally intelligent or mature than them, I'm just like them. I look at them and see myself and my friends years from now—our bond built over decades of kinship, shared memories, and acceptance of each other's lives. I see how easy it is to group us, cisgender straight men, all together, and label us with an array of stereotypes about who we are: our reluctance to be vulnerable, our resorting to aggression for conflict resolution, and, of course, our fear of commitment.

The problem with stereotypes—or one of the problems, at least—is that sometimes they're true. That doesn't mean a singular incident is emblematic of an entire group, but sometimes a stereotype is confirmed by someone. When that happens, it's easy to dismiss the individuality of the person, easy to inextricably judge them from the culture they're a part of and classify the behavior as a direct byproduct of that culture. And while that can be myopic and frustrating, the worst part about it all, for me, is how there's nowhere to hide from being labeled as *just like the rest of them*, when each one of us, even if we share an abundance of characteristics with our cultural group, has his own individual story. But the individual and the group are inextricable from each other. We need something between a wide-angled lens and a microscope, I guess, to see someone who's something between a dude and a little bitch.

Pacino wraps up his speech by telling the men surrounding him that they can either heal, now, as a team, or they will die as individuals. So maybe it's a good thing that I'm being branded as just like the rest of them, banded with all my fellow men who have theorized and philoso-phized about love, the folks who are wary of using the word 'love' lightly, the middle-aged men at the table, the brothers I grew up with, those who I went through every step of life with. Because maybe they can all help me, inch by inch, climb out of this hell that I'm in.

Maybe had Dr. McFarland not been so pedantic all those years ago, I'd have had an even better formulated argument about how the rhetoric of Pacino's speech is emblematic of the tribalism associated with male so-cialization, as well as the extremism of language and over-dramatization men apply to mundane facets of life such as a football game (using Bill Shankly's quote about life and death, which you're free to look up, as my thesis).

Maybe, though, that would've meant I would've never encountered bell hooks at that age, wrongly capitalized her name, learned from a bright, white-haired man about who she is and what she stands for, and my eyes, despite being drawn to *all about love*'s exterior, wouldn't have recognized the author's name, and I wouldn't have picked the book up from the "Lit-erary Favorites" table. Had I never picked up that book, I have no idea how I'd have started to understand the turmoil that's been engulfing my brain. Because unfortunately, despite the fact I could find a locker room full of men whose fear of vulnerability has led them to hell, despite the support we can give each other as a team, despite the advice we can be-stow, the encouragement we can offer, and the experience we can share, despite the undeniable fact that masculine socialization has the ability to be not only non-toxic, but healthy, despite how lucky I am to have friends and family who would gladly walk me through this hell, I have to heal as an individual. And trust me, I wish I didn't have to try to move on by my-self, but I do. I wish I could simply unload or vent or lean on my friends, have them carry some of the weight for me. I wish I could obtain some power by lying. I wish I could simply flip a switch. I wish someone else would give me a reason to move on; stop loving her. Most days, frankly, I wish she would give me one.

I wish she'd tell me she never felt anything towards me. That every memory I've relayed is a lie and a sham. That she suffered through every second we spent together. That she was never comfortable resting on my chest. That while my head was buried in her collarbone, she would glance over to the clock on the oven and count the minutes till she could be rid of me. That she faked having work calls because she needed a break from me. That my lips are too soft. That my lips are too firm. That my beard's lining isn't straight and my leather jacket makes me look like a fool.

I wish she'd tell me that Chipotle is wildly overrated. That she hopes Liverpool never wins another game. I wish she'd dig up my old tweets to try to cancel me. I wish I sneezed and she didn't say bless you. I wish she didn't hold the door for me. I wish she went to get empanadas and didn't get me any. I wish I never had to see the orange heart rapidly become my most frequently used emoji, parked at the top left corner of my keyboard, then gradually watch it drop a row, then another, then slide one column over, then disappear altogether—out of sight, out my fucking mind.

I wish she wasn't everything I know she is. I wish she won't be everything I know she will be. I wish she gave me one—one—reason to not. I wish I didn't believe and know that this woman can do anything to me. Anything. Except make me stop loving her.

I wish I wasn't so dramatic about it. I wish I could shrug it off and move on and be an archetypal man who treats his feelings like professional tennis players treat the balls they're offered: discard whichever don't seem appealing and have someone else come pick up the mess.

I wish I didn't want and need to keep talking. I wish I wasn't feeling like I'm making you—yes, you, whoever you are—sit across from me and listen to me unload every feeling I've ever had. I wish you—yes, you—would stop reading. I wish you—yes, you—were actually sitting across from me, just so you could lean forward, nod your head, put your palms on mine, and say, *No, keep going.*

A part of me wishes, every time I walk into a bar, alone, that she'll be in there with some dude in a smelly T-shirt who can't grow a beard and is chewing gum with his mouth open and doesn't know who the fuck Paul Beatty is nor Liverpool's starting lineup from the 2005 Champions League final and thinks Haruki Murakami is a type of dish. He'd be sitting on a barstool, and she'd be parked in his manspread, his arms wrapped around her, her back to him—because he's an idiot who's fine wasting seconds not looking directly at her face. I wish she'd lock eyes with me as soon as I walk in. I wish she'd take her palms, place them on top of this idiot's hands and, without breaking eye contact with me, wrap his arms around her even tighter.

I wish she'd put the final nail in my coffin, just so I'd be able to start living again.

(1)

I didn't drink during the two weeks I spent in Israel. I mean, I consumed alcohol, of course, but I didn't chug from a bottle of gin in order to fall asleep, which is how I define *drinking* these days. If it's at a bar with friends it's simply *being social*.

The fact I could abstain from bringing a handle of Gordon's into my childhood bedroom soothes me in a way. It slightly negates the possibility that I have an uncontrollable dependency on alcohol, and abates the probability that I've reached some point of no return. I'm not a fool (I mean, I am, but not always), and am not trying to kid myself that this means that *I can stop whenever I want to*, but there is some sort of affirmation that my sober self still has some authority and control over my drunken one. At least in preventing it from appearing.

The first few days back in New York after returning from Israel feel like being back home, which I'm sure my mother wouldn't be happy to read. I fill my days with words and miles, my nights with alcohol and conversations. The former dedicated to the long-term goals of a marathon and a book, and the latter for the short-term goals of being distracted. Every now and again, if I'm lucky, I get to go on dates, after which I nobly make sure they get home safe, then stop at my downstairs bar where the bartenders begin to pour my Guinness before I even sit down, then the next before this one's done.

I've been using the dating app on and off for the past several months. When I've felt resolute and hopeful (aka when I've heard from L), I deleted it; when I've felt weak and hopeless (aka when she'd disappear), I'd go back on. When she breathes any sort of air into being in my life, I dive back under water, stay there till I'm on the brink of suffocating, then crawl back out. I'm being unkind to myself by going through this process, and far more importantly, towards those I use to drag me out of the water, but I just don't know what else to do to fill the void. I guess that because of how much uncertainty I feel is around me, I'm chasing what is tangible and quantitative. I can see and tally the distance elapsed and the pages accumulated, I get doses of affirmation from seeing notifications from unsaved phone numbers, and all of that provides some ground to stand on. The rest of it—the void, the years that have led to it, and its ever-growing expansion—hasn't taken a tangible form yet, and since it cannot be seen on the exterior and the page, it can still be blocked, cast aside.

A few weeks before Israel, I emailed an old professor who I knew had experience with psychotherapy. I tried googling for a therapist, but all that led to was targeted ads for BetterHelp on my Instagram feed, and, no, thank you. I told the professor that I've been contemplating going to therapy for a while now, and was unsure about where to start. I told her the process was a tad overwhelming, and I preferred not asking any of my friends who I know go to therapy, so am reaching out to her. Nearly instantly, I had kind words of encouragement, names, and contact information. The rubber-banded tennis ball was back in my court. In five months or so, I'll see this professor at some agent mixer I'll attend (I'll make far, far better use of the open bar than of the access to people who could help me achieve my dream of getting a book deal), and I'll chat to her about the class we had and how things are going. I'll never say thank you explicitly for her help, but I'll think she'll know. I hope she does.

One hungover morning—a bad one, one in which my brain punishes me by giving me nothing to write—I email a contact my professor gave me, asking for help with starting the therapeutic process. Two days later, I send a drunk email late at night to the person tasked with reading my essay collection thesis, Hilton Als, acknowledging his busy schedule, but wondering if he'd mind reading a new piece I've written, "as I feel it could end up being the main essay of the collection." I add that "for some reason I'm quite confident in it," and when I sober up the next day and re-read the email, I chuckle at the phrase 'for some reason.' Three days later, I go on a date with a very cute therapist who tells me she actually works with quite a few finance bros downtown. I think the date is going decently well, but not spectacular, then she invites me back to her place for tea and we have sex twice and I spend most of the time trying to ensure she doesn't see my left forearm.

The therapy contact replies nearly instantly, wanting to set up a phone call and sending me a form to fill. I postpone our phone call for two weeks and take two weeks further to submit the form. Hilton takes two weeks to get back to me, I reply to him nearly instantly, asking again whether he has time to read a new essay, and this time he says I can send the piece along. I text the very cute therapist the day after our date, we sporadically chat for a couple of days till she says she's really sorry but will have to cut ties. She's overwhelmed since receiving funding to open a new clinic, she tells me, to which I reply saying it's no worries at all, congratulating her, and wishing her best of luck with the finance bros. A couple weeks later, I drunk text her, asking if she's interested in doing something a bit more casual, and my magnanimous offer gets left on read. What can you do.

They fluctuate in approval rating, these versions of me alcohol brings out. I'd struggle finding the courage to ask a busy and famous writer to read something I, a self-asserted masculine studies scholar, wrote, and risk imposing myself into his life and on his time. Get a couple swigs of gin in me? I'll even add a joke about fried onions to sign off the email. Sober me ended things quite cleanly with that date, and drunk me wasn't awful about it, but perhaps a tad unnecessary. Drunk me got me to finally fill out that fucking therapy form, but drunk me was also (partially) the reason that form needed filling to begin with. I don't need to say anything about liquid courage and that whole thing, I know you know. It's more so that there's a part of me that's grateful for some of what alcohol allows me to do (my first girlfriend was also a byproduct of courage found at the bottom of a Four Loko can). I love the part of me that loves and promotes his own writing when he's drunk, and I love the one that can tell someone I'm in love with them on a bench in Union Square at 4 a.m.. Without alcohol, you would have probably never read this. Without it, L may have never known. I wish I could whip out these versions of me on demand when sober, but having had twenty-seven years of experience with myself, I'm not sure if that'll ever be the case. But I will, I hope, do my best to try. In the meantime, I do need the alcohol, and if the price I have to pay is having bloodshot eyes every other morning and a few potentially regrettable texts every other night, then so be it.

Things with L have been pretty much the same. Some sporadic texting and attempted plans to go see this exhibit Hilton Als was putting up downtown that, shockingly, fell through.

Sober me made the decision, a while ago, to never drunk text her unless she does first, at which point I'm permitted to casually respond. One night, pre-Israel, I had five beers then went on a date with a really lovely girl who I mostly wanted to go out with because she self-identified as anti-Zionist and someone who hates men. I was fascinated by her interest in going out with the seemingly antithetical me, and if my memory isn't failing me, she was vegetarian, too, which further amplified the anomaly, given the fact that I self-identify as a hot piece of meat.

L texted me when I got home from that amiable and interesting date, a glass next to my open laptop, asking what I'd been up to tonight. I told her she'll probably laugh at me, but I'm drinking gin and trying to write, and she said that she loves that I can do that. I wasn't necessarily lying with my answer, perhaps just concealing some truth. It was late at night by this point, and we soon joked about how I no longer have the bedtime of an 80-year-old man. *I miss him a bit*, she said to me, and it was the warmest and fullest I'd felt in months. *If eighty year old me hadn't gone to bed at 10*, I smiled back, *he'd have said he does too.*

I was allowed to express my feelings, despite being drunk, because she did it first. The fact I've been able to uphold the ultimatum forbidding me from drunk texting her, especially anything that could be considered an exhibition of emotion, feels like another sort of affirmation that my sober self still has authority and control over my inebriated one, which feels like a good thing, but when I really come to think about it, it isn't.

My distinction between sober me and drunk me is flawed. The distinction should be between the version of me that's open and honest and himself, and the one that hides behind a performance. Who is the real me? The one that comes home from a run, sober and wholesome and full of endorphins, enters the elevator, and leans against the wall on which the elevator company's notice is taped, prepared to leave her name behind me. Or the one that stumbles into that same chamber at the end of a night of drinking alone after drinking with someone, full and empty of anger, staring at her name, one step away from slamming an open palm onto the notice, bunching it up into a fist, ripping the paper, physically coping with an emotional problem.

Both are me, I guess, but the fact that the notice is still taped to the wall, the fact she's not yet behind me, the fact I don't dare cross the line of externalizing my feelings even when I'm drunk, don't all show power, but the lack thereof. The lack of ability to move towards or away from her, not even when aided by the courage of alcohol, that thing that enhances and reveals, is a sign of my overpowering, ever-present, restraining, repressed behavior. The distinction I should be making is not the one between sober and drunk me, but between the performative and real; the one that instead of being preoccupied with how he is perceived, just is.

The (Presumed) Unheard Voice(s)
of This Woman in My Life

"I went out with this guy a while ago and it went really well actually but then he became kinda flaky and vague and I didn't really know what was going on and he just ended it. I ran into him a couple months later and then he sent me this long ass text about how sorry he was and how he still thinks about me, and then we saw each other super late at night and he told me he was still in love with me, and I was like, *damn*, but literally like a week later he said it was all too much for him and he, like, disappeared again. He hit me up out of nowhere a couple months later to say happy Jewish new year cause it was something we used to joke about lmao and we started talking again and it's been nice. Idk, I think we've always had something sort of special, and I care about him a lot, but I think we both know that anything beyond that is out the window. We've seen each other a few times but it's been like pretty casual and just as friends, I don't think either of us still has the same feelings towards each other. I like talking to him, and despite how loaded and intense things have been, and how he hurt me in the past, I think I'm fine with things being as they are, because I really do care about him. He seems to be fine with it too."

"Omg I had this thing with this guy a while back when I lived in Manhattan and it was honestly really nice but it was never like a serious thing and it sort of dragged on for a while and now he still texts me and tries to meet up and stuff and I reply because I feel so bad because I think he's still into me but obviously I'm with ___ now and I don't know how to break it to him cause I think he'll be so sad about it but like I really need it to stop and he's gotta move on."

"Oh, he's just a friend of mine."

"I don't know, really. He's just so different from me in so many ways, but instead of that making things more difficult, it makes them better.

Our existence on separate islands doesn't make me feel like we can't share common ground, but that I want to go explore his world, and he can come see mine, and until each of us figures out how to stand by themselves in the other's world, until we establish a shared one for ourselves, we can rest our heads against the other's shoulder, and lean on each other. But it's just been too difficult to reach that point. I don't know if we can get there, I don't think we've worked hard enough to make it work, been in each other's space enough to make it work. It's sad, I guess, but it's a good lesson."

"Well, he had his chance. I don't understand why he thinks he can just show up and expect anything from me, after how little he's shown. I gave myself to him, I was open and honest and invested, and he just presumed to know what would be best for me, when in reality he put himself first and he chose to hurt me. Twice. Why would I ever give that another shot, risk him hurting me again, when all the signs suggest that he will?"

"Who, E? Oh, we hooked up a couple of times but that was pretty much it. He caught feelings, I think, but I was like, no. I still text him every now and again when I'm bored lol, it's fun."

"Who, E? Oh, we went out on and off for a while, but that was it. Nothing to write home about, really."

"I went out with this guy a while back, and I've honestly never felt something so intense so quickly towards someone in my life. I really thought it was special, and could be special, but timing and life just kind of got in the way, and then it was over. A part of me still feels like I was supposed to meet him somewhere else or another time. I've told him that. But, ugh, I don't know. It sucks, but I think it's probably best for both of us to close that chapter and move on. I hope he feels the same way."

"I don't recall braiding many challahs in my life, but given the fact I grew up with a Jewish father, I must've weaved at least a handful. Most likely, I'd guess, as a kindergartner in some Jewish Sunday School activity. Two decades later, when I was living in upper Manhattan, I started going out with this Israeli guy and things were going really well, but then, out of nowhere, he disappeared. A couple months later, he opened up and apologized, and he seemed sincere, and I believed him, but then he said he can't be what he thought he could be, and I felt like such an idiot for believing him. That hurt. Time has passed, and our connection has always been unique in this very particular way, so I'm able to have him in my life again now, but that was it, for me, as far as anything romantic goes. Had I not held great disdain for emotionally unstable men beforehand, this rollercoaster would've been the catalyst.

Anyway, if I had to try to wrap my head around this rollercoaster, around who he's been in my life, I'd start simple—by telling the three strands we've had in each other's lives. I'd see if I can slowly braid the three threads together, weave them till they're combined into one. Sort of like a challah. Ideally, hopefully, by the end of the process I'd be left not with someone, but with a better understanding of how it went wrong, and who he's been in my life."

(3)

In the ether of this book (which we're almost done with, I swear) is the concept of toxic masculinity. In the early days of the subject being my theme for an essay collection, I was excited by it. I'd often get asked what I'm writing about, at which point I'd cast the phrase "toxic masculinity," and people—women, mostly—would eagerly take the bait. It's not that it ever got me laid or anything (not that I didn't try), but I think there's eternal curiosity about the subliminal meaning and manifestation of what is a rather superficial term when simply dangled out there. Not that women would need me to explain the concept, I'm sure they're all well-versed. But I think that the behavior's origins, shining a light on the emotional experiences and thought processes that take place amongst the imposers of this toxicity, is of interest to those not privy to them. Frankly, and if this has not been evident thus far, it's enticing for myself, too. That's probably why I love Jared Yates Sexton's book so much. Why the fuck am I the way that I am, is the question, and it is impossible to answer without examining the masculine environment and patriarchal thinking I grew up with, the one that's introduced me to some of the people I love more than anything, those I conceptualized the world with.

I've imposed this toxicity (which I'm aware we haven't officially defined yet) plenty in my life. I've also had it imposed upon me, I guess, to various extents. Some of it unintentionally, some of it absentmindedly, some of it performatively. Some of these instances have been detailed in this book, but a lot have been left out. Not that I feel the need to resurface every single instance of diminishing, manipulation, or belittlement, but it's good to at least ponder those experiences for myself.

"The favorite conceit of male culture is that experience can be fractured," Andrea Dworkin writes, "literally its bones split, and that one can examine the splinters as if they were not part of the bone, or the bone as if it were not a part of the body." I think that somewhere inside this quote is how I'd personally define my experience of toxic masculinity as it takes place in the ether of this book, which, I guess, is synonymous with the way toxic masculinity takes place in the ether of my life.

It's all intertwined. The fracture and the splinters and the bone and the body it's in and the body who fractured it and all the bodies that came before. Every romcom ending scene, every word that every man I've ever met has ever said about every person he's ever spoken about, every utensil in L's drawer in my brain. They're all intertwined, like the biggest damn challah you've ever seen, and the thing extracted from the metaphorical oven is myself, and every action I've ever taken.

I cannot answer the question of who I am without taking into account the value I've always attributed to 'being a man,' what that definition both connotes and dictates I do, and why it was so important that I upheld that status. It is impossible to understand or examine my story without looking at the experience as a whole, without engaging in traditional 'feminine behavior' of introspection and analysis of my own feelings and their origin. This is something Dworkin argues men don't tend to do, and instead, "Some part substitutes for the whole and the whole is sacrificed to the part." That's a brilliant line. Brilliant.

Admittedly, this argument of hers comes from a book published in 1981, and while the whole gender dynamic thing isn't necessarily resolved, it's better than it was back when Ronald Reagan began his first year in office. Even more admittedly, Dworkin's line is from a book called *Pornography: Men Possessing Women*, which I've not read. I merely read the section included in an anthology of her work, so maybe it's possessive of me in a way to use a single sentence without the entirety of the context. Apologies. Anyway. She died in 2005, Dworkin, so who's to say if her sentiments would've been different today. You'd like to think that things have improved, whatever you'd like to label as "things" when it pertains to this stuff ("stuff" can receive a similar treatment).

I wasn't around in 1981 (the sperm and egg that wound up being me were still living on different continents), but I don't think that Dworkin's claim that, "Even when faced with the probable extinction of themselves at their own hand, men refuse to look at the whole" still holds as true as it did then. First of all, for better or for worse, men aren't extinct yet. Second of all, I don't think men still refuse to look at the whole. Jared Yates Sexton, for instance, gladly does, as do athletes like Kevin Love and DeMar DeRozan who use their platform to promote conversations about athletes' mental health, as do plenty more men who are conscious of their power, space, and place in this society. Not only men who are conscious, I should say, but also those who understand that the questioning of their power, space, and place is not an attack on those same three things.

Men are like potatoes, you see: they're best when drowned in deep frying oil. Kidding. Dworkin (or Valerie Solanas) would have loved that one. I'm guessing. Men (and all people) are like potatoes in that their diversity and variety is beyond measure. The point I'm laboring towards is the "not all men" one, but I don't want to use that phrase (I'm fully aware I'm using the phrase here by pretending not to use it). I basically just want to double down on the earlier point about the wide-angled lens and the microscope: It is impossible to examine ourselves or each other without the usage of both, without looking at both the culture and the individual within it. Maybe that's just me stating the obvious, or aggressively trying to make an argument that no one is disputing, but whenever I find myself trying to talk about this stuff, I feel the need to recognize the need for both distinction and grouping. And I never fail to ramble as I do so.

Pauline Harmange distinguishes between men far more succinctly in *I Hate Men* when she talks about their manipulation of mediocrity: "Whenever I'm beset by doubt I think about all the mediocre men[3] who've managed to make their mediocrity pass for competence, by that magical sleight of hand called arrogance." She then goes on to talk about

---

3. "You know exactly who I'm talking about."

the inexplicable and unwarranted confidence mediocre men tend to have, opposed to women's seemingly inherent self-doubt. When I first read this passage, after chuckling at her lovely footnote, I made a note in which I ask Pauline what does she want terrible, mediocre, and good men to do? Not in an antagonistic way, but genuinely. The terrible are a lost cause, I presume; the mediocre ones are contingent on what type of mediocre they are; and the good are good, I'd guess, but also still have responsibility over the previous two groups. What are men supposed to do; who are men supposed to be? That's the wide-angled question around my story. Amia Srinivasan, in the ending paragraph of *The Right to Sex*, argues that the answer lies in following those who are at the sharp ends of power. In *salvation*, bell hooks argues that the answer lies in becoming self-loving as a way of challenging constricting norms. I'll combine both and argue that the answer lies in following your love. And not just on social media.

Despite my joking throughout, I don't contend to be an authority of any sorts about men, though I probably do have an abundance of unintentional ethnographical research to draw from. The only thing I sort of am an expert on is myself, hence why I'm trying to tell my story, which I know I am not able to tell without trying to tell our story, too. I'm asking myself the microscopic question of what the fuck am I supposed to do, with the hope that answering that question will give others the silly little word with which they can start their own thesis statement of an answer. Perhaps that's me using sleight of hand to feign competence, or assuming an unwarranted position of dominance, but at some point you just to need to let this self-asserted potato answer this vague question of what should men do, a question that plenty of others have answered before.

Valerie Solanas, in the *SCUM Manifesto*, argues that before males are officially replaced with machines, which will happen with the institution of automation, they "should be of use to the female, wait on her, cater to her slightest whim, obey her every command, be totally subservient to her, exist in perfect obedience to her will." Talk dirty to me, Val, why don't you.

It is a privilege of mine to make jokes like that last one. I know. I'm lucky to be able to hear an argument contending that my only purpose in life is to serve as some inhuman tool for the use of another, and just laugh it off. "Only someone in a position of dominance can permit himself to be calm and reasonable in any circumstance" Harmange writes, and I doubt her pronoun choice is coincidental. I also doubt she'd define me making that joke as me being calm and reasonable, but I guess I would. I do not take this position of dominance, offered to me on the back of millennia of a gendered societal hierarchy, for granted, nor do I accept it absentmindedly. Being aware, I guess, is how I'd open my answer for what men should do, and I'd probably include the words power, place, and space into that answer, too. And 'care.' And 'utilize.' And 'kindness.' Those are good words. Maybe something like: Men should be aware of their power, voice, and place in society, and utilize them to fill the space around them with kindness and care for themselves and others. That's too wordy. Scratch that. Here:

Men should come from love, and strive towards it.

Whether you think men should or shouldn't, and to what extent, and how, and whether you think I have any authority to say who should and shouldn't do what, and how naïve I am for saying that, that's all up to you. I said what I said. Stop yelling at me. You're the one who bought my book, anyway. Or a friend let you borrow it (make sure you give it back). Or you found a free version online somehow (at least, like, follow me on Instagram or something as a form of payment).

A good number of guys already know this stuff. I'm not trying to preach to the choir. I'm not trying to preach at all. You know how I feel about religion. But it's all intertwined. This section is the bone or the splinter or the fracture or whichever part of the experience you want it to be. I cannot tell my story without acknowledging the part that performative or toxic or ignorant masculinity played in it all. I cannot present the experience as a whole without explicitly including the wide-angled lens of my culture: the way us guys assess ourselves compared to each other, use sex as a barometer, push others down in order to bring ourselves up, and refuse to show emotional vulnerability out of fear of being mocked, leading us to being handicapped when that same vulnerability is required to make our romantic relationships work.

I have this idealistic hope that other guys will take a moment to look through that lens for themselves. Like I said, a good number of guys already know this, but it's still good to be reminded of the power that your power has. Brenda Tracy, the "Set The Expectation" founder, travels the country and tells her story of being sexually assaulted, a story she's decided will not define her and will not be her end. She tells it, she told me when she was kind enough to spend an hour on Zoom with me, to the 90% of men. 90% are good, she argues, and she tells them, *I'm not here because I think you're the problem. I think you're the solution.*

Valerie Solanas's manifesto and the arguments in it, written over half a century ago, are radical and extreme, but I get why an extreme subversion of the gender dynamics is her idea for a solution. I really do (not that she'd need or want my approval, of course). Sometimes, to get a jammed door to finally move, you need to pull as hard as you can the other way. Not because you necessarily want to jam it into the other side, but because that's the only way to get things moving.

This feminist narrative of refusing to be jammed or dominated reminds me, in a way, of when guys tell each other they can't let the woman in their life control them. I know, I know. Historically and physically and socially and circumstantially different, but still similar, for me, on some levels. An antagonism to being used, inferior, bottom of the totem pole. In men's case, a fear of being whipped, perceived as lesser, as lacking power. But whenever notions of and struggles for power are attributed to any relationship, in whichever capacity or direction, there's a problem. It is the perception, amongst men, that the accommodation of a partner, a submissiveness, and a sacrifice to their needs and wants and time, are an admission of weakness. It is the fear of being weak that leads men (some, at least) to keep the door jammed. Refuse to let it move a single inch the other way.

And there is movement. The door isn't jammed. Maybe I'm naïve, I don't know, but a lot of men aren't idiots. A lot of men aren't mean and malicious, either. A lot of men are caring and compassionate and kind and smart and loving and funny. I know many who are as such. I love them. I am grateful for them. I also know many men who aren't all those things. Maybe I'm not those things. I don't know. You'll have to ask someone else. I won't say that some men were simply dealt a bad hand—though plenty were in various ways—but instead, I'd like to say that many men were simply dealt a hand they haven't necessarily needed to look at in order to play. No one has ever told them to glance down at the cards, question them, or even ask whether they've been, in fact, losing. Ask whether the mold of 'man' they've absentmindedly tried to fit into has confined them into being something they don't want to be. No one has ever told them that they can, perhaps, play their hand in a way that enables others— including themselves—to win.

A lot of components went into me looking at the hand I was dealt and have been playing. 'Sadness' is probably the first word that comes to mind. Wanting to write something that other people would want to read is another reason. Being interesting, I guess. Wanting to make other people think, wanting to make other people—particularly those I know and love—be better is a quixotic hope that comes to mind. Around it all is my curiosity in answering the question of why the fuck am I the way that I am. What steps have I taken, in this life, that have led me to feel, sometimes, so unhappy. How did ignoring and suppressing my feelings for decades, falsely believing I can't share and be vulnerable with my friends and family, and over-valuing masculine depictions of invincibility and toughness all left me in a healthy environment, surrounded by loving people, toxic towards myself? What finally carried this forward, what finally shone a light on my hand and the way I've been playing it, was, of course, L.

Jack Nicholson's emotional awakening in *As Good As It Gets,* similarly to my sexual one, was Helen Hunt. She opened his eyes, and prompted him to tell her, "You make me want to be a better man." It's an iconic line from a classic movie, meant to convey Nicholson's maturation and growth, but that same sentence framed differently draws criticism from some. "I know that behind every man who is even slightly conscious of his male privilege," Harmange writes, "are several women who have worked hard to help him open his eyes." The answer to the question of how men may be able to open their eyes on their own is definitely not one that my-self, who needed L, can answer.

But L didn't have to work hard. She didn't have to work at all, frankly. She was just exactly who she is, which seems like it takes no effort, and that was all it took for me to fall hopelessly in love; to feel comfortable enough to show her the parts of me on either side of three and eight on the scale of emotions. Then, the person that I grew to become surfaced, messed it all up, and the after-the-fact realization of what I had done made me question how in the world I let that go. That's what opened my eyes. That's why I started writing this: to understand why my brain thought to himself, *Yeah, walk away. You'll be fine.* I started writing so I could turn all of it—the void, the years that have led to it, and its ever-growing expansion—tangible, have it seen on the exterior and the page, so it can no longer be blocked; so it would have to be confronted; so I would have to learn how to strive towards love in the future. "There is always a tension between experience and the thing that finally carries it forward," Dworkin said, and this book is it—the thing that hopefully carries me forward.

My idealistic and self-aggrandizing hope, I guess, is that this book ends up in front of the eyes of bearded men, inexperienced teens whose genetics are depriving them of facial hair, or, dare I say, people who have one of the former two in their lives and want to understand who on earth that person is. I hope that whatever I've rambled about thus far does something positive—sparks, reminds, initiates, inspires, encourages, humors. I hope this book encourages men to want to inhabit a space of love; that men read this and, like bell hooks said doesn't happen frequently enough, they "receive encouragement both to think about love and to value its meaning." I hope the book opens eyes just like Harmange says men need women to do for them; just like L did for me. I hope this book, in a way, is a woman. Maybe I should have it identify as such.

I hope that reading my experience, in its entirety, can be someone else's experience, so that they don't have to go through the same fracture. Just take the lessons and avoid the mistakes I made. It's perhaps irrationally optimistic of me, I guess, but it's also an honest claim. And if that's too unrealistic an expectation from what this book can do, then I hope you at least laughed at one of the masturbation jokes earlier. Or that you learned the difference between fiction and nonfiction. Or that you were introduced to Steven Gerrard and have brought him into your life. You're welcome.

If my rambles have aggravated, provoked, bored, annoyed, or disrespected, well, I'm sorry. Not that I've made you feel that way, but that you didn't get what I was trying to say. Don't worry, though. You can come find me, we'll have a coffee or a beer, chat, and figure this shit out. I'll pay. I am the man, after all.

(1)   (2)   (3)

It fizzles out, more than anything, really. It's barely even worth boring you with the details. I wish I had some guns blazing scene to tell you about. Some ending scene of a modern-age romcom in which the couple doesn't end up together, but at least one of the leads swings for the fences with one final grand slam gesture, which, unfortunately, strikes out.

Perhaps a scene where I hustle my way into singing the national anthem at a Yankees game, and use my childhood best friend, who's—fortuitously—the hospitality manager at the stadium, to "gift" L front row tickets. And just as she takes her seat, just as proceedings commence with the national anthem's first F note emanating from the speakers, instead of the "Star Spangled Banner," I stand by the mic, glance towards her, and exhale, with true disdain, the words, *Fuck the Yankees*. And while everyone in the stadium thinks I'm some crazed Red Sox fan, I stand there by the mound with the hope she remembers the exact barstools we were at, the beer we drank, and the outfits we had on when she said those precise words to me on the night we last kissed. And as security grabs and drags me off the field, as every white dude in the stands wearing a backwards Yankees visor and pinstripe oversized jersey wants to deck me in the face, as any shrivel of hope I had of obtaining a Green Card evaporates due to my utter disrespect for America's pastime, I look up to L, and she mimes to me, *I just don't want to be with you*.

It's none of that. It's a simple conversation that she starts by texting me saying she feels a bit more ready to talk about things. It's just before lunch time, as I'm doing some work at the coffee shop underneath my apartment. It's perhaps not the best time nor medium to do this, but she's ready, so I have to be, too. No matter how strategic I intended on being, this is it: I'm up to bat and it's time to swing.

There's a fear about admitting to having feelings towards another. A fear of the feelings not being reciprocated, the admission ruining an already existing relationship, or the exposure of the self making you feel like an absolute fool. What sometimes gets muddled into this, and I can only speak for men's side of things, or maybe even just my side of things, is the stereotype that men just constantly and naturally withhold their feelings. Sometimes—not always, but sometimes—we're withholding not because we are incapable of showing emotion, but because we're scared. We don't know where you are or how to start; we're scared of scaring you away, overwhelming, coming on too strong. Sometimes—not always, but sometimes—we're not men, but just people trying to figure this shit out.

Each relationship is its own complex thing with its own history and nuance and never-ending "Yeah, but" cycle. Yeah, but she just got out of… Yeah, but his family is in town this… Yeah, but maybe they don't want to… Yeah, but I have a big project due on… Yeah, but maybe I should wait until… Yeah, but maybe it would be better to do it in person… Yeah, but maybe I'm better off just not getting into it. Yeah, but; Yeah, but; Yeah, but. I'm not sure if this makes for a cliché or not, and pardon me if it does, but there is no right time to talk about the right thing. Just swing. The only way to get clarity is by adopting the hyperbolic and reductive slogan that's inked on my forearm. The fact I refused to do that precise thing for so long may make me hypocritical for giving this advice, but, in my defense, I'm doing it now. Right before lunch time, I'm at bat, swinging.

The conversation starts as I pack up my stuff and head upstairs, slowly realizing what absurd world I've been living in and how foolish I've been. It's a conversation where she's caught by surprise again, as if she had absolutely no clue I was anywhere near whatever feelings I admit to, which makes me laugh. This thing—this relationship with a girl who I've sort of seen but also haven't that has changed me forever—ending with her being in the darkness about the way I feel, is, more than us getting married and sitting together at a Rosh Hashanah dinner table, the most perfect way for our story to end.

We talk about why we're even still talking, a question I bring up, kind of, because I've reached a point where I truly cannot keep asking myself that question, guessing what her answer may be, then trying to drink the thoughts away; using this performative coping mechanism as if it's anything other than absolutely stupid—a realization stemming partially from talking about it in therapy, but mostly from writing about it on these pages, turning the stupidity and the void and the repression tangible and concrete.

I tell her I'm just confused about who I'm supposed to be in her life, and when I come to think of it, the last three words of that clause are redundant. She says that, now that she's thinking about it, she's not sure why we're still in each other's lives either.

I don't know, she tells me, *I guess I wasn't expecting to feel close to you after everything*, which gives me some kind of affirmation. Not in the moment she says these words, but in the moment, months and months later, when I make them tangible on this page. In the process of laying the story out, the absence of her voice, feelings, and version of it all looms large. I only have access to this voice and these feelings as they once were, as I recall them, and I've been questioning whether I'm making too much of it all—being both dramatic and dramatizing. Whether it's possible to exist in a reality that's fictional for one but nonfictional for the other. This affirmation, this reminder and reassurance that, at one point, she did feel close to me, and we did have an *everything* that can't quite be explained, that she also just didn't know, is a nod that allows me to keep going.

There's not an ounce of me that's mad at her. Not when she tells me she's not been fully honest and upfront with me (or with herself, either), not when she tells me that she knows that deep down she'll never open up to me in a way that leads to a relationship, presumably because of how I scarred her in the past, and not when she tells me she feels like she's walking away from something that she never really gave a full chance to. These words that you could guess would make me want to put my fist through a wall are actually ones that finally allow me to unclench, loosen my grip. The words are, just as I wished, not the F note that commences proceedings, but the one that ends it all—the anthem, her name, us—a C.

We have this conversation at lunch time, ten months to the day of when we first bumped into each other. I acknowledge everything. I tell her my feelings are still what they were when we met at Union Square, and add that I think I've known for a long time that she was too far gone, but a part of me was hoping to get another chance to be in her space, to build that intimacy. *I know it takes both of us wanting that,* I tell her, and resign to the fact that there's no mutuality.

You met me at such an odd time in my life, I say to this woman, which is true, but at the same time, I'll realize when I type this out into a Word doc, there's no time in life that isn't odd. I say that I know the version she met wasn't my best, but that what happened between us has taught and changed me a lot. *You know I'll always consider you incredibly special,* I type, and it's a line I'll never have to think twice about.

I tell her all of that, then go to my room, grab the Israeli chocolate that's been on my dresser by the window for thirty-three days, and hide it in the back of the bottom drawer in the fridge, where it will remain, untouched, long after I'll say my final word here. Until I'll find someone to give it to, or reach a point where I can gladly enjoy it myself.

I go to the bottom cupboard in the kitchen and extract the skillet I use every single day. I plug the toaster in and put two slices of bread inside, then get the chopped salad bowl, tahini, egg carton, cold turkey, and spinach out of the fridge. I do the exact same thing I've done for more than two years now. While the bread darkens, I pour from the big salad bowl into a small one, add a spoon of tahini, and set the small bowl on the wooden kitchen table. I twist the gas nozzle a quarter of an hour counterclockwise, pour a drop of oil into the skillet, crack three eggs, and their bottoms begin to cook while I spread tahini on the now toasted bread. My phone plays this week's Discover Weekly on Spotify, just as it does every week, and I unplug the toaster, grab it by its plastic body to make sure my palms don't get burned, and put it back in its place above the microwave. I walk to the skillet, use the spatula to separate the egg whites that have melted into each other (the stove leans so this is inevitable), and

flip all three eggs so that the yolk can harden. I place a bundle of spinach on each toast, the tahini working as an adhesive to keep the leaves
attached, then extract two slices of turkey and use one to press down on
each bundle.

I'm really sorry, my phone lights up with her name again. *It means a lot
to hear all of this.*

I pour from the Brita into my sixteen ounce cup, rip out a single rect-
angle of a paper towel, then place both next to the salad on the table.

I know you will learn and grow so much, I read, then twist the gas nozzle
a quarter of an hour clockwise.

I use the spatula to carefully flip one of the eggs, then set it, yolk up, on
one of the toasts. I do the same with the second egg, then place the third
on the plate. I set the plate on the wooden table, the skillet goes in the
sink, the tap opens, and a small coat of water soaks in the pan while I eat.

You really don't need to apologize for anything, I tell her, *it's good to have
some sort of closure.*

I cut the third egg in two, then place each part on one of the toasts in a
way that the half yolk covers whichever part the other yolk isn't covering.
I could do this blindfolded.

The last words I say, at this end, are, *I'll be here.* And I will. For her, yes,
but also not for her. I, whatever that now means, am here, doing exactly
what I've been doing, differently.

Definitely will be always wishing the best for you, she ends the conversation, *I hope you know I mean that.*

I take one of the toasts in both hands, using eight fingers to ensure everything—the bread, the spinach leaves, the turkey, the egg and
a half—stays exactly where I want it to as my teeth bite into this thing
that I made. It's the two pinkies I keep away from all the crumbs and
grease. I keep them clean so that I can tap through the YouTube app on
my phone—the one that doesn't have any favorite contacts listed, the one
that's on the table on Do Not Disturb—and find something to watch.
Something light and funny and distracting, something that keeps my

brain quiet. Some British panel show. Maybe an old *Would I Lie To You* clip. A Bob Mortimer one.

Sometimes, a part of an egg slides off or a spinach leaf tumbles as if it's the beginning of autumn. That's okay. Life will bite and things will fall. They can always be picked back up, placed where you want them to be. You just do your best holding on. Just do it.

I know you mean that, L.

I do.

Step Eight

Let Cool

(3)

A lifetime after that lazy morning in L's bed, in spatial, emotional, and mental spaces which were as far from picturesque and heavenly as I could imagine, without hesitation or contemplation, I swiped Haruki Murakami's *Men Without Women* with its yellow and pink glistening cover off the shelf at Book Culture. I wanted to know what ended up happening to Dr. Tokai, sure, but I'd be lying if there wasn't a part of me—a hopeless, hopeful part—that illogically wished opening that book would somehow send me back to that horizontal position in that vertical bed, on her duvet where one axis meets another, transport me back to that blissful origin.

I'm strict about reading short story or essay collections in order, but made an exception with *Men Without Women*. Propped on an uncomfortable, creaking, wooden chair in the coffee shop under my apartment, I dove into the book not on the first page, but where I left off all that time ago on L's bed. I didn't re-read the first eleven pages. The story of the lifelong single man, Dr. Tokai, much like mine, was still so vivid. I estimated on which page I was interrupted, in the best way possible, by the sound of hallways footsteps, the creak of a door, and a chuckle into a sweater. The confirmation for my accurate remembrance of where I stopped came in the form of the last two sentences before the line break on the page I opened on, 88: "But one day, quite unexpectedly, he fell deeply in love. Like a clever fox suddenly finds itself caught in a trap."

I was caught in a trap. Still am, in a way, frankly. But it's one I set for myself, long before L came into my life. She was not the trap, but the light illuminating it. I'm not so much a clever fox in a trap, maybe, but a dumb beaver in a dam. Every twig and branch confining me being another form of *I'm fine* I've used over the course of my life to withdraw into a secure silence. Love, as we know and as bell has told us, offers no place of safety. By the time the ray of light that is L shined through all the twigs and branches, the dam was too secure to let me out. Now, with the dam visible and tangible and spelled out on the page, I can see what's around me, and start disentangling, one *I'm fine* branch at a time.

Dr. Tokai ends up dying. Apologies for the spoiler (the story isn't really about his death, anyway, so you didn't lose much). He becomes so "lovesick," as the story reads, that he refuses to eat and work, and, by virtue, live. He withers away, loses more than half his weight, and dies. All because the woman who he fell deeply in love with tricked him; ran away with another man. L never tricked me, and even if she is with another person, she never ran off. If anything, she was run off.

There are many layers to this Murakami story, many of them this self-asserted literary critic doesn't have the pedigree or capabilities to comprehend. But titles I can do. The story's title, "An Independent Organ," is, in my assessment, its own trick. The connotation from it is that men have this organ independent of themselves—the penis—which decides for them, makes them be who they are. Murakami is much better than such a cliché (I think it's a cliché but honestly idk). The story is actually about a fictional organ women possess that enables them to lie, one men do not have. Except of course men have it. Not only can men lie, but as we learned from the bell hooks line on the page we randomly opened at Book Culture, they do so as a way of obtaining power. The power I'm trying to obtain, now, when L's chapter in my life is over, is the one to move on. The logical and alphabetical way to do that would be to move on from L to M, but logic and proportion, as Jefferson Airplane told us long ago, have fallen sloppy dead.

Murakami's *Men Without Women* is brilliant. He doesn't need my praise, of course, but I loved reading every word, all through the final story, which is told in first person and which carries the book's title. The narrator tells the story of receiving a phone call about a woman he used to be with, a woman he loved and loves and always will, who killed herself. The narrator labels himself the second loneliest person in the world, behind only the woman's current spouse, who was the one to call and break the news. He self-admits himself into a club he calls Men Without

Women. "Only Men Without Women," he tells us, "can comprehend how painful, how heartbreaking, it is to become one." The character of this woman, by the way, Murakami calls M.

And maybe that's how I move on. Not by progressing from L to M (I'm not sure dating apps offer any alphabetical predilection filters), but by accepting the fact I'm a part of the Men Without Women guild now, too. My first action, as an active member, would be to suggest a name-change. Because it's not "Men Without Women." I've been one of those for as long as I can remember. The club Murakami's narrator and I are in would be much better labeled as "Men Without *The* Woman." And it's important, I'd argue, with my minuscule understanding of how grammar and language work, that the article is "the" and not "a." Because all of the members in the club, every single one of us destined to be a middle-aged man with a receding hairline and underrated emotional capacity at a dinner party celebrating the beginning of the year five thousand and whatever, are in the club because of one woman. The one, specific one, we've lost.

In that final story, Murakami says you become a part of the guild by loving a woman deeply, then having her go off somewhere else. As simple as that. "Once you've become Men Without Women," he writes, "loneliness seeps deep inside your body, like a red-wine stain on a pastel carpet." Murakami then elaborates on the difficulties of removing the stain, and the mark that's left. It's quite a fantastic simile (I think it's a simile but honestly idk). You should just read the story. The whole book, really. I'm quite jealous of that simile. A part of me wishes I never read the book, so maybe through some stroke of luck or genius I'd have been able to come up with it myself; honestly pawn it off as my own. The paradox of this wish, though, is that me reading this book was dependent on me meeting L and perusing through her bookcase, and me coming up with any simile about the loss of love is, too, dependent on me meeting L. And I don't think there's any part of me that wants to give that up.

Murakami ends the story (and his book, essentially) by speaking to how the narrator lost the enjoyment of elevator music—something he'd always associated with M. He hopes M is in heaven now, happy and at peace, and I wish the same for L. She's alive and well, L, don't worry. Maybe she'll even read about herself—and my version of us—one day.

And I hope, with all my heart, that you do end up reading this. I hope it doesn't overwhelm you, though I'm sure it will. I'm sorry about that, and about everything else. I hope you already know that I am. I hope, almost more than anything, that you don't think I'm pulling a David Foster Wallace by iconizing myself in this book. I hope you don't think I wrote this in the hope that you come running back to me. I assume that other people will think that's what I'm doing. I assume that the fact I mentioned it now makes even more people think that's what I'm doing. I assume that doubling and tripling down on this point makes even more people think that. But, for what my pretty word is worth, which is, genuinely, the best I have to offer, that's not what I'm hoping to do. And if other people think I am, great. I'm doing my best to stop concerning myself with what other people think, so this will be good practice.

I just want you to know what you mean to me, what you've taught me, and what you're capable of. I hope this reminds you of the incomprehensible feelings you can extract out of people—a love which is nothing short of what you deserve. When Hilton Als read the very rough and early and short version of this thing, he told me, at an Italian restaurant downtown, two days after our story ended, that he's in love with you. I thought that was funny. I think that will be cool for you to know. I hope that people who know me or you read this and don't have too many questions, though I'm sure they will. I hope that people who don't know us read this and are reminded of how they can teach and learn, what feelings of love they can extract and award, and what they deserve. I hope they remind themselves and each other of the three things they love most about one another.

I hope you're resting—vertically or horizontally—on that white duvet of yours. I hope a late spring's sun is peering through your window. I hope your head is resting on something stable and warm and comforting. I hope your space is occupied by things that bring a smile to your face, make your brain think in new ways, and your eyes zoom out in that way that they do. I hope you're affirmed and appreciated and have learned to make chai that doesn't end up tasting like slightly flavored lukewarm milk. I'm quite skeptical about that last one.

You told me, in that final conversation we had as I was making lunch, that you wished me the best, and that you hope I know you truly mean that. You said you hadn't been fully honest, but you were being then. I hope you know, too, that I'm being fully honest when I say these words.

(1) (2) (3)

"Choosing to be fully honest, to reveal ourselves, is risky," hooks writes in *all about love*, and adds that "the experience of true love gives us the courage to risk." The risk I took was choosing to withhold my feelings from L, just as I'd done with many other feelings before, hoping it wouldn't lead me to an even darker, more painful place. I bet that the path to express my love, one day, was to suppress it until it's ready to be received. That turned out to be a mistake. And, I promise, I held on for as long as I could. I bottled up my feelings till there was no gin left.

When I signed up for the Brooklyn Marathon, I told myself that a month before the race, I'd cut out alcohol completely. There was never a doubt about my ability to follow through on that decision. I'd do this in college, too, and my friends would amicably jab me for it. I was known as *Wack Eyal* during the season, *Fun Eyal* as soon as the season was over and alcohol was welcomed back. I work best when there's an objective or a reason; when I have something to look forward to; when I know where I'm going or where I want to go or who I want to be; when I can make decisions that are tangible and concrete and scheduled. I say all this to my therapist, and tell her I like that part of me, the part that can flip a switch and banish anything that inhibits the path to that objective. I'm working, with the therapist, with myself, with you on this page, on not needing that something tangible in order to take care of myself. We'll see how that goes.

My knee starts acting up in the weeks leading up to the marathon. This feels like a weak excuse before I even finish saying what I'm about to say. I buy vitamins, a massage gun, ice packs, and new supporting shoes; I strengthen my quads and hammies and calf muscles; I stretch my IT band for hours a day; I do everything I can except for going to seek medical assistance, mostly because I've not had health insurance in months (please don't tell my mother, she'll freak).

I've been doing there-and-back runs along the Hudson, except, for logistical purposes, I've been running downtown first. With every increase
of the distance, I find myself deeper and deeper into Manhattan. Eventually, I assume, I'll have to cross into Brooklyn. On the day I'm scheduled
to run twenty-eight kilometers (I opt for the metric system measurement
units since the accumulation is more rapid and larger), about three weeks
before the race, after successfully and easily doing 26 the last time around,
it's cold. It's late winter, and there are barely any people along the path.
There's something so beautiful about the river when it's cold and gray
and quiet. Something so serene about spending hours running, when the
sound of my paces and the water's flow are so quiet that my brain can just
peacefully exist. I've not yet read Murakami's *What I Talk About When
I Talk About Running*, but I'm sure I'll love it. I'm sure he articulates this
feeling better than I'm doing so here. I love my brain when I run. That
says a lot, and is all I want to say.

My loving sister bought me a fitness watch when I told her I'll be
running a marathon. I've been using it to keep track of the distance I'm
elapsing, know where the halfway point is so that I'll know to turn. So,
today, my watch indicates I've hit 14 kilometers, I turn around, doing my
best to ignore the pain, and about five minutes later, my knee completely
caves in. It's inflamed, I assume, I don't think it's some serious ligament
damage. That's my self-educated diagnosis. The knee just tells me, I think,
that that's it—it can't withstand the impact anymore.

It gets very windy on the path, especially in winter. Sometimes the
wind is in my face during my trek down, sometimes it's in my face on my
trek up. I prefer having the wind in my back, the extra push, during the
second half. Sometimes, though, the freezing wind, somehow, feels like
it's in my face in both directions. My body's movement, I know, is the
reason why I feel like the wind is doing its best to make life difficult no
matter the direction. That's what happens when you try to move forward,
things naturally try to hold you back.

But as my knee buckles, as the weight of my body thrusts into the ground and gets no traction in return, as there's no strength left in my leg to bounce back up, as pain shoots into a place deep inside my knee on which I can't place my finger, it's just windy.

I'm able to walk, and I do, moving in the same direction I'd just been running. On the same path, simply much slower. It's windy, and I know that the objective is no longer feasible. I try jogging again, testing whether it was maybe a little mishap, an annoying tick we can choose to ignore, but there's nothing left. It's windy, and it's cold, and I press the watch's button to stop the workout, then ask for it not to save.

I'm wearing shorts that Dani gave me when I flew down to help him pack, and a long sleeve top given to me by my sister. It's Israeli Olympic Team gear that has the five famous rings on it. It's light gray, which is my favorite color to work out in, because it's the color on which it's easiest to detect the amount of sweat I emit—a tangible protruding and growing sign of how much effort I'm putting in and how much I'm getting out of it. People who see me wearing this quarter-zip may first assume I was in the Olympics myself (not that I'm implying I have the physique of an Olympian), but if and when they ask, I get to let out a big smile and tell them, proudly, that it actually belongs to my sister, who's a two time Olympian—something I'll never get tired of saying.

It's cold and it's windy and I have—at the very least—a two hour walk home on a fucked up knee. This thing I've been looking forward to for so long, this objective, this thing that's banished alcohol, has just been taken from me; has just been lost.

There are some people on the trail, and as I walk past them, I wonder what they think. They don't know, do they. They don't know why I'm walking on a running trail. A part of me wishes I was holding up a sign that says, *I fucked up my knee*. A part of me needs them to know that I'm not resting, that I've not given up. A part of me needs them to know that I'm not choosing to be weak. I would never—actually, I have never walked in the middle of run. Taken a break, a rest. Quit. Never. Not once. There's a little voice in my head that won't allow it. There's ink on my forearm that won't allow it. A part of me needs these people to know that I'm not as weak as I look, despite the fact I have every valid excuse to be, on this cold and windy day.

And this is the question, I guess, that I have to ponder the rest of the way. Where is the pain coming from, how can I heal, and do I even want to?

Is the pain coming from the knee, from the fact that people may see me as weak, or from my failure to reach my goal? Or, maybe, is the pain coming from the fact that this marathon was to be run in Brooklyn, and who knows who I would've bumped into there?

That's the question I need to answer at the end of this experience, the beginning of a new one. I'm in no rush to answer. There's still a long walk ahead.

Maybe my favorite ending of a book is that of Jennifer Egan's *A Visit From The Goon Squad*. I remember, vividly, the sensation I had when I first finished the book, how I remained still on a divot of a futon, basking in the admiration of what I'd just experienced. Each time I go back to that final paragraph, the words, without fail, goose my bumps.

"A sound of clicking heels on the pavement punctured the quiet," Egan writes. "Alex snapped open his eyes, and he and Bennie turned—whirled, really, peering for Sasha in the ashy dark. But it was another girl, young and new to the city, fiddling with her keys."

The whirling wind punctures the quiet as I limp uptown, thrusting the water there and back. I fiddle with the three keys in my left hand, my face numb, my throat prickled by every inhale of freezing air that I, unfortunately, have to keep taking in. I peer into the ashy gray and think of the question, *How to cool down, yet stay warm?*

The shirt and shorts, given to me with love, are all I have to try to block the gusts of wind, distract the cold, buy me some silence, some warmth, some time to think about how I want to answer.

Step Nine

Enjoy, Love

(1)(2)(3)

My life is not wholly peaceful and I am nowhere near smoothly sailing. I do, though, have a slightly better grasp of how to cope with things as they come. I no longer care if I meet my person as we both reach for the same bell hooks volume at the bookstore, as I run into them in the hallway and we both drop all the files we're carrying, or by me making a pun out of one the prompts on their dating app profile. There is—and for the final time I will ask for your pardon of the cliché—no wrong way to meet the right person. Even a blissful, joyful life will be tumultuous, pestered by grief and anxiety. I know to expect pain and affirmation, feel worthless and reliable, burden and be burdened. I'm still young and naïve and inexperienced, but slightly less than I once was, and I'm doing my best to allow my experience to encourage and embolden me to take risks, put my neck on the line. If only so that when it'll get to be late at night, and I'll be in a room dimly lit by streetlights peering through curtains, the hand that caresses the nape of my neck and the fingers that run atop my spine won't be my own.

I regret so many of the decisions I made, but I cannot change any of them. I was scared of how deeply I felt, and I fear—much like every other cliché, broken-hearted person—not having the chance to live out the same incomprehensible feelings again. In fact, I know I won't. Whatever L and I had was something only we could ever have. What I should say is that I fear not feeling the same—or even greater—level of certainty and excitement towards someone new. I fear not being frightened as I embark on a relationship that I consider to be true love. I fear not being awarded a chance to prove I've learned from my mistakes. I fear not bumping into someone new, someone I want to share a path with and who'll want to share a path with me. I'd be lying (or at least concealing some truth) if I didn't say, too, that I'm scared of this book becoming an obstacle on that path, particularly since I haven't yet read Chuck Klosterman's *Killing Yourself To Live* (pages 232-235, especially). His book, when I eventually read it, will bump all the books on my 'favorites' list one notch down. It will also rationalize for me the last fear I mentioned here, and articulate for me a new way of thinking about the love I feel (pages 232-235, especially).

Only time will tell what the next strand of my story will be, who it will involve, and which of my fears will come true.

Had I not made those mistakes, though; had I not pushed her away; had she not grown tired of my long-winded jokes and the weight of my head on her shoulder; had she traveled down with me to Florida, met my best friend, sat next to me, and rested her hand in mine in a way that appeases my mind; had we been put on the spotlight by Mr. 2-Chapters; had I not minded professing my love in front of strangers; had I felt like saying what I truly felt; had I tried and failed and experienced while growing up; had I had to give the three braids one final twist to pinch them all together; had I had to say one last thing—or, three final things—to complete the process and be left not with love, but with a better understanding of what goes into it and how it's made, here's what I would have said.

when I eventually had it; it will burn. It will leave it on my favorite flesh of notch. Jewel, it will also remind me that once, in the least felt, I made this flow.

(1̸)2̸)3)

First would be her nose. I'd gladly describe it to you, detail how it has the deftest of turn ups, maybe even analogize it to a miniature playground slide for how they both have a slight arch and the ability to spread un-adulterated joy. But it's more than the shape of her nose that would trans-fix me. Despite how objectively beautiful it is—and it is—it's more than just the physical attraction which would have awarded it a place in my top three.

It's the way the tip of my nose would touch hers. It's the way we could lie in bed in silence, sharing a pillow, our faces like mirroring profile sten-cils. My eyes unable to stare at anything but her; not wanting to, either. It's the way I'd gently run my thumb over her top lip, then let it trickle up to feel her septum—as if I wanted every part of my skin to know every part of hers. It's the way I'd scan every crevice and curve of her face, wanting to know about every dimple and beauty spot, hear about every expression this face took before it landed right in front of me, memorize its contours so that, when I would have a bad day, I'd be able to close my eyes, be reminded of the bits of bliss and beauty in this world, and smile.

And when I'd shut my eyes, alone, rub my own palm against the nape of my neck in an attempt to recreate a moment of bliss, as the parts of her I was unwilling and unable to forget—a face that's lucid, stern back I want to lean against—would materialize in my mind, as I'd imagine feeling the texture of her lip on my thumb, as I'd shift in bed and hear the sheets shuffle just as they did when we'd entwine our legs, her nose, the one that has the cutest, deftest turn up, was what everything would form around.

That's why her nose would make it into the top three. For being the centerpiece of the face that became the image of love.

Second would be the way she'd touch my collarbone. We'd stand, some-times, in front of each other, inches between us, not quite embracing. I would have my hand on her waist, threading my finger through the belt loop of her jeans, or conjoining my palm with hers to perform some improvisational, interpretive dance—our fingers' movement unscripted, purposeful. It would be in the kitchen, waiting for the kettle to boil; by the front door, begrudgingly saying a *goodbye* that's more of a *see you soon*. It would happen out in the world—under a streetlight where a block meets an avenue, standing atop a subway stop's entrance which will send us in different directions—where people would walk around us, their existence nonexistent.

What she would do was make use of my shirt's waning neckline and run her fingers along my exposed clavicle. She'd lean towards me, her arm would rise, her elbow bend, her forearm rest against my ribcage, the base of her palm land at the apex of my chest, and the top phalanx of her index finger would press into my collarbone. As if she was assessing how sturdy it is, how resistant I may be. She did this since the very beginning, since the very first night, perhaps subconsciously, as if she always knew the freedom she had to reach out and touch me, gauge how thick my exterior shell is, and feel what's underneath it.

My collarbone—because I broke it in the past, because of my predi-lection for waning necklines—feels like the physical manifestation of my conflict between exposure and withholding. This conflict, perhaps, ex-plains everything. I've spent my life trying to expose as little as possible, playing the role of the stereotypical man who's averse to showing vulner-ability and suppressing any inner human urge to share. Yet, over and over again, because of the neckline, my collarbone, the one that's fragile, is out for anyone to see. And it's out there for a reason. It's out there because I've been waiting for someone to see through the façade, recognize that I'm begging them to reach out, feel how fragile I am, and decide to stay despite it all. Decide to not budge a single inch.

It wasn't immediate, with L, that I realized I could share any and everything. As time went on, particularly after it grew more tumultuous, particularly after I lost her, I realized the safe hands I was in. The sense of security I felt about wanting to open up to her could be signified by those moments when you could barely swipe a credit card between us. When we'd talk about tea flavors and subway stops, anxieties about the future and traumas of the past. When I'd feel the denim she's wearing with my palm, and with every press of her finger against my clavicle, she'd let me know that it's okay. It's okay to soften the shell, shed the archaic, masculine layers of faux impenetrability, and reveal my true self.

What made the gentle, warm press of her hand against my collarbone so special, what would award it a place in the top three, is that it didn't only make me feel like I *can* trust, but that I *want* to trust.

And trust, as we know, is the heartbeat of genuine love.

✥

The third is a moment I noticed on our very first date on April Fools' Day, in that bar/café that's since been renovated. As we sat across from one another at the table and I told a story about being a middle-school teacher or a long-winded joke about heterosexual businessmen who were born in the 1970s, I noticed her eyes scanning me inquisitively. Her hazel irises flickered from my woolen quarter-zip to the scruff of my beard to the shape of my nose to the way I smirk whenever I come up with a joke I'm about to tell her. All of a sudden, though, her pupils, when glancing at the top of my hairline, stopped.

I was still talking, but I noticed that something else caught her attention. As if some strands of hair were out of line, as if the barber missed a spot somewhere. She slightly squinted her eyes as if she'd just noticed something that doesn't quite make sense, doesn't quite add up. As if she'd seen something wrong. The moment probably didn't last more than a second or two, but it lasted long enough for me to notice. It's not that moment, though, that would make the top three. It's what she did immediately after. I saw in her pupils that she realized what she was doing, that she'd been staring at the top of my head for some reason, and she instantly, instinctually, flickered her eyes to lock back with mine.

This continued to happen regularly throughout our time together, not only on that first night. Even months and months later, after I failed her—and myself—twice, when we met to catch up in a neighborhood Brooklyn bar she said would be chill and quiet but turned out to be rambunctious and loud, as we finally nestled into a corner high top table with our books and our beers, she did it. Even after I made her question herself and we hadn't seen each other for what felt like eons, she did it. Even when we shared god awful wings at a bar and god awful pizza on a Central Park bench, she did it.

And of the three things, this one means the most.

I know I'm flawed. We all are. Without trying to come across as too self-deprecating and craving for affirmation and attention, I'll even dare to say that I'm deeply flawed. I'm emotionally imbalanced, hide my true self from people who love me, and am unduly critical of others, and even more so, of myself. I'm just like the rest of them, Men, who have their stint being frightened of commitment, are smarter in hindsight, and whose ego makes them feel invincible when they're everything but. I gnaw at the skin on my fingers till they drip blood, drink to be able to fall asleep, and recoil away from anyone who makes a step towards me. So, when L would stare, intrigued and confused, at the top of my head, it wouldn't be a strand of hair out of place that I'd envision her seeing, but the mountain of flaws I believe define me.

One of the many bell hooks quotes I used earlier said that the process of overcoming feelings of low self-esteem must include a commitment, first and foremost, to loving yourself. We must not expect the love from someone else which we do not give ourselves. This is where I have to, for the first time, disagree with her.

Because when I was 26-years-old I bumped into a girl on a New York City street that changed the way I understand things—love, accountability, myself. A girl I'll never kiss, hold hands with, or make laugh again. A girl I'll never get to list my three favorite things about while talking in the present tense. But the love I felt I can receive from that girl is what pushed me to want to commit to loving myself. Thanks to that girl, I know how badly I'm supposed to want it. I know how it's supposed to taste and feel. I know that I have to let myself go, do my best to keep a clear mind as I let passion and intensity flow through me. I know that I have to give parts of me away, expose myself, and be vulnerable. I know that withdrawing into silence will leave me silently screaming for power. I know that I have to empty myself of performance in order to fill my life with love. I know I have to be willing to accept a pain I do not know yet. I know that I have to render myself fragile, for that's the only way I'll ever be stable enough for someone to want to lean on me.

When that girl would look at me, when her hazel eyes would fixate on the top of my head as if there's a strand of hair out of place, when I'd envision her seeing the mountain of flaws I go to bed with every night, for the briefest of moments, my body would shudder and my mind would freeze. But then her eyes would flicker back, lock with mine, and everything, with the same swiftness it takes to utter the second syllable of her name, would unclench. And the reason that moment meant so much to me, the reason it would be at the top of the three, is because I felt as if L was awarded an unfiltered view of me. A view no one else had ever gotten. A view that included every single thing that's wrong with me, and her instinctual, immediate reaction was to direct her irises back to my eyes. To look at me and let me know that whatever flaws I have, however unstable I think I am, she's there. She's there, ready to wipe my tear, kiss my cheek, string her arm around me tighter, bring herself closer to me, ink herself into my life.

It's okay if I don't have every answer for every question. It's okay if I need to lean on someone. It's okay to be weak, to ask for strength from someone else. It's okay to be the burden every now and again. In fact, being the burden every now and again is the only way someone will ever feel comfortable being my burden.

And that's what I want. For someone to look at me and feel comfortable unloading any problem they have, knowing I will always—always—respond by raising my arms, moving strands of their hair, and caressing their top lip. They'll always—always—have room to rest atop my bare chest as I'll feel the weight of their head and the warmth of their palms. And they'll do that, they'll feel that freedom to render themselves vulnerable, because they'll know how committed I am to doing the same.

I know this is what I want not because my friends have it, not because I saw it in some movie, and not because I read about it in some book. I know because I was lucky enough to bump into L and have her want to share a path with me. I know because I was stupid enough to take her for granted and cause our paths to separate. I know because I loved and lost, but instead of letting the loss spiral me completely out of control, I braided three strands together. I know because I wound up not with someone I love, but as someone I hate a little less. I know because I looked back and saw what L brought into my life: a love I did not know I had to give, a love I did not know I want to receive, and the work I need to do to enable both to manifest, blissfully coexist.

I know, more than anything, because of three things. Because of the nose, the press of the finger, and the flicker of the eyes.

ACKNOWLEDGMENTS

Ima, in a world that seems to rest on your shoulders, I'm honored you rest on mine. It will always be here.

Dad, this book is a labor (you'd say labour, I know) of love—of words, of Liverpool, of love itself. They all trace back to you.

Gili, for setting standards of humanity and kindness, not just for me but for anyone who's ever come across you, so incredibly high—ones that I will never reach but continue to strive towards.

Peta, my first and greatest teacher. No matter how many years pass, you continue to show me expanses of compassion and wisdom to learn from.

Robyn, a *royal* role model, who renders every room she enters *flush* with brilliance. You are an unmatched force, and the very best.

Dani, agent, accountability partner, brother, Willem, Toad. I do not know a life in which I don't run by your side, nor do I want to know one.

Sophie Lalani, for a friendship whose origin was as unlikely as its timing was crucial, and which is truly invaluable to my life every single day.

Al Jacobs, for the keen eye and exceptional feedback, constant support and presence, and knowing what I like throughout the journey, one pint at a time.

Danny Herz, for keeping me upright for the last decade, giving me a keyboard to type this book on (and phone to ignore people's texts), and inviting me through a door that led to all the love The Doah has to give.

Connie Shaw, for our dance of edits: your insistence or yielding, all for the purpose of making this book, and myself, better, doing all of it with warmth and patience I am privileged to have felt. (I tried to cram as many commas as I could into this sentence.)

Steven, Deborah, Laura, Emily, Marissa, and the rest of the Sentient Team. Wherever this life leads me, yours will always be the first hands I held along such a process. I couldn't have hoped for sturdier, kinder, and more capable ones.

Michele Parker Randall, for showing me that the world of writing is real, and for believing that my words could carry value within it—this would not have happened without you and your support.

Stetson University, for picking someone else to give the undergraduate commencement speech in 2018. I hope you feel stupid.

For the teachers—Brenda, Gila, Jen, Philip, Wendy—and students who helped me widen my view, rid of the unnecessary, and learn the difference between fiction and nonfiction (if there even is one amirite if any MFA program is looking for someone to teach a seminar about this I am available).

The Chipped Cup, every word in this book was written or edited at home, and by home I mean the space you've created for me and so many others. Thank you, and I'm sorry about calling your chairs uncomfortable—it's part of the beauty.

Arthur Guinness, I give you ¾ of my gratitude now, and in about 119.5 seconds I will pour the rest. Sláinte mo chara. All my love.

There are countless people whose love I've felt and continue to feel every day. Listing them all would make this book even longer, and I think we've all had enough. You know who you are, and know that your place in my heart, and therefore in this book, is indelible.

Lastly, Steven Gerrard. Just, yeah. Thank you. Always.

Michael Kushner Photography

Eyal Cohen grew up in Israel before being recruited to play Division I soccer at Stetson University in Florida. After working as a middle school teacher, he moved to New York City for his Writing MFA from Columbia University. His debut book dissects how men think—or avoid thinking—about love. Given his passion for sports, reading bell hooks, and drinking Guinness, he is the perfect person to write this book. He resides in NYC.